SUPERPOWERING INDIA

SUPERPOWERING INDIA

Air Marshal
Amal Kumar Mukhopadhyaya
PVSM, AVSM, ADC (Retd)

Manas Publications
New Delhi-110002 (INDIA)

MANAS PUBLICATIONS
(We Convert Fighters into Writers)
(Publishers-Library Suppliers-Importers & Exporters)
4402/5-A, Ansari Road (Opp. HDFC Bank)
Darya Ganj, New Delhi - 110 002 (India)
Phones: Off.: 011-23260783, 23265523, Res.: 011-23842660
E-mail: manaspublications@gmail.com
manaspublications@yahoo.com
Website: www.manaspublications.in

2nd Impression 2015

ISBN : 978-81-7049-357-0

Rs. 795/-

Designed at: Manas Publications

Printed in India at
RK Print Services, Delhi
and published by Mrs Suman Lata for
Manas Publications, 4402/5-A,
Ansari Road, (Opp HDFC Bank),
Darya Ganj, New Delhi - 110002 (INDIA)

AUTHOR'S NOTE

One of Rabindranath Tagore's poems is titled as "Kabbeya Upekshita" (neglected or ignored in epic, poetry, or in literatures), which immortalized the pain, sorrows and pathos of Urmila, the wife of Lakshman, who was left back in Ayodhya, when Lakshman accompanied Ram and Sita to wilderness for 14 years. Similarly, military with its umbilical relationship with poverty is a subject which is totally ignored, side-lined or neglected in economics and literatures of under-developed countries; only that there is no great soul to mourn for it! Economic Reforms has been one of the most significant events in India since the cataclysmic days of Pre-Partition riots and Independence. Economic reforms have touched all aspects of Indian life and society, but there is no awareness as to what economic reforms delivered for national security. The interesting part is that common Indians are not fully informed. This book is an effort to look at elementary national security and economic issues from people-relevant standpoints to decipher why there is burgeoning poverty in the land of plenty, in the backdrop of ongoing reforms and Globalization processes.

I had the privilege to observe the management of Indian economy and national security as an insider during long tenures in Defence Forces; particularly in the last decade of service in senior positions and as Principal Staff officers and

Head of the branches in commands and Air Headquarters, responsible for operation, administration, maintenance, logistics, procurement, budgeting, fund management and technical management of aircraft, helicopters, other aerospace vehicles, missiles, guided weapons, weapon systems, management and control of ground and aerospace environment systems and as Member of boards of directors of public sector undertakings. Thereafter, I had the opportunity to interact with the power elite in politics, economics, socio-cultural and socio-religious entities, which prompted an examination of matters from perspectives of disadvantaged multitude of India.

The Indian economy is always in a tailspin and crisis of confidence in the management of the country is ever deepening, with violent dissent, foreign inspired or fully indigenous, breaking out in bordering states and in inland areas also. Indians need a better deal and they deserve it by virtue of their long and chequered history and its unexcelled value systems. This book is an effort to provide theoretical basis for peoples' actions and break the circle of ignorance, hypocrisy, dishonesty, insatiable hunger for others' wealth and resources, while intelligently camouflaging these aims in economic rationality and media management, for ensuring the survival of the sterile idea of inevitability of Western supremacy.

The Indian scenario is simultaneously unique and common-place for all underdeveloped or those countries, which are still struggling to get out of foreign yoke. All unknown soldiers were agreed on one point - India is still to shake-off the foreign control over its economy, polity and culture, thanks to shenanigans of sophisticated and articulate Indian elite. We believe that all poor and deprived countries have only to substitute statistics relevant for their countries and will find that methods and procedures fine-tuned in India have been applied to their countries also with minor local variations.

I involuntarily created another unknown soldier, possibly, a combination of my wife, my son and daughter, my psychic friends, like late Air Commodore Prabhakar Gajanan Joshi of Alishan Apartments, Bhandarkar Road, Pune; Shri A C Chatterjee, of Fern Road, Kolkata, the only SCTO (senior civilian technical officer) of Indian Air Force; Wing Commander H R Seetharam, Bangalore; Air Commodore Dilip Khasnobish, Sector 25, Noida, UP and Group Captain Vimal K Jain, Asiad Village, New Delhi. All of them wanted me to succeed; but my wife is my most severe and unrelenting critic and vociferously declared many times that I shall not succeed, even though believing in heart of hearts and sanguine (God willing) that I will, belatedly, succeed. My daughter is my unabashed admirer and encouraged me along, she herself being an academic of religious studies of repute in Japan; my son, reticent in best of times, reserved his judgment and did help out as much as required; but I had all doubts myself and I transported my impatience, frustration and vision for the future to the Unknown Soldier friend.

CONTENTS

INTRODUCTION

The Armed forces are a source of pride of independent self-respecting countries. Armed forces are the 'Heart and Soul and the Iron Fist' of the nation. A nation gets its legitimacy and relevance in the comity of nations on the strength of its military. Military is the only valid currency in international interactions, all other exchange instrumentalities are facile and tentative. Weak, occupied, surrogate or dependent undeveloped (i.e. poor) countries sometimes try to create an aura of invincibility on the basis of diplomatic manoeuvres or groupings of equally weak and non-effective nations (like the non-alignment movement of Nehru and post-Nehru regimes in India) so that they could avoid taking effective steps to ameliorate poverty and increase military strength. In fact, the historical truth is that all the so-called non-aligned countries (particularly India) tried to hide their capitalist exploitative inclinations behind brave and belligerent posturing against capitalists but on the quiet accorded free run to the big and super powers in the management of their countries and their economies. These countries tried their best not to understand the significance of military mobilization of the country and preached the value of Peace, when their countrymen were always restive, often, violently.

The march of civilizations has always been accompanied by division of the militarily weak composite countries by less cultured monotheistic but militarily more powerful countries. With the growth of the currently running western civilization, poverty of undeveloped countries and militarization of the rich (by exploitation of Asian and African countries) has assumed menacing and sinister dimensions without any indications of reversal of the trend.

The problem of unmitigated poverty, however, has been the greatest concern of some people. Although widespread poverty has been a fact of life in India from about the eighth century AD when foreign conquest of parts of India became passé, poverty grew by leaps and bounds as the duration and sophistication of the colonization of India advanced. In incidental poverty, the choices of the people are not restricted by other humans. In organised poverty, the victims have no or limited access[1] to opportunities or choices due to action or inaction of other humans. India suffers from organised poverty mostly.

Though poverty has been an ever-pressing phenomenon in India for long, and political and economic discourses recognized this fact, but when the Indian leaders had independent choice of action after 1947 they did not recognize that India basically suffers from organized poverty due to human actions. The Indian elite started behaving as if it was a natural thing. The issue of poverty has always been examined from very narrow perspectives, even though Prof. Amartya Sen tried conveying the multi-dimensional features of poverty. Of course, he restricted himself to socio-political-economic-cultural factors, expecting succour from the same power elite which created the unviable situation in the first place. Citing the examples of the austerity and penury, which Indian ascetics accepted as a matter of their faith for attainment of their highest goal, Indian leaders were not even reluctant to depict poverty as a means of attaining 'Moksha" (salvation). Independent Indian government's one of the first proactive (socialist?) actions was to reduce the pay of the military personnel drastically in 1953, after having got a foreigner dictated constitution accepted by a constituent assembly dominated by kulaks and elite indebted to foreigners, which made privileges of civil administration and ministering to British interests sacrosanct with constitutional protections.

Poverty in newer forms is generated and perpetuated by the power elite and they displayed inability, hypocrisy, and studied unwillingness to do anything concrete to improve matters. Since, what the economists or their political supporters (or vice versa) decided for India's future turned out to be dismal failures, attempt was first made to educate the political and other leadership class. But we did not have funds like what Enron Corporation (for the, now abandoned, original Dhabol Power project in Maharashtra, India) had for the "Education" of the politicians and bureaucrats, we could not motivate a single MP of any of the national or regional parties, or leaders of religio-cultural, politico-cultural or religious entities to agitate national interest or national security issues intelligently in Parliament or in other public fora. I was introduced to an MP of a regional party in early 21st century; the MP seemed quite aware of the shady dealings in procurement of a British AJT (Advanced Jet Trainer) for the Indian Air Force. He, as characteristic of such people, asked for a write up for taking it up in the Standing Committee of Parliament on Defence and that was sent, but nothing happened. He, once on the phone itself, demanded to know how much share he would get and how much I could give him straightaway. It was assumed that it was an aberration of a single MP of a regional party, till the 'Cash for Questions' scam broke and about a dozen MPs had to be thrown out of the Parliament in 2005. I once got totally exasperated with one top leftist political leader but could not slow down his monologue. The mistake I did was to ask him as to why his party did not oppose the "Insurance Privatization" Bill as strongly as they agitated and made the

Government bow down to their protests against Gujarat Government allowing public servants to join the RSS (Rashtriya Swayam Sevak Sangh) 'Shakas'[2]. When I kept on asking why his party did not obstruct the proceedings of the Parliament as they did for a protracted period on a non-economic issue only a few days earlier, he, continuing his monologue, just mentioned that his MPs had walked out and had not voted for the measure! This will give a partial picture if some instances from right or centre etc. are not quoted for balance. I had concluded that the MRTS (Mass Rapid Transit System) for Delhi had been conceived, designed, approved and is being executed by a set of congenital morons. I rang up the concerned Urban Development Minister and told him of my serious reservations. He heard for a few minutes and told me to give him a note. I protested, as my experience with leaders was that they either do not read or understand or find my briefs contrary to their interests. He assured me on all counts and after keeping my briefs on MRTS and direct method of 'tackling recalcitrant bureaucracy' pending for some time, when we met again it appeared that he had not read my brief and had to call upon his personal secretary (an Indian Administrative Service officer, who was equally articulate and colourful, as he was operating an NGO even when he was still in active service) to retrieve the papers. He could not readily retrieve the papers, but on seeing the headings of the papers, which I helpfully presented again, he trotted out the stereotyped arguments that underground Metro will be costlier than over ground Metro as per the experts. I mentioned about the inadequacy of mental calibre of experts to take into account the massive social costs of dislocating people from their habitats, utter dislocation of transport and civic services and inconvenience of travelling public, the Minister mentioned such issues might have been considered and accepted as inevitable. When I queried what the experts had opined regarding underground Metro system doubling as very low cost nuclear shelter for the teeming millions of Delhi residents, he and the Minister confirmed that this aspect was not considered, as India does not expect to be attacked with nuclear weapons. Requirement of multiple crossing lines for Metro, which was only possible through underground Metro, was not considered feasible by administration and politicians. As regards taming the bureaucracy, the Minister mentioned that he proposed to take it up in the cabinet. Since the whole discussion appeared to be verbal diarrohea, I got exasperated and started diligently questioning the personal secretary on urban renewal, (like, keeping in mind the extremely high population density in India, Urban Development Ministry could prescribe that ground area coverage cannot be more than 50%, and no DDA, public or corporate building should be less than 50-storied tall, no building for rental for residence can be less than 25-storied tall, and that every building should have minimum four underground levels for service facilities, including rain water harvesting/filtering before recharging the underground aquifers, and adequate government subsidy being directly provided to the land owners or to their co-operatives, sufficient open spaces and play grounds around every residential, or partially residential building, and sufficient recreational area around each high rise building etc.), as the Minister was sitting pretty as a doll! When the secretary was feeling uncomfortable, the Minister intervened that he was helpless as the decisions are taken by the GOM (Group of Ministers) under a more senior and powerful Minister and the empowered committee under Cabinet Secretary. The picture will be somewhat clear if I mention the outcome of my interaction with a long-surviving and very articulate Minister (temporarily out of office then) of a proclaimed (then) left of centre party, which ruled India for many years. When a serving Chief of Naval Staff and Chairman of Joint Chiefs of Staff Committee was summarily dismissed, without any investigation or trial, for the unpardonable crimes of protesting too much (on what he thought was) in the interest of the Navy and the country, the concerned leader and his party suddenly became very conscious of corruption and shenanigans in the bureaucracy and the armed forces and made me write a paper and we discussed the nuances several times. It was reported then that the dismissal order was intimated by some low level secretary to the Government of India even before it was got signed, sealed and issued by the President, as propriety demanded. Incidentally, secretaries to the government have no locus standi in the matter but he was operating under the inappropriate protection of the SC verdict on Wing Commander Hazara Singh vs. Union of India and some clause 18 or 19 of Navy Act which does not cover the Chief of Naval Staff or Chief of Joint Chiefs of Staff Committee and was, prima facie, illegal. As time passed, the poor admiral was left in the lurch and the leaders, this leader in particular, unabashedly talked on these points exactly opposite to what we agreed upon. These points were again resurrected during written submissions and oral presentation to the 'Tehelka' Commission (headed at that time by retired honourable Judge of apex court, Shri Venkataswamy), but this must have again been sent to the waste bin or hidden in mountains of papers generated by the venerable Commission! This same leader, and possibly his leader, kept a non-official top secret offer for supply of nuclear weapons by a collapsing state pending long enough, so that the other party was forced to back out complaining of breach of trust and bitterly complained of pressures from a foreign country alerted by Indian high party.

I had the opportunity of attending a seminar in FICCI auditorium in Delhi in July/August 2003 to eulogize a new book, 'Development as Freedom', of Prof. Amartya Sen, but in actual fact, to co-opt him to the capitalist fold. One of the five simultaneous seminars was chaired by Dr. Manmohan Singh, then an opposition member in Rajya Sabha. I asked him why must India limit currency in circulation to 15% or so, when America and China put currency in circulation many times more than the GDP, he kept hedging about parity, international obligations, international accounts settlement requirements, which I assiduously tried to demolish, but to no avail. Then I asked him why can't India have parity exchange rate of $ 1 = Re.1, which is actually the only realistic exchange rate. When I tried to dispel his disbelief with some revealing statistics from World Bank Reports, he launched into an elaboration of the intricacies of exchange rate fixation in his tiring monotone, but I kept on interjecting to bring him back to the main question and he kept on in his unhurried monologue impervious to all logic. When this carried on for some time, Prof. Amartya Sen, who was moving from one seminar room to another, shuffled out and the gentleman sitting on my right, who I later came to know was secretary general of some federation of some chambers of commerce, murmured in my mother tongue, 'you are wasting your time, he is not going to understand or answer your question'. I gave up. After the chair prattled on for some more time without interruptions, next question was taken up.

There is convincing proof that poverty in India (or in other countries for that matter) is not because it is God's wish or a natural phenomenon or that it cannot be remedied within the existing framework. I was reasonably unimpressed with such bottom-up approach (without in anyway deprecating the necessity or effectiveness of mass/popular movements), as I was fully convinced after observing the history of freedom movement, partition holocaust, and recent upheavals in India that people can be roused mainly on communal, religious or ethnic issues and not on political or economic issues, especially where the attack to the system is through creeping invasion with local support. However, it has been repeatedly noted that people, even without political mobilization, give their adverse verdict within the current venal system of governance.

Every nation has four basic interdependent, with complex interconnections, supports/props/pillars viz. Culture, Politics, Economy, Military. A nation can be strengthened or weakened effectively only by a sequential effort at these supports. Thus, if culture is to be debilitated, politics must first be debilitated; for debilitating politics, economics must be debilitated before that; and for debilitating economics, military must be debilitated first of all. This is a universal truth unrecognized by the economists and other liberalized thinkers. They cannot afford to. Decline and fall of USSR started with the withdrawal of military power projections in Afghanistan and now rump Russia has been reduced to a non-strategic, non-effective nuclear power, with a crippled economy, without any power projection willingness or capability. Western jazzy culture has more or less over-run Russian traditional cultures. Modern economics and its complementing oligarchic democracy were used to debilitate USSR economy. How crippling modern economic concepts and practices can be has been demonstrated once again in September 2008 by the collapse of the great American showpiece investment Banker Lehman Brothers, AIG, Wachovia Mutual, etc.!

All systems and factors, which keep a country going in its existential route, operate in varying degrees in debilitating military and perpetuating poverty in undeveloped or developing countries. Culture, religion, national and international politics, trade, articulated national ethos, defence capability and last, but not the least, the judiciary and the administration, especially, the apex courts and the central secretariat of the country, all play their unassigned roles. Economics is used as the cutting edge for ensuring delivery of unending stream of poor, deprived and dispossessed humanity to smoothen the path of profit-propelled private enterprises. Since a militarily strong nation cannot be kept poor, the heart and sinews of the nation – the armed forces – are kept marginalized in poor countries, so that people can be made to internalize the concept of powerless nation without much freedom of action in national interest issues. Lack of strategic capability in national security and sovereignty issues is so acute that a Prime Minister, like Dr. Manmohan Singh, could openly claim that what applies to India cannot be expected to be applied to America or vice versa or another Prime Minister, like Atal Behari Vajpayee, after promising a decisive outcome, could keep the Army standing on the international border for one whole year and after punishing two General rank officers (one Corps commander and one Air officer commanding-in-chief of the major operational command) who inadvertently crossed the LOC, a line lying wholly within Indian territory, shamefacedly withdrew the Army to peace locations without achieving a single demand made to Pakistan. This needs to be critically appraised to get answers to the question as to why India is poverty-stricken amidst plenty, what is essential, necessary, feasible and practicable, even within the existing State and power structures, and without too much violence to the economic framework.

The mythology of western economic and technological superiority and their conceptual purity has struck deep roots in India[3]. The economically and militarily powerful nations have been able to impress the Indian elite, and through them the Indian vocal gentry, so much that even ordinary people have also started accepting that India is poor as India does not have enough money. When a charismatic young leader from Bengal built up a movement and a party from scratch and won eight seats in Parliament (House of the people) in 1999 elections from Bengal, a communist fiefdom, her reputation was sky-high and she got media and popular encomium in great abundance. She got the cabinet post of the important portfolio of the Indian Railways. I called on her to congratulate her and commiserate with her for taking over the charge of the accident-prone Railways. But when I suggested that she immediately take steps to make every single Railway level-crossings manned within a year and demand immediate tripling of the Railways budget, she was aghast. Fortunately, at that point of our discussion, her senior, apparently friend, in her erstwhile party and the then Chairman of the powerful Public Accounts Committee (or Estimates Committee, I am not too sure now) of Parliament walked in. The Minister explained the gist of our discussion and my ideas. Both were silent for a few minutes and then in one voice they uttered, "Where is the Money?" My answer was as prompt, "Print it". The Minister gave me such a look of compassion and pity that I thought a Leonardo da Vinci or Michelangelo could create another memorable painting or sculpture of "Pieta"! This young leader had possibly disdain for scholasticism or ecclesiasticism, had no worthwhile economic idea and though she made a splash for some time, had a first shock in municipal elections in west Bengal in 2002 and nemesis for the fledgling party came in 2004 general elections to Parliament. To my mind IQ has three components: (a) Animal, (b) Functional and (c) Spiritual. Animal IQ is concerned with survival and procreation. Functional IQ is concerned with the use of fire, natural and human created products, wind, water and energy in different innovative ways. Spiritual IQ is concerned with the use of spirituality, imagination, intellect, cooperation, selflessness, self-sacrifice etc.

Greatest impetus for writing this book came from my abiding faith that destiny of mankind cannot be decided by part-time bit actors on the world stage, however much they strut, fret, huff or puff to impress the innocents. I always take heart from the statement of our guide, "How frail are prophesies of the mighty!" While recounting the horror and senseless murder of the innocents in Hiroshima on that fateful day in August 1945, he, inter alia, mentioned that the attacker had claimed that 'not a blade of grass will grow' in Hiroshima in 76 years after the explosion of the first Atomic Bomb. Mother nature and human ingenuity proved to be more powerful than the mightiest in the world: first scorched and stunted maple tree flowered in three months, and the first Tram from the city centre to port was made functional by the Japanese within one and half days after the catastrophe!

The horrors of Hiroshima and Nagasaki did not have any effect on the big powers and they are demonstrating their great capacity for mischief by brandishing arsenals of nuclear weapons, missiles and computers of bewildering variety, while still cowering in the corner in fear that India can easily convert Indian ocean into an Indian lake, where access and transit of all other states will be at the whims of India. The outside powers are resting comfortably for the time being in the knowledge that the current crop of leaders in India has no stomach for any decisive action in economic or national security matters. This book is an attempt to bring some sense to the aspiring power elite so that they act as per the potentials of India.

Although it will be claimed that poverty has been a way of life in India for centuries but then Indian people did not have opportunity for exercising free options. The question why must India wallow in poverty in the midst of abundance of economic resources needs to be thoroughly examined from analytical and rational perspectives.

This book can be taken as a charter for renaissance (not the European labour-exploiting variety, but the reawakening and rejuvenation to foster real equality and equity) of India, particularly, in political, economic and national security measures. If these aspects of the nation are taken care of, cultural revival of India to which the various groups of nationalists are giving lip-service may also be achieved. We know that Shri Aurobindo[4] and Swami Vivekananda[5] have clearly defined what culture implies and how it is extremely important for self-respecting independent people and we are also aware that Indian power elite are reluctant to agree with Shri Aurobindo. We start with the premise that culture is essentially different for nations, countries, regions, societies, groups, families and the individuals. We should also keep this point in mind while analyzing any system like economics, religion, state or world.

A lot of people try to highlight the influence of religion. Religion has always been used to divide the people for ease of manipulation. The picture and the type of renaissance we are thinking of cannot be visualized or actualized unless we internalize that the so-called religious or cultural synthesizing groups or those who swear by 'Qaum' actually attempt preservation of the status quo ante or facilitate anti-native economic policies or for perpetuating weak military and poverty of a section of the native population.

This book is the result of our deep conviction that India

can be made the principal super (not the soft variety at the cost of or on the corpse of military) economic global power in ten years, even surpassing China, Japan and the current super power by order of magnitudes, provided China and Japan and the super power continue in their pursuit of progress on the basis of current western economic and business models and paradigms. Indian people will ensure in their non-demonstrative manner that there cannot be recourse to 'monarchy', dictatorship of any type or 'aggressive rule' in India without damage to the State and social and the 'cozy' constitutional structures.

Once the economic levers shift to the national entities, the raison d'etre for 'brain-drain, immigration, resources' transfers from India will get curtailed due to operation of the fundamental laws of economics. Productivity of labour in Western countries is so low – much lower than that in India – that their economic growth is critically dependent on skilled and unskilled immigrant labour. Any reduction or shift in immigration will seriously affect the economy of these developed countries, which they will endeavour to prevent. Western countries have highly developed military apparatus and have all the theoretical foundations built over centuries and they will be able to strike back in a graduated scale of violence to thwart all move for any reordering of the world, particularly, economic order. Western civilization understands that without alienation of the people from their roots, culture, religion, society and family, individuals cannot be totally controlled. It is also odd that such aberration was fostered most in the so-called free democratic country of the world. For the western countries, it is not enough to divide the people within a country or region and increase the total tension in the community. They are now looking for theoretical basis for generating some sort of clash-situations amongst the countries or different ethnic religious/ cultural groups of people.

The author of "Clash of Civilization"[6] has presented elaborate data of exploitation of non-European states (see table on p.23), but draws the conclusions that demand for equality or redistributions of world wealth can only lead to serious conflict. Another great thinker,[7] after analyzing the data similar to that of Huntington came to the conclusion that very high productive efficiency and superior management techniques of westerners is at the root of their affluence and ability to control other bigger countries!

Table 4.4

Shares of world output by civilization/country 1750-1990.

Country	**1750**	**1928**	**1990**
West	18.2	84.2	57.8
China	32.8	3.4	5.0
Japan	3.8	3.3	9.1
India/Pakistan	24.5	1.8	2.3
Russia/U.S.S.R	5.0	5.3	21.1

The following data is taken from an article in *The Economic Times*, New Delhi, 29 January, 2008, titled, "The return of India & China: Large corporates need to abandon the safety net of resource allocation and replace it with one of corporate stewardship. Big corporations also need to encourage entrepreneurship, says Jaspal Singh Sabharwal".

SHARE OF WORLD'S GDP*

	India	**China**	**Japan**	**USA**	**Europe**	**Rest of the World**
1 AD	33	27	1	0	14	25
1500AD	25	25	3	0	21	26
1820 AD	15	33	3	2	27	20
1870 AD	12	17	2	9	38	22
1913 AD	8	8	4	21	39	20
1950 AD	4	5	3	28	31	29
1973 AD	3	5	8	23	29	32

2001 AD	4	7	8	23	21	37
2008 AD	6	13	7	21	19	34

* (In %)

Sabharwal has noted the basic facts: 'From around the common era until the early 19th century, China and India accounted for around half of the global GDP. For much of this period, China and India were independent countries and technological leaders. Until around 1450, China and India were technologically more innovative and advanced than Europe. Both the countries were very well knit with rest of the globe but both countries went downhill between the early 18th century and the late 20th century'. Sabharwal cited western propaganda for the downhill march of these mammoth and magnificent countries except mentioning the most important ones, viz, colonization, ruthless and savage exploitation of the natives of the unfortunate countries and massive transfer of wealth.

Possibly unknown to Indian scholars and elite, there is strongly perceptible undercurrent of social/political churning in India in spite of the rising share of world GDP. If only Sabharwal or someone concerned with the reality of GDP story examines the matter closely he will notice three major debilitating factors, viz. a) Disproportionate percentage of GDP in India, and in similarly disadvantaged countries, in recent years is provided by 'Service sector' dedicated to the service of foreigners and affluent in the country, b) Highly skewed distribution of available GDP for the benefit of affluent in the country, c) Unacceptable level of poverty and destitution in spite of higher GDP share. (300 million or so of Indians still go to bed hungry in spite of 8% share of world GDP).

In the period 1913 to 1973 (i.e. sixty years continuously), western countries like USA and Europe had grossly disproportionate share of world GDP (namely 50% to 60%). During this period colonization was at its peak and two World Wars were fought for the benefit of USA. No wonder USA has assumed the mantle of super power with unquestioned privileges. USA is necessarily a very highly militarized or mobilized state.

Many people are aware that 'Development' and Controlled/oligarchic Democracy in India has been as divisive as poverty, but stalwarts are giving India-specific solutions, but when confronted with reality, claim inadequate knowledge or data. These elite seem to be unaware of their inadequacy of knowledge or data relevant for India while sermonizing government leaders and hobnobbing with business magnates in India!

This small effort is not a handbook on security and poverty or a treatise on the all pervading, all important questions, "Why Insecurity? Why Poverty?" People, including all the sects of Buddhism, have either forgotten or misread the futuristic words of ninth Avatar, Gautama Buddha: "Violence Begets Violence". If the import of this message were taken to heart, the scene in this world would have been different. We hope and pray that resurgent India will not mimic the current barbarism of the West!

The other unresolved question (with apologies to Ricardo, other eminent Western economists or latest addition to the creed, viz Dr. Raghu Ram Rajan of Chicago Business School, Chief Economist of IMF and currently in 2008 an economic adviser to the Government of India etc) which we tried to grapple was: Who is owner of the fruits of output-surplus of labour? The labourer or the hirer of the labour? Does labour lose all claims on the output-surplus of his labour in exchange for the remuneration (however small that might be) given to him by his hirer or master? Also, whether 'Profit' or profiteering is really not the main force behind development in the West? Profit, if any, in the operations have to be shared with the only other human element viz. labour, fairly, with access to judicial recourse.

One observation which becomes important repeatedly is that in the world and, in India particularly, the evil never dies. It gets resurrected from time to time in spite of the efforts of saving humanity by the Nine Incarnations (Avatars of the supreme Preserver of the Universe, the Vishnu, of the trinity of Hindu supreme Gods).

But, what is most disconcerting is that a system like capitalism which is imploding is being attempted to be brought back to its pristine glory by some people. One great man (an IITian) and his colleague appeared with much fanfare with the aim of "Saving Capitalism from the Capitalists"[8]. The most interesting aspect is that the authors have distinguished between the system and the operators or beneficiaries of the system. From the time economic reforms were heralded in, one scam after another surfaced in India and in super developed and developed countries regularly because the perpetrators had all the alibis, particularly, the legal ones. Collapse (conveniently as bankruptcy) of Fannie Mae, Freddie Mac, Lehman Brothers and AIG – all American financial institutions controlling the world economy – proves the point that any amount of irregular and criminal acts can be carried out with impunity in capitalist countries, still staying within legal limits and no auditor or Regulator ever finds out anything before the crash and wiping out of the funds of the common investors and of dependent countries like India. The Indian and world experience is that scams are a constant companion of capitalist system of production and distribution, as the system is permissive enough and tolerant of evil-doing by the elite. The question remains whether capitalism and financial markets can thrive concurrently with equity to all (including aliens), social justice and equal access to opportunity without prior benefit of extra wealth gained improperly or through heredity. Also, financial development appears as a cruel joke where very little capital is in circulation for production purposes (a prime example being India) and where distribution of wealth, means of production and income flow is always to the affluent. GINI index has become worse for the major countries in later periods indicating heightened inequality and inequity. Capitalism and its companion, the financial markets, as a matter of course, ensure transfer of wealth from the poor to the rich regions, from the poor people to the rich people and must destroy or distort the production processes, native technologies, native talent, the native cultures and the military of the captured or subjugated lands so that capitalism can flourish in the dominating country. Some talented people would like us to believe that capitalism is really very beautiful but misunderstood system but still the question remains how can surplus be taken out from the productive systems if there is no unrealistic withdrawal of wealth from the production system, captured lands and client states. No average prudent human can really object to financial revolution, individual economic freedom, financial development, but will these ever come about if irrational decision-system in economic matters and in surrogate political, legal, constitutional and religious domains persist? What intrigued me most was the convergence of views between Karl Marx and these two authors (singing praise of capitalism) of the necessity of limiting state power, as much as possible. But it is suspected that these authors could not be thinking of reducing state power with regard to control and policing of the people at large. On the contrary, all lovers of capitalism want a very strong and directed and committed police force and massive law and order machinery, as, otherwise, people's discontent and contempt for power cannot be kept contained within reasonable limits.

One seminal study I came across in *The Economic Times*, Delhi edition, which clearly demonstrates how economic policies affect the political outcome in voter choices in general elections in India. This was an article by Dr. Surjeet S. Bhalla, director of some organization 'Oxus etc.' published in August, 1996 in India. I normally do not expect to see any coherent, logical or rational article in mainstream newspapers in India. After analyzing the voting percentage secured by the Congress Party of India in different elections in several decades, Dr. Bhalla, concluded that Congress will secure 108 to 124 seats, with the median value being 116. Congress in those elections secured 112 seats I was amused at the forecast of Dr. Bhalla that Dr. Manmohan Singh, the father of economic reforms (unrecognized father or surrogate mother being V P Singh) who was fighting elections from South Delhi (where I belong) constituency in 1996, will win. This was exactly contrary to my heuristic forecast, after studying his paper and general state of the economy, about electoral prospects of Dr. Singh. If the honourable Dr. Singh had won, my assessment of Indian economy and my confidence on shifting public choices would have been proved wrong. Incidentally, Dr. Singh lost by a wide margin.

But this article exerted a very great influence on me and I explained the significance of this to all leading lights of India and expected them to initiate a U-turn in management of Indian economy or at least start a debate. Around mid-2003, a reporter of a national newspaper with head office in South India came to see me. We discussed many points and I offered to contribute my economic ideas in his newspaper. During our discussions, I made a forecast that BJP (Bharatiya Janata Party, the main force behind the ruling combine then) might expect to capture 95 (most pessimistic estimate) to 120 (most optimistic) seats in the next general elections in 2005. I had based my inspired guess on Dr. Bhalla's genuine conclusions and my estimate of the effect of liberalization and economic reforms on people of India. With the elections preponed to 2004 and at the height of the media hype synthetically created by the party in power, the forecast was adjusted to 85 (pessimistic) to 135 (optimistic). The BJP secured 138 seats in the general elections of 2004.

Developed countries invented the threat of communism, Nazism, fascism, and terrorism to mount their attacks on the wealth and resources in the target countries. This attitude of impatience with people of other countries manifested by the elite (i.e. the predators) of western countries has hardened the souls of the western people almost completely now so that they can, at the slightest provocation, wage war and atrocities on non-western countries, torture their prisoners with ever newer savage methods, bring untold miseries on the victims. The gory stories of torture of prisoners in Abu Gharaib, Guantanamo, and other secret and non-secret prisons operating for the western powers and the super power now are only the tip of iceberg of depravity of the dominant countries. Germans and Japanese have also internalized their guilt of trying to assert themselves in 1940s and have made themselves completely available for free use by the major victor of WWII. How super modern and super developed people can be so gutless! This narration is important because we want to caution well meaning Indians that if they adopt capitalism or its variants as growth models, they are becoming candidate members for being the cause or victim of WWIII/WWIV. Fastest the path to current economic reforms in capitalist mode is traversed, fastest will be the progress to initiation of WWIII, as India is too big, too diverse, and already too divided to react uniformly to any elite-orchestrated media hype or inputs. Of course, we are almost convinced that the economic reforms programme on current models will ensure dismemberment of India as we know in 2006.

Some beautiful conventions, like the series of Geneva conventions on treatment of POWs, ethics of war, etc. and some international organizations, like the UNO, FAO, and many other subsidiary and associate organizations, International Red Cross organization, Human Rights Commissions, IAEA etc. have been created mainly to control the uncontrollable unfortunate people of Asia, Africa, Latin America, Eastern Europe. These conventions and organizations have uniformly failed to deliver on their original aims and objectives.

We are not in a no-win situation. Alternative Indian models are always available. How was ancient India treating their defeated enemy or the vanquished? After Ravan was felled by Ram, he made Lakhsman, his younger brother and constant companion, to pay obeisance to Ravan and seek his advice on all matters of life and statecraft. Earlier responding to Ram's prayer, Ravan had carried out the Puja and the Goddess Durga was pleased to bless Ram to be successful in battle against Ravan! Can you imagine a similar situation in modern times? Ram had not annexed Lanka to his kingdom (unthinkable in modern times!) nor obtained war reparations from the defeated country. Victors in ancient India did not ever constitute War Crimes Tribunal and such other sham shows.

All those who agonize a lot about the state of Indian Republic cannot accept, like other officially recognized intellectuals that it is either God's wish or that poor are only responsible for their poverty. After cogitating long and observing in close quarters how the economy is managed, it has been concluded that the present dismal state is due to:-

(a) Common Indians have infinite capacity for acceptance of pains and they have infinite capacity to rationalize their deprivation.

(b) Indian leaders have ready capacity to be compromised and infinite capacity to rationalize inaction.

Thus, India even in the 21st century AD is in a piquant situation created by modern development economics as understood by the rulers. Purchasing power of the people is very low due to all pervading unemployment. Nothing gets done satisfactorily due to shortage of labour; there is no job for the people as there are no vacancies. All vacancies have been surrendered as there are no funds. There are no funds with any one, as there is little money in circulation. More money cannot be put in Indian economy as there is no reserve. There is no reserve, as bulk of the reserve is in FE and these have been parked abroad (for use by foreigners) on the advice of the mandarins of the powerful countries. Hence the circle of poverty and insecurity is complete in India. How can anyone in India find some funds for the military then?

If the market were such a leveler, then introduction of market economy would have been a *sine-qua-non* with elimination of disparity in resources allocation, income distribution, wealth distribution etc. The market economy has accentuated these in country after country in all time periods, other than introducing some newer and more virulent evils of misuse of minor children of both sexes, increasing crimes against women, crimes and deterioration in general safety standards and introduction of pornography as a mainstream economic activity and big business etc.

Although mobilization in appropriate scale is a national necessity, Indian governments of all persuasions have convinced themselves that their grip on power and perquisites is secure so long there are enough poor people to justify inaction on national security issues, with the plea, 'where is the money for military when we should better be looking after the poor'. If poverty vanishes how will they justify strangulating the military?

We have to study the nature of conventional Super Power (SP) or Global Power before we can get a tentative definition of Soft Super Power (SSP) or Soft Global Power. A SP (Super power, i.e. Global Power) is one which has large population, large geographical area and has some natural protection and is preferably rich in natural resources, has no religious or cultural constraints in unnecessarily harsh use of punitive powers and has a historical tradition of vulgar display of masochism; can interfere or intervene in the affairs of all other nations and countries at the time of its own choosing and has national willingness and readiness for it always. It can intervene and destroy or debilitate armed forces of any chosen target country, nation or state in all media -- land, sea, under the sea, air, space and outer space, if necessary. It always maintains overwhelming military strength; its mobilization state is invariably very high; it maintains technological edge at all times and is ruthless in maintaining its superiority at all times and erects elaborate denial, sanctions and control regimes and gets international accords for banning all competing technological research or manufacture. It also is invariably very rich or gets to be so – wealth and military strength grows simultaneously; it is most iniquitous inside the country and fosters inequity in all countries controlled directly or indirectly by it. It directly transfers wealth and resources from subject countries and extracts undue advantage by monetary, fiscal and by administrative measures enforced through international agencies; it closely controls all international bodies. One of the principal instruments is to impose very adverse foreign exchange rate on all client states. It is the world consumption leader; inward flow of low-cost goods and services are facilitated by its own highly favourable FE rate and other contrivances like getting the topmost leadership of the target country mesmerized with its aura power of punishment and simulated excellence in all fields.

In contrast, an SSP (Soft Super Power) is a mirror (convex at that) image of SP. Everything is reverse or negative (that is what we call *ULTA* in Hindi) for SSP. It never tries to do anything in national interests and if by mistake or involuntary action some good comes of any policy decision, then it changes it as soon as SP or a some big power point out the deleterious effect of such policy on SP or big powers. It maintains low mobilization and totally ineffective military for its national defence. It accepts only advice of SP in economic matters, however much those decisions might be deleterious for the country. It starves the nation of money and resources and never produces enough goods and services. It withdraws from primary and secondary sectors and concentrates on service sector to service the SP and big powers. It always eulogizes the service sector and diverts maximum wealth and resources to the service sector so that cheap goods and services can be provided to the foreigners. The worst of the SSP (like India) get a foreigner to rule his country. Our elite are enthusiastic about being a powerless soft super power!

We do not want to mimic the current super power and we will be soft in dealing with common indigenous population and aliens alike. But we will be highly mobilized as we are convinced there is no other alternative!

1

RATIONALISTIC ASSESSMENT OF INDIAN ECONOMY AND MILITARY

Chambers (20th Century) revised edition dictionary defines poverty as "the state of being poor; necessity; want; lack; deficiency". All these are really economic terms and ought to be taken note of and addressed to. But the aspect of unsatiated want is only treated as a matter of profit laundering or from supply management considerations. Indian elite have also internalized the doctrine of powerful countries that military debility of the natives is essential for controlling them. Have you ever wondered why Indian economy is always in a tailspin and why Indian leaders do not do anything about it? Has anyone even wondered why Indian labour is so unproductive? Have you seen any race-horse winning the Derby when hitched to a hackney carriage?

FUTILITY OF SEEKING RATIONALITY IN INDIAN ECONOMICS

We have noted that study of economy books, published articles etc. cannot be of any help in understanding why poverty gets perpetuated for so many centuries and why has it accentuated due to introduction of currency, first, as a medium of exchange and gradually, as the determinant of expression of economic prowess. What is most intriguing is that economists, big or small, are reluctant to examine this aspect thoroughly. Further, although poverty afflicts a major portion of the population of a country, the intellectuals of the country do not seem to be aware of it or are treating it as a good subject for preventive analysis for foreclosing all possible viable outcome or treating it as a non-economic issue. Even Nobel laureate economists are reluctant to treat it as a subject central to economics. The problem of poverty stands neglected with great detriment to society. This issue comes out vividly if we examine some published data given hereunder.

THE REALITY

Data culled from World Development Report 2000-2001 and other published sources show that real economic facts and data are being hidden or twisted for presentation to the general public in India and the other poor people in the undeveloped segment of the global family.

Indian Rupee is the most undervalued currency in the world. Indian Rupee has the highest Internal and lowest External Purchasing Power in the world. Compared to Market value of Dollar, Indian Rupee Market value is about 20% of its real Purchasing Power Parity (PPP) Value, even as per the faulty calculations of the World Bank. In respect to currencies of other major G-7 countries, it is devalued by 5.2 times to 6.7 times (that is, market value is only about 15% to 19% of the real PPP value). Even the Malaysian currency is overvalued compared to Indian currency by two times! No wonder, Indians are poor!

RBI keeps on devaluing the Indian Rupee continuously by using the latest 'Market value' as the Reference Rate, instead of the Exchange Rate established by 'Bretton Woods' Agreement, for their calculations of REER (Real Effective Exchange Rate) and NEER (Net Effective Exchange Rate), of course, without any theoretical or economic rationale. The only rationale is that it keeps the strength of the US Dollar always high in India, of course, at great detriment to India's interests!

India maintains very high proportion of FE and SDR (Special Drawing Rights) in its Reserve, much more than what is maintained by USA or other G-7 countries. With bulk of the Indian Reserve in FE/SDR, India maintains unnecessarily very large 'International Reserve'. As against Indian Reserve of the order of about $ 35 Billion in 1999 (it was more than $ 350 Billion in first quarter of 2008), USA maintained (1999) hardly $ 60 Billion and UK (1999) less than $ 30 Billion in 'International Reserves'. How excessive is India's 'International Reserves' can be seen by comparing the imports by the respective countries and the extent of their International Reserves. India imported about $ 40 Billion and in the same year (1998) USA imported more than a Trillion Dollars worth and UK about $ 387 Billion worth. Apparently, our RBI thinks "what is sauce for the (Indian) Goose is not sauce for (American/British) Gander"! Thus Indian FE Reserve is only for the comfort of US Banks and US Dollars and is grossly against Indian national interests.

Indian FE/SDR is kept in foreign countries (mostly in US Banks), of course, without any economic rationale and without the specific approval of Indian Parliament. USA, UK and other major G-7 countries maintain Reserves mostly in their own countries or small amounts in a few other countries as *quid pro quo* for reserves maintained by other G-7 countries.

Although in US Dollar terms Indian gross GNP is 11th and *per capita* GNP is 162nd in the world but in "Labour Output equivalent of gross GNP (GNP divided by the Statutory Minimum Hourly Wages for Unskilled Labour of the respective country)", it occupies the first place in the world and about three times that of the super developed mightiest economy of the world, i.e. USA.

In terms of Productivity, as defined as the ratio of 'Output to Input', Indian labour, including Indian agriculturists, are the most efficient in the world.

USA consumes about 17 times more 'Commercial Energy (Kg of Oil Equivalent)' per capita as compared to India.

USA is the least efficient user of energy and the criminal Polluter of the Environment, since it releases 20 times more "Carbon Dioxide Emissions Per Capita Metric Tons" as compared to India.

India produces about six times more "GDP Per Unit of Energy Use (Per Kg of Oil Equivalent)" compared to USA.

USA consumes about 33 times more 'Electric Power (Kilowatt Hours) per capita' compared to India

ENSURING INDIAN POVERTY

In spite of these efficiencies of ordinary Indians, management of Indian economy has been *very Bad* all along! It is apparent that external sector was managed in such a way that all benefits flowed to USA (and the western nations) at the cost of Indians. Thus the comparison of Indian "GDP Deflator (Ratio of Current to Constant Price GDP)" with America shows that whereas, in 1980-90 decade, Indian 'GDP Deflator' was just about double of that of USA (Indian being 8.0 to USA's 4.2), in the decade of 1990-99, Indian position drastically worsened, it being almost five times that of USA (India's worsened to 8.6 to USA's improved position of 1.8). The decade of Indian liberalisation (1990-99) [the period dominated by the so-called administration and economic giants like Sarvashri Yashwant Sinha, Manmohan Singh and Chidambaram], being a period of unmitigated gloom!

India saves and invests more than the Americans. Thus 'Gross Domestic Saving (% of GDP 1999)' in India was 20% to USA's 17%. and 'Gross Domestic Investment (% of GDP in 1999)' in India was 24% to USA's 19%.

But the most telling Statistics unwittingly provided by the WB is that the economic activity in USA is funded by outsiders like the supplicant Indians. Thus "Domestic Credit provided by Banking Sector: % of GDP 1999", it is 170.1% in USA, whereas, it is only 44.9% in India. Even China has almost three times more (130.4% of GDP) from Banking Sector.

India maintains all its Foreign Exchange (FE) Reserves in foreign countries, mostly in USA (and that also in private Banks and not in government Treasuries). USA and others utilize these reserves as any other ordinary deposits and the USA and other such developed countries only benefits from Indian FE reserves. We have already noted above, as to how US banking sector helps their domestic sector with the funds received as reserve from dependent countries like India!

Data given above also shows that "Income Velocity of Money (i.e. GDP versus Money in Circulation)" is less than 'Unity' in America and in most other G-7 countries. Notwithstanding this experience from developed countries and not withstanding the fact that Income Velocity of Money is still more than 'Unity' in India, Indian RBI and Ministry of Finance (MoF) insists on keeping very little money in circulation and forecloses adequate GDP growth. Although it is a well established fact that with M3 (Broad Money) growth limited to 15%, only 3% to 5% GDP growths have been achieved over the years, RBI (in order to pass on the advantage to America and other developed countries) maintained tight monetary policy and thereby thwarted adequate GDP growth. India is not monetizing the potential GDP growth! India follows a very very self-defeating currency and monetary policy. In case India really wants 10% or so GDP growth rate, money supply must grow to around 30% or 50% to 400%. Since Income-Velocity of Money is still above one, more money supply can only lead to more GDP growth! Indian economists are loathe to accept this, as they are afraid additional money supply will also go to sectors which gives least Income-velocity of Money, viz. Infrastructure/ Import-intensive sectors which already have liquidity surplus! India follows an allocatory monetary policy, whereby some sectors can starve of funds and other sectors can have Liquidity surplus! More funds get allocated to the sectors, which give least Income-Velocity of Money! Peripheral and indirectly relevant sectors always get comparatively better allocations! Defence force personnel gets a pittance compared to the finance ministry. There is no theoretical, practical, analytical, economic basis or argument for keeping limited money supply and starving different sectors of essential financial support. RBI/MoF failed to provide financial support to the Potential GDP growth. Their allocatory policies ensured 'Liquidity Surplus' and 'Liquidity Starvation' simultaneously. RBI/MoF ensured excessive money supply to the inefficient (i.e. where the 'Income Velocity of Money' is less than Unity and Capital-Output ratios are very poor) sectors, like the so-called foreign-funded Infrastructures, Open Cast Mining, IT, Modern Manufacturing, Petrochemical, Road Transportations and foreigner dominated Services sectors etc. and starved the Public and Social sectors, Defence, Railways, Underground mining etc. which invariably turn in better Income Velocity of Money.

India keeps its FE Reserves abroad and is always begging for some FE investment and gloats over when some foreign investment comes in. Economy managers never spell out that foreigners and enterprising and well connected Indians (with cover from the requisite state authorities) only re-circulate a small fraction of the Indian FE kept as Reserve in their Banking system. Foreigners impose exorbitant interest charges on the basis of the 'Ratings' of their own Rating Agencies for the deposits for which they pay a pittance as interest to India.

Another source of exploitation of India by foreigners has been conveniently made available by the Indian Economy Managers. RBI and Indian Banks are authorized (by some vested interests, obviously) to only hold a few millions Dollars (i.e. FE) at any time and the excess is required to be transferred to US or other such foreign Banks within 24 hours or so. Thus, a foreigner need only bring in a small amount of FE and then repeatedly re-circulate the initial amount by making arrangements with the American Bank which is the "Correspondent" Bank of the Indian Bank. Our Ministers and economy managers are either ignorant of this or are a party to this charade of FDI or foreign investment, which are only 'Paper Investment', so far as Indian economy is concerned. After government authorities permitted importers, exporters and some businessmen to park their FE earnings or ECB (external commercial borrowings) etc. abroad, this channel of diversion of Indian wealth has increased manifold. No wonder, with the introduction of ECB, Indian foreign indebtedness and distress level in the economy has increased by order of magnitudes.

RBI and MoF are quite oblivious of the fact that "Incremental GDP versus Investment" is always better for Public Utilities and other Public Corporate Enterprises as compared to Private Corporate Sector.

Our economy managers are always gloating over the fact of large IT sector Exports, but always forgetting to mention the even larger corresponding Imports. Further, the great IT Super Power in South Asia collects the least per hourly rate for their professionals. *Business Today* Magazine (28 October 2001 issue) has quoted that Billing rate by Indian organizations varies from $ 22-32 per hour, corresponding figures for Japan $ 90, Australia $ 50 and Singapore $ 40. Indian organizations have been paying salary rate of just $ 2 per hour, whereas Japan has been paying $ 19-27; Singapore etc. from $ 12-19: even South Korea and Malaysia pay better than India, from $ 6-9 per hour. Incidentally, Statutory Minimum Hourly Wages for Unskilled Labour in America (where Indian IT specialists have mostly been working so far) is $ 6 per hour (in 2007). No wonder the super rich IT labour exporters in India have always been in the forefront for ensuring continuous devaluation of the Rupee; otherwise, they will not get away by paying Slave rate of wages to the super-skilled Indian IT specialists.

It is high time Indian policy makers convince themselves that America will never stop immigration of super-skilled IT specialists or BPO (Business Process Outsourcing). All the noises which American entities are making is mere posturing to cut back on Indian Billing rate further, as the economics of these two businesses are so profitable for the developed countries (of course, totally counter-productive and costly for their populace) that they cannot afford to let go of these. Indian IT exporters have already started cutting back on payments to specialists. Their position will be seriously compromised if India at any time tries to up-value the Rupee. No wonder, market intervention of RBI has always been directed to keep the Rupee-Dollar exchange rates adverse for India. The market rumour is that market interventionist's gain to the extent of $ 3-5 millions per Paisa devaluation of the Rupee as India loses several hundred million dollars per Paisa of devaluation. The poor can wait and national security be damned!

Our IT exporters are freely giving away the 'Source Codes' along with the dirt-Cheap softwares and our importers do not get the Source codes for their super-costly engineered Softwares. IT manpower is and is treated as 'bonded' or 'indentured' labour only; of course, some private parties benefit from this arrangement. IT Ministry was requested to form a dedicated "Source Code Holding Organization"[9], but that suggestion was treated with undeserved neglect.

Supply of cheap software after massive imports of IT products, leads to double capture of India. India pays heavily for its IT Imports. With the help of cheap Indian software, America and other developed countries can comprehensibly control all facets of Indian life. Although vested interests are crowing that India is a great IT power in the world, the fact is, and this has all along been known to leaders, that India is one of the least developed country, even inferior to Malaysia, Thailand, Singapore, Korea, Indonesia and et al (puny countries in terms of economic and human resources) so far as IT production and usage is concerned. The great Indian IT entrepreneurs, IT and management whiz-kids have ensured, in connivance with the power elite and permanent bureaucracy, that India remains a backyard so far as IT environment is concerned. The compulsion was that export of natural beings (that is, super-skilled or unskilled Indians for sustaining and servicing the economy of the super developed country) had to be maintained. After all, slavery, having proved uneconomical, a more sophisticated substitute was necessary for the labour-short, in fact, super-inefficient but with very high animal and functional intelligence and military preponderance from the beginning, super power. Indians, since independence in 1947, have fitted the bill admirably. Have any economists ever noticed that Indian Rupee's down-slide relative to the US dollar started in earnest since the so-called independence and accelerated from the time direct British control over Indian economy ended?

FDI: In 1998, India got a little less than $ 3 Billion, China got a little less than $ 44 Billion and USA got about $ 2 Trillion.

Subsidies and other current transfers (% of total expenditure of Government): Although, our economy managers moan the great subsidy burden on the government, the real picture is different as seen by World Bank. In 1997, subsidy and other current transfers were 40% for India (a decrease from 43% in 1990) and 60% for USA (an increase from 50% in 1990)!

Social Services: % of total expenditure of Central Government on Social services, 1998: Capitalist America spent 53.8% (up from 43.4% in 1990) as against expenditure of 9.2% (up from 8.1% in 1990) by Socialist India! In spite of these facts, economy managers and media-savvy personnel are constantly haranguing the Government in India to raise the cost of social services accessible by the poor and low income-earners! No wonder social services are in complete disarray in India.

India collects very little Direct Taxes, as the Taxation is highly regressive. As per World Bank, high Income earners (top 20% of the population) capture about 46% of GNP (i.e. about $ 200 Billion in 1999, with a Tax liability of about $60 Billion at 30% peak rate of taxation). But these high Income-earners actually pay less than $ 3 Billion of tax only (thereby resorting to massive, apparently legal, tax non-disclosure or evasion). Our economy managers are turning a blind eye to this and are busy bringing petty traders etc. into the tax (i.e. harassment) net and busy inflating the fiscal deficit!

Liberalization and economic reforms have been counter-productive on the FE front so far. After that Mondal Messiah (the unrecognized Father of Economic Reforms) initiated his LREP (Long Range Economic Plan), the Net Inflow of FE started going down. In 1988, the Net of all flows was a positive Inflow of about Rs.1000 crores. In 1992 the Net Inflow became Zero and by the time the great recognized economic reformer relinquished office in 1995, it became a net OUTFLOW of about Rs. 900 Crores. This trend is continuing with greater vigour. Net Outflow of FE in conjunction with massive devaluation of the Rupee is having a crippling effect on the Indian Economy.

It has been reported (*HT*, New Delhi, 25 Oct 2006, *HT Business*, page 20; "FDI outflow may exceed inflow") that FDI outflow was $ 10 billion due to FE investments abroad by Indian private corporations, whereas, total FDI received by India during Jan-July 2006 was a mere $ 4.74 billion. It is the doyens of private sector who are mortgaging Indian future to the foreigners. We would have welcomed foreign investments abroad by Indian entities if the investments were in Indian Rupee by export of Indian manufactured goods and high value added services. It really needs a dedicated economist's mind to comprehend the logic of begging for FDI abroad (and consequently give innumerable concessions to foreign inimical entities) and simultaneously making outward FDI investments abroad by profiteers of private business. India is a net loser in such investments.

Much vaunted steps of "Divestment", by sucking out liquidity from the market, VRS (Voluntary Retirement Scheme), by paying out for not working and encouraging wrong investment avenues, running down of the PSUs, thereby undervaluing the investments made therein and increasing the run on the public finances, excessive allocation to so-called Infrastructure facilities, thereby allowing high-cost import and killing of Indian job-market, excessive brain-drain and body–shopping, virtual Slave-trade by Software companies, allowing excessive high-cost Imports by IT sector, much above their much vaunted Export performance, etc. - is acting as massive disincentive for job-creation in India.

Example of the gospel truths assumed to be very much applicable for India by the leaders and economists (the most despised lot in India) can be summarized as follows:

a) India is economically backward because Indians are not exerting enough!

b) Some bold decisions, of cutting the t's or dotting the i's of the present economic policies, will make honey and butter to flow in abundance in India, given some more time and if the indolent poor could bear some more pains for some more time!

c) India has no option ('TINA') but to follow the leads given by American Federal Reserve Systems or by American advisers!

d) Money supply in the Indian economy is sufficient! (*In spite of evidence to the contrary*), India does not need sufficient Currencies Per Capita! It is of no significance that a small country like UK used (in mid 90s) 23.7 Tons of Currency Notepaper per million populations, whereas India used about 15 Tons of currency notepaper per million populations! To Indian power-elite it is of no economic significance that per capita money supply is much higher in UK than in India. Japan and particularly USA, has much higher currency supply per capita, but Indians should not bother as American advisers say that higher currency supply is bad for Indian economy!

e) Constant Devaluation of the Rupee is good for Indian economy and value of Rupee must be adjusted for comfort of the Dollar!

f) Since Indians are poor, they need less per capita Resources and other supports, such as, less of per capita Customs Duty, per capita BOP (Balance of Payment), food, electricity, or covered accommodation, doctors/nurses, hospital-beds, drugs supply, teachers, engineers, scientists, professionals etc., to name a few!

g) Standard economic parameters, like, Sectoral or Gross Income-Velocity of Money, some sort of relationship between External and Internal Purchasing Power of national currency, Statutory minimum hourly wages of Unskilled Labour, Productivity (Output-Input Ratio) in different sectors, etc., need not be rigorously taken into account in India while taking economic decisions!

h) Though Centrally Planned economy is bad, central/RBI allocatory money/resource supply to different sectors is very much required!

I) America and western countries cannot help but impose crippling Denial/Control/Sanctions regimes against India from time to time and India is duty-bound to proclaim that these do not badly hurt India! India must not erect any such Denial/Control/Sanctions regimes against the USA or other western countries or their entities, as those might help India directly or indirectly!

This sort of mindset has permitted the power-elite to give effect to a policy-set which has thrown up the aberrations in the Indian economy, an illustrative example of which can be summarized as follows:

Unquestioning acceptance by India of American violation of the Basic tenets of Breton Woods Agreement, viz.

i) Par value of Dollar with respect to Gold Not ® not being maintained by America and America successfully transferring the Dollar devaluation load to Indian Rupee, whereby Indian Rupee suffers but

Dollar thrives! US Dollar was to maintain $34 = 1 troy oz Gold. (1945: IMF Articles of Agreement effective. Par values established for all members based on gold value of US Dollar on 1 July 1944 (o.888671grammes of fine gold). 1 oz of gold is now selling at around 700-800 Dollars, almost fifteen to twenty five fold devaluation, the amount of devaluation which Indian Rupee is facing vis-à-vis Dollar! USA has been able to transfer the burden of devaluation and mismanagement of their economy and polity to unfortunate countries like India. India leads the pack of nations carrying the white men's burden!

ii) Although Dollar is the Reserve currency, India is not allowed to transact dollar directly or directly deal with US treasury!

iii) America has prevented Indian Banks from directly participating in American Banking Clearing System!

iv) Prevented India (and, of course, some other backward and supplicant countries) from carrying out FE arbitrage!

v) Enforced on India (through IMF/WB) a FE-management regime in which any amount of devaluation of Rupee is possible but no UP-valuation (more than a few fractional percentage points)!

Generation of jobs is predicated on a growing economy. A collapsing economy (as evidenced by sale of public assets and forcible retirement, unannounced retrenchments and shrinking of manufacturing bases) cannot generate growing rate of employment, if there is no intention of changing the basically anti-national paradigm of planning or economic policy thrusts. Indian economy cannot grow unless it breaks out of the American economic control and follows independent monetary/fiscal, currency and gold control systems.

INDIAN ENTREPRENEURS AND FDI

In this context we are examining closely an FDI deal by Tata Empire. We want to clarify that Tatas may not be the worst case, but Tatas have long experience of land-grabbing. There is, of course a significant difference with other land grabbers in that they never violate or bend any laws or rules – they just get the administration and ruling political establishment to change or amend the constitution, laws or rules as required! Land grabbing has continued with more ferocity in independent India with the help of suitably reformed and gratified governments of different persuasions – capitalist, centrist or communist. Another unique thing about Tata Empire is that its headquarters are in coastal western India, but its depredations are vigorous in resource-rich eastern India – particularly, in the dispossessed states of Bihar, Orissa and West Bengal. Violent protests had broken out in West Bengal and Orissa in 2006 and 2007 but Tatas are unfazed. They ought to be, because in case of land grabbing in Singur of West Bengal, the communist government is funding the so-called industrialization ("Tatas land windfall gain from Singur deal", *The Economic Times*, New Delhi, Wednesday, 21 March 2007), even though the government has acquired the land by giving pittance as compensation to the poor farmers. Tatas can call the shots with any state or central government; they have been able to acquire enough assets, wealth, political and economic clout from British days to soften up any state or central government. Poor 'Yukos' (of Russia), they could have taken some lessons from the Tatas, who have been able to build up a reputation of being the best in labour relations, albeit at the cost of poor of India.

We consider that such land acquisition was unconstitutional and we beg Supreme Court to either recall the decision of the then SC on Zamindari Abolition Act or strike down West Bengal government decision on land usurpations (reminiscent of colonial practices). The court ought not to allow the SC decision to exist in records when West Bengal government is blatantly flouting constitutional right to property (Article 300A) without any let or hindrance from the judicial system. A two judge bench of SC (in September 2008) refused to take action on a PIL regarding land usurpations on the plea that Parliament should consider such issues.

We happened to examine the Corus deal closely as interesting data on this deal are on hand. We always hold that it is for the public investigation and regulatory authorities to protect Indian national interests, which they are constantly failing to do.

Some interesting snippets brought out in this news item are:

- Tata Steel acquired US-based Energy Brands for $677 million
- Tata Steel bought Singapore's Natsteel for $486 million
- Tata Coffees acquired Eight O'Clock coffee for $220 million
- Of course, others are active as well: Ranbaxy paid $324 million for Romanian pharma firm Terapia earlier this year (2006).
- Of course, the newspaper forgot to mention much extensive exposure abroad of Reliance group of companies – of both the siblings!

None of these great Indian enterprises or their still greater and noble entrepreneurs are aware that when they strengthen the manufacturing facilities abroad, they are delivering the death penalty to Indian industries and businesses, which are already languishing to the point of collapse. The enthusiasm with which investments abroad are being embraced by the Indian elite, it seems they (like the rats) have premonition that India is doomed and are in a hurry to be the first ones to leave the sinking ship.

Newspapers in India (for example, *The Economic Times*, New Delhi, 21 October, 2006, Page 1) ran Banner headlines something like:

- "Tatas take over UK national icon (Corus)
- $8-b deal vaults Tata Steel to fortune 500 club"

This deal is unique in many respects. A complex funding arrangement has been made for this deal. The Tata group is raising over $10bn for the Corus deal (final deal was at more than $12 Billions). Of this, 8.04bn will go in buying out the shares, and the balance will go towards refinancing loans of Corus. Indian public sector banks may take a lesson, as these banks refinance loans mostly gratis, in the fear of losing all loaned amounts through the mechanism of NPA (Non Performing Assets), as Indian industrialists and businessmen consider running up NPA as their birthright. This entire financing structure is broken up into two parts - $3.5-3.8bn infusion from Tata Steel and another $5.6bn through a leveraged buyout structure. (If you don't understand what it means, rest assured common people of India will carry the can)! Tata Steel is putting in $2bn (whose money?) as its contribution into the Singapore based (why Singapore, why not India?) SPV (god only knows what Special Purpose Vehicles mean, except, possibly, wheeling dealing), Tata Steel Asia Holdings and thence to UK SPV, Tata Steel UK. Newspapers reported (*ET*, 21 October, 2006, page 14, with the heading, "And now, to raise the funds.......") that Tatas were raising very high cost loans (of course, depending on the perspectives). The interest rate on the senior term loan is reported to have a spread of 200-225 basis points above Libor, while that for the high yield loan would be at around 400-450 basis points over Libor.

Whereas, Tatas in one deal with Corus could commit national wealth to the extent of Rs. 50, 000 crores, with the government encouraging them along, the PM offered a few hundred (or is it a few thousands?) crores of Rupees of relief package to agriculturists with such a thick envelope of administration and with so much of conditionalities that suicides continued unabated; but media lost interest as the PM lost interest in such a minor issue, when he had to deal with more serious issues of Corus and many others like that! One central cabinet Minister and the Chief Minister of the state where maximum suicides of farmers took place had the temerity to describe the farmers as lazy, indolent people, as these great characters could not countenance offering of any concession to the poor or agriculturists!

Ratan Tata, Chairman of Tata group of companies, clarified the purpose of the deal as, 'We are looking for strategic fit'. (Front page news of *ET*, 21 October, 2006). The nature of 'fit' has been explained in the newspaper to mean Tatas will be supplying from India steel slabs and raw steel (i.e. after converting the iron ores in essentially ecologically and environmentally damaging conditions in the lax regulatory environment in India) to Corus for high value addition, under ecologically clean environment and principally to meet the European/US needs and supply back to India at exorbitant prices, thanks to very adverse FE exchange rates (which, under present dispensations, can only mean ever worse exchange rate) and there being no rational pricing formula.

The strategic and sordid dimensions of TATA-CORUS deal and the real purpose of the 'fit' was revealed in a news analysis given in a mainstream newspaper (*HT 2 Business & World*, Page 23, 04 December, 2006) under the heading

"Global Steel M&A still hot as input costs pinch

Raw material control turns business driver"

The newspaper elaborately explained the purpose of 'vertical' and 'horizontal' consolidation of steel business in the world is control of raw materials sources. The paper reports, "The consolidation will allow the steel producers to have a greater control over the demand–supply balance and ensure stability in steel prices". Nature of 'stability' has been explained by quoting the example of Arcelor-Mittal which closed two of its units in Europe citing annual maintenance needs, but industry analysts saw in this the accompanying gain of controlling inventory levels in the continent" for ensuring high profitability. After quoting the instances of manipulation of 'HR steel coil prices' to make for abnormal high prices of more than $600 per ton, the newspaper concluded, "Therefore, whenever HR (hot rolled) coil prices go below $400 per ton, the players who are not integrated will suffer losses". Liberalized government of India has ensured that private steel producers have captive mines, and their profitability is always ensured. In case of public steel producers, private interests are ensured through Mines-Mafias, existence of which is always denied by responsible ministers, of even cabinet rank.

Tata's deal can only hold provided Indian labour keep getting abysmally low wages. Also India will have to continue to be supplier of raw materials or low value products to Corus in UK, as otherwise this deal will collapse. How neatly Tatas have organised perpetuation of Indian poverty and backwardness. From the funding arrangements elaborated above, it will be clear that Tatas will be scrapping the bottom of their financial and company barrels and will be required to scrape some more barrels of public sector banks and public banks, FI(s), IDBI, ICICI, SBI (State Bank of India, a public sector behemoth faithfully serving the interests of private big businesses in India and abroad); other public sector banks, when they do not contribute directly, will give investment reinsurance and other secondary covers. If the deal goes sour, public banks and FI(s) will take the maximum hits, like in the case of that infamous Enron deal. Incidentally, Ratan Tata was heading (in 2007 also) the Investment Commission constituted by the Government of India. We are not surprised that such a deal, so disadvantageous to India, could be conceived! A third world country, rich in raw materials and labour willing to work with slave-rate of wages, like India, fitted the bill perfectly. Tatas walked in where an industrial angel like LN Mittal dreaded to venture! *ET*, New Delhi, 18 Nov, 2006, reported.

Chairman of Tata group Ratan Tata with Corus chairman James Leng

HOW THEY STACK UP

	Tata Steel	Corus	Combined
Sales	5,007	19,367	24,374
EBIDTA	1,480	1,962	3,442
Net Profit	840	861	1,701
Crude Steel Production*	5	18	23
Current M-Cap	6,510	8,227	-

Source: Tata Steel and Corus ($M) *(MT)

Heavy Metal

Top Global Steel Producers

Company	Production
Arcelor-Mittal	109.7
Nippon Steel	32.0
POSCO	30.5
JFE	[illegible]
Tata-Corus	23.0
Baosteel	[illegible]
US Steel	19.3
Nucor	[illegible]
Riva Acciao	17.5
ThyssenKrupp	[illegible]

Source: IISI, www.etintelligence.com

From above data two things ought to have been clear to all that: a) Corus was in a better position to take over Tatas, b) what is the secret of Tata's vaunted efficiency. Whereas, production in Tata is less than one-third, but gross profit and net profits are astronomically high. Even economists with minimum visual acuity should be able to discern that Tatas (like all other businessmen in India) are fleecing the helpless consumers. The market capitalization analysis also tells a sordid tale of betrayal of common people. Massive m-cap has only been possible due to massive investment of public funds, including FE accruals (in whatever nomenclatures conveniently assigned) in market for converting public money into private profit. Do you still wonder why common Indians are so poor? Do you get an idea why Indian GDP and growth impulses are so low? Do you still hold the fond hope that economic reforms will some day deliver the goods? The possibility of 'clash of interests (and propriety) never bothered the government of Dr. Manmohan Singh or the industrialist concerned. That all rules and regulations were tailored to suit the requirements of TATA Empire and other industrial empires is vividly brought out in a news item:

- "Tatas line up $ 1-billion exchangeable bonds
- Bonds To Give Access To TCS Stock On Conversion,"
- *The Economic Times,* Delhi, 3 May, 2007.

The accompanying write-up clarified matter somewhat. "...If the group decides to go ahead with its plan, this will be the first time an Indian company will issue exchangeable bonds to investors". It adds, "They are therefore somewhat different from ordinary convertible debentures. .....If the legislation is passed this year, there is likelihood that the group will issue the bonds in next few months".

This is an instance of how the government can anticipate even outlandish wishes of the industrialists, even though they fail miserably to prevent starvation deaths or suicides by indigent farmers and the poor in Kalahandi or Vidharva and other regions!

After news of Tatas deal broke in the newspapers, others have gone public with their various hare-brained diabolical (but profitable proposition for them) schemes at the cost of Indian well being, national interest and national security

Samples of other stories of betrayal of Indians are given hereunder.

"Exposure to Troubled GM & Ford Puts US Cos out of Focus

Indian auto parts cos. go shopping in Europe" (*ET*, New Delhi, 20 July, 2006)

More Indian labour will lose jobs and more Indians will commit suicide (of course, thereby the businessmen and others are helping in population control in India). How many are aware that suicide deaths due to pecuniary circumstances is more than deaths due to AIDS in India, but more money is spent on AIDS control than on lightening the debt-burden of the Indians, especially of the farmers.

"IT major plans to continue with inorganic growth" (*ET*, New Delhi, 20 July, 2006)

The report referred to ** (a software firm – i.e. a slave trader and manager) plans for focusing on growth through acquisitions abroad, (instead of investing in India by having proper facilities relevant for India). Government of India having agreed, albeit without a proper law, to allow private entities to squander hard earned FE abroad to strengthen manufacturing facilities abroad for strengthening foreign countries, no one should expect any patriotism from such software behemoths.

This is a sample narration of exploitation of common Indians by legal means helpfully provided by the power elite. There are other innovative means of exploitation.

TRANSFER PRICING

Transfer pricing is a system under which related but separate companies assign prices for goods and services transferred from one company to the other. Because these are negotiated prices, asset-stripping of a company by its parent or major share-holder(s) is possible and happens in un-regulated markets.

There was a well-publicized transfer pricing case in Pakistan. 'Pakistan Lawsuit: Transfer Pricing at the heart of Pfizer Case', *MINT* (magazine), July 24, 2007, reported this. In Pakistani case, 'Ernst and Young', which was asked to examine Pfizer practices, noted huge mark-ups by parent Pfizer for its Partner in Pakistan, in some cases as much as 70 times. For example:

	Charged to Pakistan By Pfizer	Market price at the time
Amlodepine besylate	$ 30,000 per Kg	$ 500
Piroxicam	$ 8750	$ 125
Vibramycin	$ 700	$ 65

It is safe to assume that all companies –– indigenous or

foreign — carry out transfer price manipulations/frauds as a matter of routine and the governments of all the countries of the world are fully aware of this. The very fact that entrepreneurs and businessmen of India and other countries have multiple (or innumerable) separate companies, sometimes in the same premises, is to hoodwink the people about the honesty of their purpose, which is anything other than that! Indian Government has given some convenient techniques for filching the common consumers by their 'arms length (or is it leg length)' norms of transfer pricing and all involved have heartily joined in the kill. One of the main sources of profit of businessmen in India is transfer price manipulations, though Indian Government and private enterprises have many other tricks in their bags of entrepreneurship.

Above cited *MINT* also reported that in Nigeria the government is planning a lawsuit claiming $ 7 Billion damages for illegal drug trials on children. In India, the Government has liberalized all drug trials, so that nothing is illegal any more.

FISCAL DEFICIT (Aamnie, Aamnie?)[10]

A lot of officials and the committed economists are beating their breasts on the fiscal deficits in India. The prognosis is that the fiscal deficit can only go on increasing, if the present set of policy-thrusts in economy is to be continued.

Fiscal deficit in layman terms is the difference between government earnings and expenditures, assuming, of course, that what the government does is not essentially unethical, illegal or unnecessary! In Indian context, the definition of Fiscal deficit is quite a flexible matter depending on whichever items of receipts, expenditures or Outgo's from and into the government till is counted or excluded. The items of income and expenditures for calculation of fiscal deficit have been changed several times by several finance ministers and no universally accepted definition of fiscal deficit is really available or recognized. Again, it is the government and big business, which can start the year with a budgeted fiscal deficit.

Thus fiscal deficit is warning to the discerning people that the worst can be expected. That the common man and even the 'protectors of the proletariat' (the celebrated Communists) never seriously protest the fiscal deficit, goes to show how ignorant and credulous the people can be! It is forgotten by most of the people most of the time that: "You can fool all the people all the time". It seems Indian people particularly can be kept fooled all the time, as an elite group of Indians think that legacy of foreign domination must be sustained at all costs. Fiscal deficit is a legacy of foreign domination and the continuing practice of passing on the benefits to the affluent at the cost of the common man. The bulk of the expenditures of the government are cornered (directly or indirectly) by the affluent through different budgetary heads. Social or military sectors or items of mass or popular consumption always get a short shrift or is accorded token recognition only and token budgetary support. An allocatory banking and fiscal policy shut out the social and public consumption sectors from essential fiscal support. It is support to the social and military sector that is ultimately shown up as fiscal deficit because after upkeep of Government apparatus and incentives and impetus through Government investment for support to private industry and business, hardly any funds are available for the social or military sectors, as Government is still faithfully following essentially same British colonial policies on budgetary support to different sectors of the economy.

Public officials, committed economists/intelligentsia are always bemoaning the subsidy to agricultural and rural sectors, but it is never highlighted that the subsidy is actually paid to the secondary manufacturing (fertilizer, for example) and industrial/business sectors and not directly to the agriculturists or primary producers! Even in rural sector, the bias is in favour of the cash crop at the cost of food production. No wonder, rate of growth in food production is lower in the decade of 90s as compared to the decade of the 80s. No wonder, per capita calorie supply has gone down since the grip of Liberalization tightened in the decade of 90s. Lack of growth of food production has been a bonanza for the exporter/importer/business class, bureaucrats and ministers, as then government unabashedly goes about massive imports of wheat, sometimes as much as five million tons or so at exorbitant prices, as in 2006-7. The domestic wheat/rice growers are forced to sell their produce to the government or traders at most non-remunerative prices, always well below the international prices at the relevant time. Even Karl Marx could not imagine how venal the so-called popular democratic governments would turn out be in 21st Century AD in exploiting their toiling masses and passing on the largesse to the affluent unashamedly. Is anyone entitled to ask the governments why they do not treat the agriculturists at par with producers and marketeers of Petro-products in respect of fund availability, profitability, pricing of the inputs, raw materials and products? We presume agriculturists will have to wait for 4th millennium or till the fury of Kalki arrive!

Conventional wisdom dictates that public finance (of government, banking sector, financial institutions, foreign financial institutions, non-banking finance companies etc.) will be applied preferentially into those sectors which are most productive. In economic terms, those sectors are considered productive which fulfill two basic criteria, viz.: a) Generate more employment for indigenous people, b) Generate the highest "Income Velocity of Money" (that is, give more GDP per unit of money supply).

In terms of employment and Income Velocity of Money, social sectors, railways, and defence are the most productive. On the other hand, import-dependent sectors, (to name a few: Infrastructure, IT, Oil/Naphtha-based Thermal Power, Modern manufacturing, Open Cast Mining, Services sectors) are inefficient - moderately to grossly – inefficiency being directly related to import-dependence and dependence on foreign funding. It is a surprising fact of life that public funds are applied preferentially to the most inefficient sectors. Thus, gross Income Velocity of money has continuously fallen since the commencement of liberalization. Even if all funding to social, Defence sectors and Railways is stopped, the fiscal deficit will not go away, but will accentuate further as the cushion provided by these beneficial sectors will then be removed.

Another criterion of economic efficiency is the savings Rate. In India all savings are made by the domestic sector. Private corporate sector is notorious for not saving enough. This sector was saving even much less than the (much-maligned) Public Corporate sector prior to onset of liberalization around 1984. Savings in private corporate sector is more than balanced by non-performing assets run up with public sector banks and financial institutions, under direct patronage of the government. Private corporate sector performance was so scandalous that Government economists have now started combining the private corporate sector data along with domestic sector so that public corporate sector can be pilloried. Annual Economic Surveys of Finance Ministry and RBI are now fudging the saving rate data so that no accusing finger can be raised against the private corporate sector.

Again, there is another measure of economic efficiency is the criteria of "Incremental GDP vs. Investments" in different sectors. Till the 7th Five-Year Plans, this data was being separately shown for public and private sectors. 7th Five-Year Plan document (Vol. I page 32) gave data for different broad categories, viz., Mining/Quarrying, Manufacturing, Railways/Transportation and Agriculture/ Animal Husbandry etc. This document gives very interesting and unconventional data. Incremental GDP vs. Investment is uniformly bad (rather pretty bad) in private corporate sector compared to public corporate sectors. No wonder such data has been missing from subsequent plan documents or economic surveys. Incidentally, private corporate sector gets the lion's share of the investible funds of the economy.

When private sector consumes more and produces less, the effect has to reflect somewhere and fiscal balance (in the shape of fiscal deficit) goes into a tizzy.

The most telling factor of the economy is the "Employment vs. Investment". RBI and Economic Survey blandly give statistics about the employment vs. investment but this issue never comes for any serious critical comment. Private corporate sector, after gobbling up almost all investible funds has been showing negative rate of growth of employment generation.

It is not easy for average Indians to understand the logic of the RBI and Government restricting the money supply to around 15%. It is, of course, forgotten conveniently by the power elite that all developed countries and even the "Pussy Cat" (the so-called Tiger) economies of Asian countries have per capita money supplies much more than that of India. The real fact is that money supply only caters for the requirements of industry and big business. High (rational) GDP growth will automatically control inflation and fiscal deficit.

Any discussion on Indian economy starts and ends with the moan about lack of Rupee funds ("Where is the Money?"). Powers that be never explain what is the difficulty in putting more money in circulation for sectors where GDP/Investment ratio is high. When I mentioned to a FM that none of the highly developed countries of the world hold back GDP growth for lack of local currency, he could mumble something incoherently. I had a feeling he was also victim of "Advanced Gujralitis Syndrome" (AGS – a disease more dangerous than AIDS)[11]

Misutilisation of Rupee funds is being compounded by mismanagement of hard-earned Foreign Exchange assets of India. Whereas Indian entities are always hankering after foreign, our FE is being invested abroad (mostly in America) at nominal interest rates and then same FE is being borrowed back at much higher interest rates. Also an artificially low FE exchange rate is being maintained at the behest of IMF/

World Bank for benefiting the foreigners and Indian exporters and importers. This sort of management of FE is putting serious strain on Indian Fiscal balance. Further, Indian Government officials and intelligentsia, for reasons unexplained,

a) Do not monetize (in Rupee) the FE reserves

b) Do not bring the Gold held by the public into RBI reserve, nor monetize the 'Public Gold reserve'. A self-defeating scheme of gold deposit has been started for benefiting some banks and foreign "Hedging Agencies". This measure has further worsened the fiscal deficit.

c) Impose un-scientific self-defeating restrictions on FE accretion to Indian Banking and other sectors but allows free outflow of FE even to the extent that virtually free 'Capital Account Convertibility' is provided to foreign Banks and other foreign entities for converting their profits and surpluses earned in Rupees into FE although this facility is not available to average Indians.

d) Practise restrictive Banking Reforms whereby foreign Banks have a free run of the Indian economy, but Indian Banks operate in foreign countries (USA especially) by first depositing Dollars in American Banks. RBI and Indian officials are happy that Indian Banks act as subsidiary to American Banks while operating in foreign countries and lock up precious FE in foreign countries.

e) Unlike other independent Central Banks, our RBI (acting as a subsidiary, first of Bank of England and now of the American Federal Reserve System) do not carry out FE arbitrage. In fact, only American Banks carry out FE arbitrage on behalf of RBI and keep all the profits to themselves.

f) Whereas Indian Banks, like SBI etc. cannot directly participate in American "Banking Clearing System", but American Banks can fully participate in Indian

"Banking Clearing System". Thus, India has to pay in dollars as commission for getting clearing facility in Banks in America which facility American Banks are getting for free in India.

The pernicious effect of these policies is that Indian economy never benefits directly from FDI as the actual inflow of FDI is always a small percentage of our own "forced" investment abroad. Indian economy is always starving of Rupee funds. Further, in the name of making FDI, foreign entities capture sizable amount of Rupee funds thereby denying other Indian entities of Rupee funds and accentuating fiscal deficits.

The story of fiscal deficits reminds me of a story. A young unmarried Bengali girl went to the doctor for a check up. The doctor carried out a perfunctory check and enquired softly, "How did it happen?"

The girl demurely replied in Bengali, "Aamnie, Aamnie" ('just like that')!

The doctor exploded, "This is one thing that cannot happen without your connivance or knowledge"! Is fiscal deficit occurring without connivance or knowledge of our economy doctors?

DIVESTMENT

Private sector cannot be expected to delve in green-fields; hence, they are always eyeing the functioning public enterprises for take over at low price and earn immense profit. Our anguish and disgust at the mindless divestment was communicated (30 Aug 2002) to a very powerful cabinet minister of government of India, who is an acclaimed socialist and an erstwhile member of 'Socialist International'.

The heading of my letter was "PRAY INTERVENE, OTHERWISE DIVESTMENT WILL CRIPPLE THE COUNTRY". It seems our cry was in the wilderness!

"Newspapers have reported that you have taken a stand against so-called strategic sale of BPCL and HPCL (major oil distribution companies). The country was wondering when would socialist $$$ come alive to the looming dangers to the National Economy by the mindless pursuit of policies of Liberalization, Divestment, and VRS!

Municipal Corporation of Delhi Elections 2002 have confirmed the belief that: "Indians Vote with their Tummies". The MCD elections 2002 can be construed as giving a sample of the "Order of the Boot" to the ruling elite for their self-defeating management of national economy and civic affairs. Voters like to take pride in the Economy and National Security but the ruling combine has disappointed them thoroughly.

Conventional economic wisdom would specify that when the economy is in downswing and employment growth rate is falling, the Government would increase Investment for increasing employment. But the Government is just doing the reverse by simultaneously initiating Divestment of PSU's/ PSE's and providing for VRS (Voluntary Retirement Scheme). Government reduced Cash Reserve Ratio, CRR, and Statutory Liquidity Ratio, SLR, (contrivances to prevent profligacy of the banking sector) and increased fiscal deficits to increase the fund flow to the Private corporate Sector. By Divestment, the Government is taking away investible funds of the Private Sector, which in turn, is reducing the liquidity in the market and investment and job-creation opportunities. Also, in the name of 'Restructuring' before Divestment, the Ministry of Divestment has loaded the exchequer with the liabilities of the entities earmarked for divestment, as private sector was not willing to touch an outfit with all its liabilities. Thus, by divestment, the Government is left with the 'liabilities' and the ownership/control of the 'Assets' has passed on to the Private Sector. A more economically unviable measure could not have been thought of!

You could kindly ask him what the aim of Divestment is and see how he (***) fobs you off! [If he tells you about contribution by PSU's and PSE's to national exchequer, quote to him the Table 17 of World Development report 2000-2001- **In developed countries nothing is contributed** to exchequer by public enterprises, Indian PSU/PSE have all along been contributing 9% of GDP to the exchequer; **Labour**

efficiency - Indian Labour is most efficient in the world in terms of Output/Input Ratios: Indian Labour **consumes less than 4%** of his per capita production per year - foreign labour consumes about 20%; *Economic Times*, New Delhi, 01 Aug 2002 reports - **Labour gets lost in Reforms rush**: Cost of production goes up six fold but share of wages dip to 5.6% during 1989-2001 from about 11% earlier.

In terms of Employment vs. Investment, Output per labour, Output-vs.-Investment, Product Price etc., Public Enterprises beat Private Enterprises hands down! Many more such gory details of gross mis-management of Indian Economy (of course, published data of World Bank or the Capitalist Press being only considered) is available for your scrutiny, if you so desire! Some additional facts about divestment are given in the enclosure, which you may kindly read if you have the time and patience.

DIVESTMENT AND THE NATION

Divestment of public enterprises for private profiteering touches the core issues which are connected with economic and political survival of the nation, national security and constitutional propriety. You are aware that private entity is not recognized in the constitution, excepting individual's rights and liberties. Assigning of state enterprises to private entities and empowering these entities with sacrosanct punitive and sovereign powers of the state is a direct attack on the constitution. Specifically, ordinary Indians have following caveat on divestment:

a) Divestments (especially, foreign advised ones) have been a disaster so far as Soviet Union/Russian Federation is concerned. Production in Russian Federation is 25% now of what it was in 1992. India will face the same fate if Shri *** succeeds fully.

b) Divestment will increase Fiscal deficit instead of correcting it.

c) Divestment has never succeeded in any country where the national currency is highly overpriced internally and highly under-priced externally.

d) Divestment has never succeeded in any country where the National Central Bank (like RBI) has not got full freedom for Exchange Rate fixation or, for prevention of market manipulations or, where full FE Reserve is kept in Foreign Banks.

e) Divestment cannot succeed where the "Statutory Minimum Wage per hour for Unskilled Labour" is low (say, less than US $ 4 per hour).

f) Divestment cannot succeed where the full potential GDP is not monetized and where "Per Capita 'Money in Circulation' M3" is kept artificially low, as in India.

Divestment cannot succeed where public facilities and utilities are in disarray, as in India.

g) In the absence of favourable factors, divestment reduces the country to the status of Client State. National Security is invariably extremely adversely affected by divestment. Rump of Soviet Union (the Russian Federation) has been reduced from a Super Power to an Insignificant (virtually, Zero) Power!

h) Divestment cannot succeed where Trade Balance (Export/Import) is always negative with respect to major trading partners.

i) Powerful countries do not go for distress sale of PSU's (even below 'Reserve Price', where, even the co-called 'Reserve Price' is artificially set without any nexus with the total current market value of the assets or with respect to the capital already invested!).

j) All powerful countries like USA, UK, Germany and France give budgetary supports (both in Quantum and Percentage of Budgeted Expenditures) to the PSEs or public utilities, much in excess of what Indian Budgets do.

k) Countries that collect less than US $ 40 per capita in Customs Duty cannot benefit by divestment.

l) No article of the constitution permits divestment of state functions on non-state entities. You could use the good offices of the President of India to get an authoritative determination by the Supreme Court of India.

But these are not the economic criteria that the foreign advisors will consider or stipulate, as their aim is to do India in. But my interactions with Shri *** has convinced me that he will not stop or ponder, till he has achieved what has been "laid out for him!"

ACTION PLAN

Knowing that our power elite are always crying that 'There is No Alternative' (TINA) to their mischief, we drew up an action plan to show that 'There Are Many Alternatives' (TAMA). We could persuade some marginalized powerful people to send this action plan to all sorts of ruling elite. The outcome will be Zero. We are giving hereunder the action plan for consideration of the victims and of those who claim to be champions of the depressed and deprived, with an assurance that we shall not give up.

ACTION PLAN

TO CONTROL THE FISCAL DEFICIT AND

KICK-START THE INDIAN ECONOMY AND

ASSERT INDIA'S RIGHT TO INDEPENDENCE OF ACTION

(NON–INVASIVE NON–INTRUSIVE MEASURES)

BANKING REFORMS

1. Indians and foreigners should be permitted to deposit Rupee and FE in Indian Bank Accounts without being asked about the source of funds. The account will only be accessible to the account holder/

declared beneficiary/nominee/accredited attorney of the beneficiary (account holder) with an access code only.

2. TDS will be on withdrawals and not on deposits or Interest Incomes.
3. Only Indian Banks be permitted to carry out final transactions in Rupee. Foreign Banks or foreign entities handling Rupee funds or transacting Rupee should be required to deposit equivalent FE in "NOSTRO ACCOUNT" in authorized Indian Banks. This FE will be in RBI reserve and Banks will get accommodation in Rupee from RBI.
4. Foreign Banks will be permitted to take part in "Indian Banking Clearing System" as subsidiary of authorized Indian Banks only after paying suitable commission and other charges. Later foreign Banks may be authorized to directly take part in 'Indian Banking clearing System' after reciprocal facilities are provided to Indian Banks in foreign countries.
5. Repatriation of FE deposited in Banks will be freely allowed up to 75% or balance of FE deposit minus CRR and SLR, whichever is less, without concurrence of RBI. Remaining FE can be repatriated on closure of account, with concurrence of RBI.
6. Account holders will be allowed FE arbitrage facilities, as per their desire. Similarly, Indian Banks may carry out FE arbitrage without hedging, but without erosion of asset value to the detriment of the depositors or the country.

FE MANAGEMENT

7. All FE received in India or by Indian entities to be retained in Indian Reserve systems **in Indian soil only**. Stop further transfer of FE to America or to other foreign countries
8. Gradually withdraw all FE reserves (including SDR, ECB, and Gold) from foreign countries and keep these in Indian soil.

9. Commitment or other charges, commissions etc. to be paid *only after* the ECB, other loans, grants or any receivables have been credited in authorized Indian Banks in India.

FDI AND INVESTMENT ABROAD.

10. All FE brought in as FDI or in Indian Bourses or other foreign investments in India are to be deposited in authorized Indian Banks in Indian soil only. This FE will go into RBI reserve and Banks will get accommodation in corresponding amount of Rupee from RBI.

11. Only FE deposited in Indian Banks in India can be converted into "Equity contribution" in India by foreigners. FE expenditure in the donor or investing country or expenditures by the donor cannot be part of "Equity Contribution".

12. Foreigners will be allowed to freely repatriate declared profits and surpluses. This repatriation will be through export of Indian goods and services and not through repatriation of cash FE, as 'Capital Account Convertibility' is not available to Indians and, hence, cannot be claimed by foreigners.

13. Indians or Indian entities or foreign entities on behalf of Indians will be entitled to freely invest abroad in Rupee and not in FE, i.e. through export of Indian goods and services, technology, know-how, consultancy etc. No cash FE be permitted to be invested abroad under any circumstances by private or semi-private entities, except by national entities for furthering national purpose or national security. Privatized profit motive cannot be deciding factor in any foreign investment.

REFORM RBI

14. RBI to carry out all functions which a Central Bank or Reserve System carries out in USA / UK / France.

RBI must carry out FE arbitrage itself. RBI must exercise full control over FE exchange rate fixation.

15. RBI must hold in Indian soil all FE reserves, SDR, Gold and other international monetary instruments acquired by India. Investments or any deposits abroad must be in Indian Rupee only.

16. Redraft RBI Act of 1934 to bring it in line with the requirements of independent India.

17. RBI must immediately bring sanity in FE market. All FE receipts and mandatory or contractual payouts by Government of India or RBI will only be on "Purchasing Power Parity Exchange Rate" of Rupee relative to respective foreign currency. RBI will sell FE at "Market determined Exchange rate" provided that is above the PPP exchange rate. Private transaction in FE can only be in PPP exchange rate.

17. All Exports and Imports will be valued in PPP exchange rate for purposes of taxes/duties/subsidies etc.

GOLD DEPOSIT SCHEME

18. Gold deposit scheme in existence in a limited way needed to be expanded to include all household gold, especially ornaments, of middle class, 'not so affluent', families, who are already aware of the benefits of safe-keeping gold in Bank lockers and who will see the benefits of keeping their gold in Government/ RBI reserve through the Bank lockers, especially when the gold (ornament) will be retained in original form and they will also get liquidity. A full scheme on "Gold Locker and Banking System" is available with Shri Yashwant Sinha, the former FM, since 11 May 1998, and can be easily implemented.

19. Public gold accepted by Indian Banks must not be 'hedged' with any agency located outside India or whose head office is outside India.

20. Public gold must be held in RBI reserve to provide liquidity to Indian economy and it must not be hedged or pledged in any way with any foreign agency. This reserve of 'Public Gold' must not be used as a means of profiteering by banking sector.

These measures could easily be incorporated in the Budget 2002 proposals (or in subsequent budgets) and these would have drastically reduced the fiscal balance and improve the overall liquidity in Indian economy. The guiding principle should be that "Economic Reforms is for the benefit of the Indian people first and it must not be allowed to be dictated by foreign interests or their collaborators, as at present."

LIBERALIZED POVERTY

Market economy under the garb of economic reforms and liberalization was introduced in India in 1991 (but it had already displayed its dark countenance from 1984 under the stewardship of the then finance minister and that 'Mondal Messiah'). Indian economic problems multiplied by leaps and bounds in absolute and relative terms and increased progressively thereafter. We could not convince a single top leader of any of the political hues or any noble laureate or media-savvy economist to kindly read the economic surveys ritually published by the Government of India, Ministry of Finance, and compare the economic parameters of 1990 and with that of 2003. Our observation is that India ('Bharat Mahan' of Congress or the 'Shining India' of NDA) has deteriorated in majority of economic parameters or parameters which basically touch 80% of the population.

Nonchalance of great economists and charismatic leaders for low down (low earning) population is astounding but we shall analyze elsewhere in this book how this could come about. I am quoting hereunder a verbatim critique of liberalization written long back (1987) but seems to be equally pertinent today also.

FOR WHOM THE 'LIBERALISATION' BELL TOLLS[12]

The slogan of "Liberalization of the Economy" is in crescendo now. With Gorbachev's Russia and Deng's China embracing liberalisation as a central doctrine in their economic management, this word has assumed added significance for the Indian Economists and the political cheer-leaders with the committed industrialists chortling gleefully in the sidelines. Of course, another party, the toiling masses, are at a loss to know; what is being liberalized and for whose sake? These fundamental questions raised by the commoners bear closer scrutiny.

Competition and Technology

What is liberalization? As it has evolved over the last two years or so, liberalization has literally meant freedom to import whatever you like at whatever non-competitive basis without much question or scrutiny. Repetitive imports have been the order of the day and 'kit-culture' has been raised to the status of big 'entrepreneurship'. The bonanza has been so good that all sorts of foreign companies have got access to the Indian economy which they would normally not have, Liberalization is supposed to promote competition. It has only succeeded in promoting competitions in India amongst foreign firms.

Thus, in scooter and LCV (light commercial vehicles) and other vehicles, we are seeing multiplicity of collaborations with many 'duty-concessions' cadged by various stratagems where competition is virtually non-existent as the different companies have conveniently divided up the market amongst themselves. Can you imagine any prudent businessman starting an LCV line for production of a few thousand vehicles a year?

And where is the fabulous productivity of those developed countries, especially of Japan? A Maruti car should be considered as a running shame for India. Maruti's so-called fuel efficiency has been achieved by cutting down on structural weight, fitting toy-wheels and at the cost of structural safety and replaceability/repairability. Can you imagine this car running on the gutted roads of Indian cities/ villages other than in the Velvet roads of Delhi or Bombay? (of course, socialism has been brought in, as roads in these super metros are also in horrid condition now in 2009). Incidentally, money spent yearly on Delhi or Bombay for roads is often close to what is spent for a big state like Madhya Pradesh or Rajasthan.

Liberalizing the already Liberalized

So much for technology and competition. At another level, things are curiourser. Not many people will believe, but Indian economy has been extremely liberalized from the beginning. The public sector-private sector debate has always been a contrived device to keep public gaze fixed elsewhere. The aim of both the sectors have been identical - to convert public finance into private profit; only that private sector did it directly and public sector indirectly. How many know that the doyens of private business were at the top in most of the major public sectors in their formative years. The management structures, manpower policies, inventory control, financial and administrative apparatus were built up by these leading lights of private industry and these have been the mill-stone around the neck of the public sectors. Elites from private sector have been sitting in the Board of directors of Public Sector enterprises including RBI and other financial institutions and constantly trying to strangulate these, 'like the Old Man sitting on the shoulder of Sindabad, the Sailor'.

Look at the structure of plan expenditures. From pre-Independence days, it was known that food-security is most important for India. But agriculture (especially food production) always got the lowest deal in Plan and Private Sector expenditures. Even in 7th Plan, out of a total Plan outlay of Rs.1,80,000 crores, agriculture gets Rs.10,573.62 crores, i.e., 5.8% of the total allocation. Everyone knows agricultural products are unconscionably low priced but even then, agriculture provides near about 37% to the Gross

Domestic Product (GDP) in India. Thus, the sector which provides more than one-third of GDP gets less than one-sixteenth of the Plan allocation (Seventh Plan Vol. I, pages 26 to 29 refers). This has been broadly the picture in all previous plans. The bulk of the plan expenditure is in providing low cost infrastructure to the private sector. Thus, in current Plan, 30.45% of allocation is to be spent on energy which is mostly consumed by the private corporate sector and mostly by top 40% of the population. Petroleum gets more than Rs.12000 crores and most of this petroleum will be used by private sector and personal vehicle owners. Whereas, there has been a fillip to private car and two wheeler production, there has been no significant thrust for development of Public transportation system. Whereas Railways development is languishing (because it is in public sector), Road haulage (which is costly and devastating to ecology in more than one way) is being pushed hard as this mostly generates private profit. In a country where road communication in rural India is suffering due to lack of funds and unimaginative use of local resources, Air travel is being expanded rapidly. Thus, in a short span of time, third line Air Service, helicopter services have all been introduced. It is, of course, not mentioned that these highly subsidized services equipped and maintained with imported equipment is primarily for providing better transportation for the private sector.

All sorts of high-tech communication systems are being imported (directly or surreptitiously through the C-DOT of Shri Sam Pitroda) for benefiting the elite and private corporate sector but vast areas of the country must go without communication. It is never-articulated that improvement in communication or introduction of modernization or sophistication in communication in the principal metropolitan cities like Delhi or Mumbai has necessarily to mean diversion of resources from other metropolitan cities and the rural and semi-rural areas. The think-tanks of telecom have been found to be extremely evasive when pointedly asked when whole of India can be covered with ordinary telephone connections. One peculiar thing is happening in India. All opinion-leaders, intellectuals and professionals know what ails India and what needs to be done. Different studies have shown that there is a direct correlation of the extent of economic development to the number of telephones per hundred populations. Thus, if telephone connections go up, economic activity goes up and vice versa. Knowing this empirical fact, what we would expect to see is massive expansion of telephone connections in rural, semi-rural and semi-metropolitan cities. But no, not that what happens. Rural India, watch out, you will have to remain incommunicable for a long time to come!

Terms of Trade

That India is a highly liberalized economy ought to have been apparent to all knowledgeable personalities. If liberalization means more import or contact with the Western market economy, that has been happening for a long time. Government of India, Economic Survey 1986-87 brings this out clearly. This Survey shows that since 1970-71, at least, India has been importing excessively from some countries than exporting to those countries. Thus, during the heyday of liberalization, i.e., in 1985-86, Indian imports from EEC countries have been 2.6 times the export and in trade with Japan, Indian imports were 3.96 times more than the exports. This is only one side of the picture. During this period, Indian Rupee got continuously devalued with respect to the currencies of these countries. Thus, in terms of goods, these countries have been able to capture much more than if liberalization was not all that pervasive and if Indian currency was not tied so intimately and dis-advantageously to these market economy currencies. This 'double capture' of the Indian economy has been responsible for its low growth rate.

If liberalization was beneficial for the Indian economy, then the terms of trade with the Western trading partners would have improved in favour of India. But contrary has been the effect of liberalization over the last few decades.

If with all the accumulated experience, someone wants to liberalize Indian economy then the motivation is other than helping this stagnant economy.

Again, most of the liberalization has been directed at benefiting the private corporate sector. It was to be expected that this sector will be vibrant and will generate more employment. But table 3.2 (Employment in the Private Sector-Industry) of the Survey 1986-87 shows that employment in industry has actually fallen in 1985 below the figure of 1984 which itself was much below the corresponding figures for 1982 or 1983. So, liberalization is actually shrinking indigenous employment opportunities. Of course, some people must make sacrifices if the economy is to progress! Then, this sacrificed humanity may ask whither liberalization? Incidentally, employment in Public Sector (Table 3.1 of Economic Survey 1986-87) has consistently gone up. Is it because public sectors have not been touched by liberalization as strongly as Private Sector?

Superiority of Private Sector?

The thrust for liberalization has been based on two-pronged attack:

a) A pseudo-debate about lack of competition

b) Relative merit of private enterprise compared to public enterprise.

We have already noted that the debate about lack of competition was generated not with a view to increase in indigenous production by competitive application of Indian talent and Indian resources but in actual fact, to cut out Indian element from the enterprises. We have already noted private corporate sector has been successful in reducing employment.

Also, this has been accompanied with additional application of scarce resources like capital and imported equipment and materials. If nothing else, on this count itself private sector has proved to be least cost-effective. The inefficiency of private sector has been revealed in various other ways as well. Seventh Five-Year Plan Vol. I page 32 [Table 3.4(d)] gives some devastating statistics which clearly shows that ratio of Incremental GDP (IGDP) at factor cost to investment is invariably very low for private industry compared to public sectors or government-run concerns.

Similarly in savings also, the 7th Plan Vol. I page 47 (Table 4.1) reveals that private sector has been able to show 1.7% saving as against public sector saving of 4.2% in 1984-85 out of total-disposable income. In gross domestic saving also (Table 4.2 of Plan document ibid), Private corporate sector contributed only 9.5% as against public enterprises' contribution of 19%. On the one hand, private corporate sector was not saving enough, but on the other hand, they were cornering the Bank advances. Thus, Economic Survey 1986-87 Table 4.1 (Page 70) shows that all along, net Bank credit to commercial sector has been much higher than net Bank credit to government, including public sectors. Outstanding as on Jan 2, 1987, for private sector has been 128% more than that for the whole government sector (Rs. 90089 crores for private sector as against Rs. 70146 crores for government sector).

If liberalization implies procurement and utilization of external assistance, then it will be seen that apparently the external assistance is not fully utilizable. Again, the Economic Survey points to an unsatisfactory picture of utilization of external assistance. Infrastructure for useful utilization of foreign assistance is lacking. Incidentally, external debt servicing liability has steeply risen in the last few years.

There is another dimension to the collection and utilization of indigenous finances. Along with the liberalization drive, a Long Term Fiscal Plan (LTFP) was announced. The way the LTFP was framed and implemented, it transpired soon that the whole purpose of the LTFP was to keep the Indian financial market open for private business. Of course, the LTFP targets got violated from the beginning as can be seen from the following data culled from National Accounts Statistics of Central Statistical Organization:

Tax Revenue (net of States' share)

1985-86		1986-87		1987-88	
LTFP	Actual	LTFP	RE	LTFP	RE
a) 1.5	1.5	1.7	1.5	1.8	1.4
b) 6.3	7.2	6.5	7.4	6.9	7.8

Direct taxes do tend to lead to some sort of egalitarianism whereas indirect taxes invariably militate against the interests of the under-privileged. But the effect of the implementation of LTFP was to impose additional load of indirect taxes and reduce the proportion of direct taxes.

Skewed Distribution

Thus, the answer to the first question is that an already highly liberalized inequity in economic order is being made more susceptible to manipulation by extra-regional economic powers which are not non-inimical to Indian financial health. Benefits are again getting distributed to those who have had prior access to capital and resources. This also gives answer to the second question, i.e., the millions of those who are below the poverty line or are on the margin, have no visible stake in the liberalized economy as this economy is not addressing itself to attacking the real problems of food, shelter, clothing, quality of life and education for them. The call for liberalization is the call for legitimization and strengthening of the non-egalitarian forces.

If we do not want to keep a large segment of our population below the poverty line, we must give them jobs. And where better to find jobs than in Armed Forces. Then economists will say "I have been telling you all along, it is in armament or related production only that an economy thrives. I wonder why it took so long for Indians to understand this after seeing the example of America where the economy is principally dependent on defence and related production. If America ever cuts down on security and related production, its economy will face a recession compared to which the recession and depression of 1930s will look like a Banquet to the hungry".

'This is all very well!'

'Now let us start our negotiations for import of some Hi-tech Defence equipment from one of the Western countries which is in some financial straits because of falling Defence related sales!'

The above statement represent the mindset of our elite. The dénouement of this is that Armed Forces of India are in retreat mode.

WHERE IS DEFENCE MONEY GOING?

The Budget (taken as an illustration) for 1986-87 made an allocation of Rs 12,512 crores for Defence which marked a rise of Rs 2,318.45 crores over the revised estimate of the outgoing year and Rs 3784 crores over the budget estimates of 1985-86. This steep increase was noted by all concerned with a touch of concern and dismay. That time Doordarshan (the national TV channel then) had organized a live commentary on the Budget on 28 Feb 1985 with a panel of specialists. When the budget flash about Defence outlay came out, the remarks were rather muted except that a lady in the marketing field wondered where exactly the money for Defence was going. But, neither the moderator nor the Economic Adviser to the Government of India cared to take note of the point and add to it.

A study of the book 'Military Balance 1986' what struck me as most intriguing was that India was spending then more than China for Defence although China was having more than double the manpower under arms. Then a comparison with USA was made. The data on various parameters are rather startling.

Expenditure on Defence

This statistics also make interesting reading when compared with other countries. Please see the statistics given below.

Sr. No	Country	$ Million			% GDP		Numbers in '000		
		1981	1983	1984	1981	1984	1981	1985	1986
1.	India	5022	5683	6907	2.7	3.9	1104	1260	1260
2.	China	6000	6326	6455	1.7	1.6	4750	3900	2950
3.	USA	169888	217198	237052	5.8	6.4	2049	2152	2144
4.	Pakistan	1649	1871	1957	6.1	7.1	451	483	481
5.	Hungary	2095	1942	2136	4.1	3.9	101	106	105

In 1984 India apparently spent more on Defence than China. Rather surprising when India is buying much less defensive and offensive capabilities. Further analysis reveals some more interesting data.

Note: All statistics are taken from 'The Military Balance – 1986-87' (ibid).

Dollars per soldier

Dollars per soldier computed for 1984 and 1985 Armed forces personnel gives the following in current US dollars. These figures are subject to exchange rate fluctuations and do not represent the true value.

Country	Military Expenditures (Dollars per soldier in 1984)
India	5482
China	1655
USA	110154
Pakistan	4052
Hungary	20151

India spent more than 3 times that of China per soldier and about one half times more than Pakistan. But India spent only one twentieth of that of USA. Hungary is a special case. It is a member of the Warsaw Pact but has close link with World Bank and IMF and gets loans from these organizations. It has reasonably more contact with Western countries compared to other Warsaw Pact countries. You might have noticed that its mobilization state is very high (it ranks 5th in both active and overall mobilization). In fact, of all the Warsaw Pact countries, it has the highest status of mobilization. The economic status of the Warsaw pact countries could not be compared; but it is safe to assume that Hungary has the highest development status also.

In defence, a large share of the expenditure is spent on procurement and upkeep of the materials of war, like, aircraft, ships, submarines, aircraft carriers, ballistic missiles, tanks, troop carriers, fighting vehicles, armaments, rockets/

missiles, ammunition, fuels, oils, etc. A relative comparison of only the main delivery vehicles like ICBM, aircraft, ships, Tanks and major fighting vehicles indicate the following :-

Country	Offensive missiles/vessels/Aircraft/Tanks and other major items (approximate figures only)
USA	781,598 pieces.
India	10,864 pieces.
China	52,937 pieces.

Thus USA has about 72 times more number of delivery vehicles compared to India and China has five times more major equipment than India. One word of caution, in computing above figures, we were interested in getting a broad order of magnitude. Thus in the list of USA and to some extent in China are included ICBMs, Nuclear Submarines with missiles, AWACS, etc. India has none of these. The list also includes smaller items like guns and artillery pieces or combat vehicles listed in "The Military Balance 1986-87". If we consider these disparities, USA has at least 100 times advantage in delivery vehicles and similarly China has at least 10 times advantage over India.

We have not included in the above tally the Air Defence and space defence radar systems, Nuclear warheads, C^4 I (Command, Control, Communication, Computer and Intelligences) systems and the vast array of bombs, rockets and ammunitions of various degrees of sophistication and versatility. Considering all these, the conservative estimate is that USA has 100 x 100 =10,000 time's superiority over India and China has 10 x 10 =100 time's superiority over India. If we apply these factors then Dollar expenditure per soldier works out to as follows:-

Country	Military expenditure (Dollars per soldier) before adjustment	Military expenditure (Dollars per soldier) after adjustment
India	5482	5482.00
China	1655	16.55
USA	110154	11.02

It hurts to accept it, but accept we must that a poor country like India is maintaining the highest cost military in the world – at least 300 to 500 times costlier than China or USA. Most galling aspect is that in per capita expenditures China and USA are in the same league. The next question which agitates most economists is the pay and allowances of the vast population of the armed forces. Let me reiterate and this needs to be reiterated ad-infinitum that India has the smallest Armed forces in the world vis-à-vis its size and the population. And the Indian Armed forces personnel are being paid pittance compared to other countries. In 1986 USA spent 67.7 Billion (data taken from 'Maintenance' magazine of USAF) in current Dollars for personnel which constituted 24.30 percent of total DOD spending. Thus, for USA, expenditure per soldier as pay and allowances works out to $ 22,949 per annum. In the Revised Estimates for 1985-86, a provision for 2.067 Billion dollars was made for pay and allowances and transportation for personnel including personnel in R&D and Ordnance Factories. In terms of per capita expenditure, it is 1640 Dollars per soldier per year (actually much less, if pay etc. of civilian component is removed, say, may be less than $ 1000 per year). Thus an Indian soldier gets less than one-twenty third in Dollar terms (and if we consider the actual purchasing power, then it is much less) than that of an American soldier. So much for looking after the Indian soldier!

If we subtract the payment to personnel from the expenditure on defence then we find that comparison of other countries with India still remain skewed against India.

Country	Defence expenditure Less expenditure on Personnel (Dollars per soldier) before adjustment	Defence expenditure less expenditure on personnel (Dollars per soldier) after adjustment
India	5482 – 1640 = 3842	3842
China	1655 (Personnel expenditure not known and figure kept unchanged)	16.55
USA	110154-22949 = 87205	8.72

Payment to personnel is a significant proportion of Indian army budget but not for the Air force and Navy. The position is as follows :-

Service	% age of service budget spent on personnel
Army	49.04%
Navy	27.70%
Air Force	17.50%

The above data and the conjectures behind those data are so much in violent conflict with the line generally purveyed by our elite, I would expect some economist or thinker of repute to contradict me with relevant data. How long must I wait for that?

Not only that defence money is being wasted by the government of the day, they are unconcerned and are negligent in managing the biosphere. This comes out vividly when we examine the response of the Government of India in combating global warming.

GLOBAL WARMING

The effect of global warming has already manifested in the most dramatic way in India in the melting away of the Ice Shiva Linga in the cave in Amarnath. Retreat of the glacier, responsible for natural formation of the Shiva Linga, was ascribed as the most important reason for non-formation of the Linga. The yearly pilgrimage to Amarnath caves in winter (in 2007) got disrupted arousing the wrath of hundreds of thousands of pilgrims and support personnel, cutting across religious divides. Authorities concerned created an artificial Linga with ice then. When this information broke, it started being reported that all the Himalayan glaciers have retreated significantly in the last few decades due to global warming. Authorities concerned, as is the usual practice, pleaded helplessness in the face of evolving disaster. They have no plans; at least they have not articulated as to what countermeasures they wish to take. This is the same situation for which the Indian government is famous for, viz. they have admitted defeat even before joining the fight. Global warming is the outcome of the excessive consumption and exploitation of the natural resources by the Western powers. All those who should be concerned are reticent in admitting that Global warming is the outcome of relentless pursuit of profit by use of ever rising quantum of energy and toxic substances in production processes. In this case also, India (with other unfortunate people of South Asia) paying penalty for crimes against Nature committed by Western powers. Indian Governments have gone still further; they found the experiment of creating an artificial Linga with ice to be too costly and cumbersome. Our Government in 2008 has created an artificial Linga of glass and prohibited entry of pilgrims to the sacred cave. Indian governments, whether independent or dependent, have come to the conclusion that they can get away with any amount of affront to Hindu religious beliefs and practices with possibility of the Hindu worms turning and striking back being remote.

We are seeing the same type of charade being played out in destruction of Ram Setu, bridge built by Ram to cross over from India to Sri Lanka for his campaign against Ravan. Britishers called this as 'Adam's Bridge'. The case is in court now, but every one can rest assured that a shipping channel will definitely and ultimately be made across the Ram Setu for ensuring private profit of foreign and Indian businessmen and shipping companies. We consider that the construction of a shipping channel across Ram Setu is an example of avoidable heinous crime against ecology and India, whatever fine logic that might be proffered by the courts.

You cannot expect Indian leaders and all-powerful bureaucrats to comprehend that you cannot prevent Global warming without restraint on use of energy for worldly functions and by committing crimes against ecology. Our recommendations are for the Indian government to implement and enforce a plan.

No personal or public vehicle will have more than three horse power (HP) per passenger for which the vehicle has been designed. For example, a car designed for carrying total of five persons (including the driver) will not have more than 15 HP engine. Maximum permissible speed of vehicles moving over:

- Land will be 80 kilometres per hour,
- Water or under-water will be 40 kilometres per hour
- Aerial vehicles will have only sub-sonic speeds and only Turbo-prop engines will be permitted after 5 years, that is from 1st January, 2014. Transonic or Super-sonic speeds for aerial vehicles to be prohibited before 1st January, 2010. All turbine engines to be 'de-rated' so that aerial vehicles fitted with such engines do not exceed subsonic speeds.

These restrictions will not apply to military vehicles provided military of any country involved does not consume more than 25% of the total power consumption of the country concerned.

No country will be entitled to consume (fossil fuel or thermal) energy in excess of 20% of the world average consumption of such energy. Similarly, temperatures and toxicity for industrial processes cannot be more than 20% of the world average in any country of the world and cannot be more than that in 1960.

Super and big powers must revert back to the average level of temperatures and toxicity in the world in industrial processes prevailing in 1960 in the next five years. We are aware it will give undue advantage to the super and big powers. We are regretfully convinced that super/big powers will not be allowed by their big businesses to reverse Global warming. If the world community could accept the suggestions elaborated in this book regarding social security and distribution of national wealth, then only reversal of Global warming would be feasible.

Getting the world powers to agree to these recommendations will be well-nigh impossible without some proactive action from Indian government. India will mandate and implement the above restrictions and will forthwith prohibit operation of higher powered vehicles and also prohibit all imports from countries which do not obey the restrictions in their own country. All exports will be as per the energy-consumption standard specified earlier. No foreigner will be allowed to operate in India, including in Indian economic zones outside the land borders, or in Indian or Indian-controlled air space, any vehicle, machinery or equipment beyond the standards laid down. India will be able to reverse the Global warming once it gets appropriately mobilized, as then India will be able to unilaterally enforce its 'will' and/or its regulations.

2

ECONOMIC FOUNDATIONS FOR MOBILIZATION OF INDIA

Examination of current economic, politico-economic, socio-economic theories and practices indicate some trends in management of economy towards converting India into an SSP (Soft Super Power) of the servile variety. It is common knowledge and belief that India is poverty stricken, the land of naked Fakirs, even though it is endowed with vast natural and other resources. But intellectuals, especially the renowned economists are not unanimous on the extent and cause for this poverty in the backdrop of the surfeit of economic resources. So far as the extent of poverty, the economists and leaders have successfully created all round confusion as to whether poverty line in India rests at 40% or 36% or at 26% of the population. As if it is any consolation for those men below the poverty line that he has company of very many or fewer men and women. Also it is never explained as to why there must be poverty in the midst of plenty of resources if it was not profit motivation of some powerful interests. Economists, at least, in respect of India (or other undeveloped countries), did not display any historical perspectives. Further, the poverty measures themselves create doubt about purpose of such data. For example, for assessing the number of persons below poverty line (BPL), a non-resident Indian origin economist, specified 30-day recall method by substituting the earlier 7-day recall method, and thereby drastically reduced the number of BPL families. If some NRI or foreign economists recommend a 365-day recall method, government, in all probability, will accept that, as the BPL family data might turn out to be just 3%! Massive improvement in economic prosperity can then be claimed!

Other non-financial impediments restrict the access to opportunities for those on the lower levels of the economic and social totem pole. But the great economists or thinkers have not clearly delineated the economics of why these deficits of access to opportunities persist even though there have been claimed developments in economic, social, cultural and religious fields.

CANARDS AND MYTHS

We can dispose of a few misconceptions about causes of Indian poverty at the outset. Large population and pressure on available land are cited as the most important of all causes of poverty. As "Timeless India, Resurgent India"[13] shows, pressure on land is lowest for India. Number of people per hectare of arable land is lowest for India - lower than that in USA and in other Big developed countries. Although, India is having 16% of world population, and only 2% of world's geographical area and is having very high density of population overall, but, thanks to bounties of nature (vast and very fertile continuous flat lands, with ever renewed fertility, vast and adequately deep and full and placid river systems, abundant rainfall and sunshine throughout the year, mild weather in most parts of India for most of the time, mountains and oceans acting as necessary guards and suppliers of essentials) more than 60% of the land surface is cultivable and hence density of per hectare of cultivable land is lowest among the Big countries of the world. Of course, abundant non-agricultural land is available for implementation of those grotesque ideas of special economic zones and such like other capitalist devices to deceive and deprive the hapless poor, which majorities of Indians are.

It is a pet theory of all economists that unbridled growth of population in India is the cause of poverty and destitution. Dr. J.K. Bajaj and others have shown[14] that till about 1700 AD, 50% of world population was in India (of course undivided India is meant). Now world population is more than 6 billion, out of which only 1/6th (16%) is in India. Thus population growth in India is the lowest in the world. During British and colonial rules, population of India reduced significantly. Successive Indian governments since independence are bending all their energies to ensure that invidious colonial rule continues in India. This bogey of excessive population is coming handy to Indian elite and western powers. Of course, no scientific explanation of population growth ever appeals to administrators. Everyone likes to ignore evidence from animal world. Weak, defenceless animals have large population. In case of human species, their natural enemy is always another group of humans only. Humans are the only species which systematically kill, maim, deny, deprive, deceive and make otherwise unlivable, without any escape route, another class of humanity. By long experimentations and experience gained thereby, the more enterprising humans have concluded that simplest way to control another class is by creating and perpetuating newer and more sinister forms of poverty. There is another distinction from animal world. The predators among the humans always strive to increase their population.

Religion really has been used as a factor of the economy by the USA and Western Europe. (We will use the term 'western countries or powers or entities or Anglo-Saxon' to mean USA and Western Europe, barring where the context otherwise suggests). Those who lament large population of India, may I remind the great saying of Voltaire "God is always on the side of the biggest battalions".

Inadequacy of agricultural production has again been cited as the reason for Indian poverty. Of course, it is clean forgotten that Indian agricultural production came to the current dismal state progressively as the grip of colonial, especially British, rule tightened over India. Indian agriculturist is not to blame for Indian poverty; blame should be apportioned to consecutive central and the state governments, especially the communist government of West Bengal, for perpetuating the state politics of exploitation of colonial and British rule even after creation of Indian Republic. How many economists are aware that Indian regions and provinces (now states) were producing 17 to 19 tons of rice (and other cereals) (Timeless India etc.) per hectare before British started their exploitation and expeditionary enterprises. Incidentally, the Best Rice Farmer in Japan does not even now produce more than 9 tons per hectare, after investing more than 10 to 100 times more inputs than Indian farmers. Modern economists have flexible definitions of productivity (output/input ratios), it seems! Many economists do not see much difference between productivity and production per unit of selected factor of production. Otherwise they would not have made unsavoury statements about Indian agriculture or Indian farmers!

INDIAN LEADER'S PSYCHE

The problem why Indian intellectuals and leaders are so unconcerned and rendered themselves to so much of irrelevance for India's national interests and national security interests, well-being of the populace and even to the important *raison d'etre* of modern state viz., sovereignty and territorial integrity, has bothered common people like me all the time. The elite are so confident and so sure of their current pet theories on economic problems of India; it is difficult to believe that they can be so shallow and callous when confronted with the reality of Indian situation.

While cogitating on the problems of poverty I recall the story narrated to me by a friend[15]. My friend had mentioned that just after the great Indira Nehru-Gandhi poured gallons of milk on the head of Mahabali statue in Shravanbengola in Karnataka from a hovering helicopter (Mahamastakavishekam celebrations), he, with his extended family, visited Shravanbengola and one day he was sitting on top of a hillock (high ground). The picture of waste and destitution was so clear in the summer mid-afternoon that he understood how inadequate the power elite are and visualized why must Nehru-Gandhi and others display such vulgarity of pouring tons of milk on the head of the unresisting stone statue of a supreme creation of god, when the children and calf around might not have tasted milk in sufficient quantities in their lives! All liberated economists have also rationalized their distances from reality and created their theories and practices on similar barren fields of economic irrationality. Examples of irrationality amongst economists of super-developed country are galore.

Prior to Independence, Indian national leaders suffered a lot of torture and deprivation and, by choice, led a life of austerity and penury. The sacrifices of the top leadership inspire great awe and respect. In India, ascetics and denouncers of the worldly possessions always generate respect and following. Mahatma Gandhi understood this very well and chose the path of renunciation of material benefits but, possibly, renounced on the way Indian basic values also. Ascetism and renunciation of worldly possessions, however romantically associated with the mass/ charismatic leaders, did not necessarily demonstrate any good economic, social, political, cultural or religious outcomes for the average Indians. Gandhi–Nehru duo did not display adequate political or sociological knowledge or concepts and were too easily manipulated by the British. They were so dazzled by the prospect of exercising absolute powers (like the Britishers) without responsibility, they were willing to partition India into two and if required they would have agreed for three or more fragmentations of India. In fact, the Britishers retained control over Burma and Ceylon in the Instrument for Partition of India although British Governor General continued to control these two segments of British India even after handing over of power to India and Pakistan. The horrendous riots, massacres and destruction of property and social upheavals which followed the decision to partition and partially implement that most absurd decision of exchange of population could not be anticipated by the leaders of non-violent movement. The British appointed Governor General or the Indian leaders did nothing to use the military to quell the riots quickly. Failure of administration and Indian leaders (ignorant novices in exercising newly acquired power) were total and condemnable. They allowed covert British control of Indian polity and economy through subservience to emperor-appointed British Governor General to continue, even after Independence, and provided the spiritual basis for saddling India with a constitution designed to perpetuate foreign control over India.

PERPETUATING POVERTY AND STRANGULATING MILITARY

Straightforward techniques are used by Government of India, RBI, other constitutional authorities and the legal system, business/industry, power brains and the con-men, to keep Indians poor and thereby strangulate military. It is always depicted that the rich are necessarily more gifted, talented and efficient and they have a natural flair for control and domination. Controlled democracy of the Anglo-Saxon variety has been found to be a handy tool but actual levers of power and capacity to dispense favours are strictly kept out of bounds for the poor. The legal system has been made innocent of logic or rationality and expecting justice is almost impossible now. Judges are selected, promoted, glorified or publicized by a small coterie of power brokers. Monetary system has been designed in such a way that foreigners, colonizers and exporters of Indian wealth have the first lien on the Indian wealth and resources - natural or man-made.

First step in perpetuating poverty was taken by our venerable founding fathers when they eternally bound the Indian majority into bondage, by ensuring that their freedom of belief or action in economic, religious and cultural affairs could always be called into question on the plea of a weird version of secularism. Indians have been foisted with a totally foreign, illogical, non-phonetic language (fit only for barbarians) as the official language, thereby perpetuating Macaulay-advised education system, which can only be accessed by the affluent and ensuring that nothing called the Indian culture can subsist after some time. The great founding fathers and the so-called fathers and mothers of Independent India kept harping (latest votary being our venerable PM, in 2006, Dr. Manmohan Singh) on the unavoidable necessity of English-medium teaching to make India relevant in international milieu. In hindsight it can be surmised that India never became a major player in the world, whereas, tiny and unimportant countries became "Tigers", even though they continued with their less developed languages.

Distribution of wealth is kept highly skewed in favour of the well-to-do. Here again the virtual masters residing outside India have the final say in matters important or significant. It is depicted that consumption by Indians is a heinous crime, whereas excessive consumption by outsiders helps in increasing the volume of production in India and efficiency of labour (never of the production process as a whole or the efficiency of the managers). Again regional distribution of production or wealth creation is kept skewed with calibrated inducements and penalties. Who will tell the powerful that the "Freight Equalization" of the natural produces of Eastern India (without simultaneously mandating such equalization for all other produces and services of other regions) started by the Nehru regime in the morrow of Independence was the first step in distorting the production processes and increasing inefficiency in production in India? This single so-called egalitarian step had swelled the ranks of the dispossessed in India. After the failure of previous schemes to generate enough profit for the private entrepreneurs, the governments are now moving in to directly attacking the life and livelihood of the poor agriculturists and land-holders with their obscene schemes of acquiring massive stretches of land in the countryside, especially in the poor states of West Bengal, Orissa, Uttarakhand, Chattisgarh and even in some comparatively affluent states like Haryana, Maharashtra and Punjab for setting up mega steel and power plants and for industries for producing goods for the super affluent by the so-called devices (totally illegal and unconstitutional) SEZ (Special Economic Zones). It is incomprehensible how leaders of (so-called?) independent India could so blatantly fall for colonial techniques of taking control of land from poor of India and then plead surprise that common Indians are still so poor. Land proposed to be acquired is, in every case, much in excess of (as much as 10 to 1000 times more than) the legitimate technical requirements of the enterprises. Our political and business leaders get vertigo when they think of high-rise buildings or factories or get claustrophobic if they are advised to build underground structures! This urge to deprive the poor Indians of their (perpetual assets) lands by independent Indian ruler is exact replica of the methods and rationale presented by the Britishers for introducing Indigo, Jute, Tea, Coffee, Rubber and such like cash crop cultivation in India. All concerned have forgotten that 'right to life' is still a fundamental right whereas 'right to property' is only a constitutional right; the executive still considers, knowing the ambivalence of the judiciary, that any British period colonial rule/law supersedes the Indian constitution, as otherwise 18th or 19th century laws could not be invoked to take away the land from the poor farmers forcibly in spite of Article 300-A of Indian constitution!

Allocatory monetary policy is invariably used so that wealth and investment can be directed at the undeserved entities and sectors. Whereas agricultural subsidies are never given to the Agriculturists directly, but Export subsidies (much more than Agricultural subsidy) directly helps the importers in foreign countries. Indians are kept starved of materials, means of production, and money so that these can be exported out at a low price. The matter has reached such a shameful level that most of the major items of Indian exports invite 'Anti-dumping duties'. These duties are imposed when the importing countries suspect that exported items are being sold at prices lower than that prevailing in the exporting country markets. Knowing that Indian cost of production is invariably a fraction of the cost of production in developed countries, it is a miracle that Indian goods and services should encounter 'Anti-dumping' duties in developed/super-developed countries, unless the consumers in India were being penalized by export subsidy, which distort the export price. Obviously some one is stealing! Indian economic authorities never seem to question the exporters as to how they could achieve the miracle of supplying goods and services at below the national prices ruling at the relevant time.

SOURCE MATERIALS FOR STUDY OF NATIONAL SECURITY AND POVERTY RELATED ISSUES AND THE LURKING NOOSE

If anyone is seriously concerned to find out what ails India, he will not be required to search around much. The gory details of problems afflicting India and other undeveloped countries are elaborately and diligently laid out in every single government document in public domain, especially, the annual economic surveys, budgets, and routine reports of the Reserve Bank of India or of other countries; only one is required to have a perceptive mindset. We did not have to depend on Karl Marx, Engels, Hegel, Trotsky, Lenin, Stalin, Gorbachov, Yeltsin, Mao Zedong, Che Guevera or Ho Chi Minh to know the debilities of the undeveloped countries with compromised or subverted leadership, modern economists like Amartya Sen, Joseph Stiglitz, Dr. Raghu Ram Rajan, Bhagwati, Soros, or thinkers like Samuel Huntington etc. have done commendable job of comprehensively documenting the problems of unfortunate countries like India. We accept in full their findings on problems and are refraining from devoting much space of this book to these matters. They have also elaborately explained their ideas of changes and necessary reforms of the world order. We just want to caution the poor people of Asia, Africa, East Europe, and Latin America and also the poor people of developed and super developed countries that if they accept and implement even a single recommendation of these economists, the noose around their emaciated necks will be tightened by a notch and two and already poor people will be further pushed into obscurantism, destitution, corruption and prostitution.

DISTORTING DEMAND-SUPPLY RELATIONSHIP AND SUPPLY CHAIN BY PRICES

All economic books – whether elementary or advanced – will invariably quote or allude to the demand, supply and price relationships and the inevitability of their umbilical relationships.

Our economics books and primers always make out that the demand curve starts at some high point on the vertical Price axis and falls off as supply starts flowing in. Economists devote considerable talent and energy in creating a 'Consumer Surplus (CS)', as if the consumer gets more than what he should rightfully claim. This CS is conceptualized as the area on the left of the demand line bounded by the demand line on the right, price line on the left and an imaginary horizontal line drawn from the so-called equilibrium point (i.e. the point of intersection of demand and supply lines) to intersect the price-line at right angles. How neatly economists present their illogical and irrational case!

Also, traditional economists are unaware that equilibrium point of demand-supply curves is really the meeting point of the elasticity of demand and supply to price determined by the supplier or the point of congruence of demand-supply hysteresis under price pressure.

Also it never appears as funny or make-belief theory that demand should fall with rise in supply and with falling prices! To economists such unreality is a natural thing. We would solicit economists to consider that demand-supply relationship can be better explained by interchanging the names of the demand–supply curves, as that will be more realistic. With fall in prices demand will rise and supply will increase tc take advantage of rise in volume. Ultimately, the marginal utility for the supplier of increased volume will tend to fall and supply restraint will increase and an unstable equilibrium point will be reached which will be always in a flux.

34 MICROECONOMICS

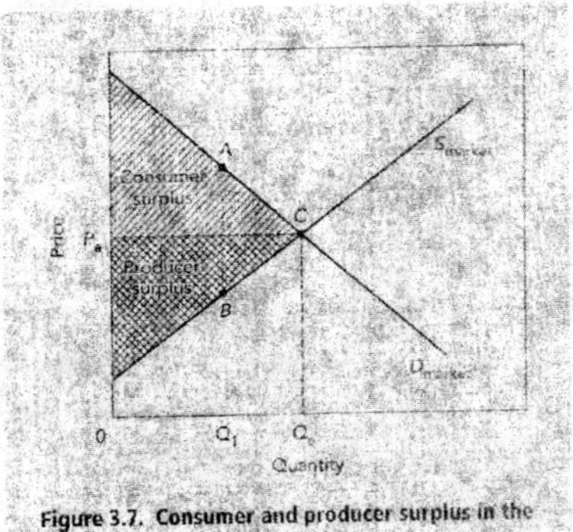

Figure 3.7. Consumer and producer surplus in the market equilibrium

This, in fact, is the reality, but, alas, unrecognized by mainstream economists! Proof of our concept is vividly provided by the price-demand relationship in case of Mobile Phones in India. When these under-designed contraptions were introduced in India, prices were astronomical. Handsets were costing tens of thousands of Rupees and per minute call-charges were Rs. 16/- or more initially and consumer response was necessarily poor. To push sales, entrepreneurial brains of the big businesses conjured up many schemes; one of these was introduction of CPP (Calling Party Pays) in addition to the called party paying the massive call charges, obviously, to increase the profit-margin of the big businesses. CPP was prevalent in low cost land-line calls, where the called party does not pay anything. The idea was that the hapless caller from landline phone will have to bear massive call charges to have the privilege to make call to mobile phones, in addition to the landline charges. There was a hue and cry and the case landed up in Delhi High Court. We, under the banner of "India Defence Foundation" (a non-government, non-profit organization, hence having no funds other than those provided by the chairman and secretary general, two retired Defence service officers, with lofty ideals and action plans unmatched by the resources) got impleaded in the case. Our brief called for not only rejection of the demand of the mobile phone (cell phone) operators but also mentioned about a thorough investigation into the legality of the introduction of super high cost cell phones in a contrived manner with total dependence on land-lines for their functioning and imposing additional loads on the already stretched land-line systems. We also highlighted the absurdly high prices of the handsets and call charges by quoting prices and practices in other developed and super developed countries. CPP ultimately came as claimed by the interested parties, but things had changed considerably by then. Government made sure that DOT (department of telecom), instead of becoming a contender and competitor, became a subset of the business models of the affluent and powerful private entities. Also supply demand interactions led to fall in handset and call charges and there has been an explosion of cell phone usage since then, of course, by deft management of government and demand impulses by the interested parties with their ready-made profit calculations always handy.

This diversion from the main theme was necessary to demonstrate how economic decision matrix turns out in real life in an undeveloped country like India, which cannot boast of captured foreign markets. India also lacks relevant economic theories or models. The concept of price is a very intelligent innovation by economists to hide the stigma of exploitation of the poor consumers. Economists use price and factor costs as freely interchangeable items.

PRICE

Price is always higher than the factor costs. Price is generally explained as the amount essential to be recovered from the consumer, of course, without any mention of the amount spent or deemed to be spent for paying for all the factors of production. Even in case of administered price fixed by government or other agencies, a difference is always catered for the final price and the total factor costs at the production stage. Flexible state policies of accommodation to entrepreneurs by tax and other assorted concessions and rebates lower the factor costs but help in increasing the hiatus between price and production costs, with price always winning. Who benefits by increased price? The answer has been devised by economists so that entrepreneur takes the entire production surplus as 'Profit'.

PROFIT

The idea of profit evolved in the fertile brain, full of diabolical schemes, of the economists and other thinkers. These great minds failed to provide a valid definition of profit. The only valid definition of profit acceptable to us is: 'Unauthorized/unregulated extraction of labour and production surplus for private gains' and this is highly condemnable. Profit and profiteering had a social stigma attached to it in pre-Christian/Islamic era in India. No one is sure what really profit means; it has been defined as the remuneration of the entrepreneur, ignoring the fact that all entrepreneurs take payments and wages as sponsors, CEO, COO, Chairman of Board of Directors, member of Board of Directors, as part of top management which are reflected in factor costs. Then common men, like us, always wonder what other entrepreneurial skills or attributes remain to be compensated by an undefined/unregulated element called profit! Profit and price has an umbilical relationship. Higher the price or lower the costs, higher is the profit. Profit adds no value to the production process; in fact, it distorts and disturbs the production process and creates all-round uncertainty and confusion and destabilizes polity and military, as we are seeing under the black veil of gloom in liberalized India. Profit always, unnecessarily, increases the amount to be paid by the consumer. Higher the profit, higher is the cost to the consumer or to the nation, if consumer is protected by administered prices.

The concept of profit is *ab-initio* absurd and illogical. We have posed these questions to many, including serving/ retired judges, that if you allow the private entrepreneur the privilege of earning profit, then how can you prevent profiteering by serving Armed forces or employed persons without violating the constitutional provisions. Apparently, the controllers of US forces have come to terms with this concept profit. One report indicated that millions of pieces of armament sent to Iraq during and after Iraq II conflict are missing and unaccounted for. USA did not acknowledge that but we cannot ignore that the famous 9/11 attack was conducted by America-settled men with American resources and training in America. If and when the next attack comes that also will be with everything American. We shudder at the prospect that malcontents can easily get nuclear and biological materials and ready-to-use lethal equipment freely in the highly profit-propelled privatized markets in America. *HT*, New Delhi, 27 June, 2008, in a London datelined report mentioned that: "Security lax at US N-bases in Europe" and added that "after the US air force lost track of six nuclear cruise missiles last August it was found that support buildings, fencing, lighting and security systems were in need of repair. In some cases, it was found that conscripts with less than nine-month experience were being used to guard the nuclear weapons. Elsewhere private security guards were used to protect the bombs." Almost every function of American military and security agencies have been privatized or has significant civilian/private involvement. Although privatization has not taken deep roots in Indian military, but Indian experience with civilian/ private interface with military is neither uniformly smooth nor harmonious. If USA could not keep track of a small quantity (in American norms) of armament sent to Iraq II, how can anyone be sure USA has full and valid account of thousands (or hundreds of thousand) tons of nuclear materials and lethal and other equipment of bewildering variety along with other massive quantities of technical and non-technical equipment, stores, accoutrements dispersed all over the globe with highly complex and intertwined logistic and maintenance webs with computerization in different stages of evolution. Obviously, some enterprising civilians and service men have, on the quiet, made or are making some profit at the cost of USA; of course, USA is none the worse for that. Bulk of the armament used by Al Qaeda, Taliban and other terrorist organizations in Iraq, Afghanistan and other places are provided and maintained by Americans or people in their command and control. After 'Glasnost' and 'Perestroika' had been give a free run by those dedicated democrats, Gorbachev and Yeltsin, in USSR, the armed forces got decimated and were rendered totally non-effective in taking control over national security matters. The surgical precision with which USSR military took over Hungary, Czechoslovakia and Afghanistan are completely missing in Russian federation military. They are struggling for many years to control and over-power a tiny fragment called Chesznia. It has been mentioned elaborately that Russian armed forces are making quick profit by selling armaments to the rebels than fighting them to submission. So long problem in Chesznia continues, profit will keep flowing to Russian armed forces and other personnel in the conflict zone. Has private profit something to do with the ever lasting, illogical and irrational problems in Indian Kashmir and North Eastern states, particularly the ones with Christian and Muslim majority (attained by ethnic cleansing and aggressive conversions)? We can confirm to all and sundry that tension in Indian polity (and for that matter in all countries of the world) is in great measure due to tolerance by state apparatus of private profit by some selected sections of the state and abroad. If the courts consider profit as constitutional then they are duty bound to quote the specific clause of the constitution; this cannot be the product of their fertile brains or highly developed conditional imagination.

GDP AND GROWTH CONUNDRUM

Governments of all developed, developing and undeveloped countries publish GDP statistics. When these statistics are not available or are highly undependable World Bank/IMF or other UN Agencies make prognostications of the GDP and expected growth rates. Defence sector is completely ignored for GDP calculations in India, which is not the case in all countries. This exclusion is another example of conditional exercise of economic judgment/prudence. Defence sector in totality is kept out of GDP calculations in India by the entrenched administrators and their consorts, so that these can be indicated as unnecessary and nonessential expenditure, best avoided (of course, it is of no significance that freedom to exercise of state power gets debilitated thereby also). The political (theoretical) masters, with the sole purpose of presenting defence as a net consumer of resources and should be suppressed at all costs (national interests can go to hell - of course, never verbalized!), are always justifying their dedication to peace. They allow reduction of national security, thereby facilitating attack on territorial integrity or sovereignty and then plead helplessness. Further, weightages given to socially-relevant sectors are not same in all countries and depiction of GDP in Dollar terms hides a major portion of the deprivation which an undeveloped country, like India or other surrogate or captured lands (overt colonialism having gone out of fashion) suffer. The contrived F.E. exchange rate is one of the main culprits, as we have examined elsewhere, for keeping some countries perpetually poor.

GDP in India is around $450 or 500 (in 2000 AD) billion Dollars, GDP growth rate around 3-5% (Occasionally touching 6-7% or so) and share of world trade has continuously gone down from about 5-6% before Independence to about 0.2% now. But, such dismal figures of share of world trade, especially after liberalization and Reforms have taken deep roots in India, is quite embarrassing. World Bank uses a contrived measure for arriving at PPP measure of GDP. World Bank compares what one Dollar can buy in USA with what a Dollar can buy in the country under review. This of course ignores a small issue that dollar cannot buy anything in most other countries, as dollar is not a legal tender in most foreign countries. This is not uniform in all countries. World Bank/IMF instinctively assumes some exchange rate between the currencies for arriving at the PPP value of GDP. Further, there is no consensus as to what constitutes the essential consumption in a country.

WB FOLLIES

Whenever the WB thinks of capturing the economies of the third world, they start a slogan and keep repeating that ad infinitum till the aim is fulfilled. Thus WB eulogized economic reforms and structural adjustments till the people of third world became structurally adjusted and starving more. Almost simultaneously they started pushing for privatization without a single rational argument. Now they are giving a big build up to their version of perverted form of oligarchic Democracy. Thus Afghanistan and Iraq have become democratic to the fullest satisfaction of WB after these countries were ruthlessly occupied and suppressed by the big and super powers.

WB/IMF has committed economists who sometimes use the PPP value of GDP to compare the performances of selected countries for the purpose of hedging and to keep their conscience clear. Such an attempt has been made (in *E.T*, Delhi, 24 Nov 03) in "Growth in India - a longer term view") where the GDP story has been retold on the basis of percentage growth in selected Asian developing countries and compared to those with the results achieved by developed countries. Though as per Economic survey of Government of India, Indians share of world trade is around 0.2% but in terms of 'Share of World Output', it occupies the record place, next only to China. The contrast between China and India (incidentally, a so-called democratic country) is striking: whereas China's share grew from 3.76% in 1982 to 12.67% in 2002 that of India was 3.0% in 1982 and 4.77% in 2002. The conclusion drawn was that third world countries are doing very well with regard to share of world output and by implication in consumption. A different picture of share of world output is obtained if market exchange rate at the relevant time is used. For example, India's market exchange rate is about 5 to 10 times more adverse than the PPP exchange rate and Japan's market rate is 0.75 to 0.8 times (that is, better) vis-à-vis dollar. If these exchange rates are used, then the picture for India and Japan works out to:

SHARE OF WORLD OUTPUT 1992-2002

	Market Rate	**Corresponding figures (PPP Rate) in Newspaper**
India	0.090	0.477
Japan	22.09	8.89

So much for the realism of the IMF World Economic outlook Data Base! It is relevant to recall that India's consumption expenditure is in the lowest band. India has one of the highest percentages of unemployment. In absolute numbers of unemployed or grossly under-employed labour, India can boast of the highest figure in the whole world. In fact, the number of unemployed in India exceeds the combined population of Western Europe and North America! The employers collect full payment but pay only a small portion of the statutory minimum wages to the children and often to the women and many times to the (illiterate) men folk as well. But such a poor, underdeveloped country like India with one of the lowest consumption expenditure in the world turns in second highest share of the world output! Who benefits from India's output is the question agitating the minds of the common Indians.

If anyone thought that the bulk or proportionate share of world output is consumed by India, he will be devastatingly wrong. FAO has reported that nutrition level of Indian populace has fallen. In fact India can boast of the highest number of malnourished/undernourished children and population in the whole world, because, the food has been exported out to the affluent West! Even livestock population is absolutely undernourished. Actually, India's share of world trade is low, because Indian produce is lowly priced in world market and India's imports are super-costly in both Dollar and Rupee terms. Indian Exports and Imports are both geared to reduce domestic consumption in India and India's economists always find some theoretical basis for passing on the benefits of India's production to the foreigners. This also explains the phenomenon of persisting poverty in India. This also brings in the question: "For whom the growth bell tolls?"

INEFFICIENCY OF SUPER DEVELOPED COUNTRIES

The inefficiency and un-conscionable high consumption and lack of international competitiveness of the developed and super developed countries are also involved in another set of data culled from the published documents. This is what we can call as "Standard Man Hours Equivalent of GDP". This is arrived at by dividing the GDP (in the currency of the country) by the Statutory Hourly Minimum Wages for Unskilled Labour in the currency of that country. Some countries have specified Statutory Hourly Minimum Wages for Unskilled Labour (SHMWUL) and some countries do not have a statutory basis of the minimum wages. But in such countries, especially in the developed ones, sufficient data to determine what is the minimum wages for 67% of the unskilled labour is normally available[16] (For example, ILO reports) and that can be assumed as statutory wages for comparison. We have taken a super developed country like USA, which incidentally has also the highest GDP in the world and compared that with India. The result of such analysis is rather startling.

For USA the SHMWUL is $6 per hours and for India it is now Rs. 6/- [i.e. 6/44=0.136 dollars, Rupee-Dollar exchange rate being Rs. 44 in end quarter of 2005] per hour. Assuming that data given in W.B. Development Report 2000/2001 is correct, the GDP data is as follows :-

GDP 1999 Billion US$	
USA	8381 (Approx.)
India	450 (Approx)

Then Standard Man hours Equivalent of GDP for USA is about (8381/6=) 1397 billion man hours; whereas, for India it is (450/0.136=) 3309 billion man hours.

Thus, half naked starving Indian labour produce two and half times more than the super developed, super consuming, super mighty USA! If we take even the faulty PPP exchange rate of Dollar-Rupee (which is about 5 times more than the market exchange rate and market exchange rate itself is one-eighth to one-tenth that of realistic PPP exchange rate of $ 1 = Re. 1), then the hiatus decreases depending on what exchange rate you assume for comparison. Will it be wrong to say that a very large part of the might of America is provided by poor Indian labour? Will well-meaning people still continue to nurture the belief that USA is more efficient producer of goods and services?

Rational pricing formula is necessary for international trade. Some fancy concept of 'arms length distance' pricing of products between the principal and subsidiary have been devised which is to fool the weak nations by the stronger ones. A straightforward pricing formula can be:

Price of the product/service in the supplying country in the currency of that divided by the minimum statutory wages for unskilled labour in the currency of the supplying country = Price of the same product/service in the importing country in the currency of importing country divided by the minimum statutory wages for unskilled labour in the currency of the importing country.

This is the most rational pricing formula, as TRIPS and TRIMS agreements of WTO enjoins all countries to provide

"Own country treatment" to aliens. Since there is parity of the statutory wages, the above ratio can only reflect the correct international relationship in trade matters.

BLOCKADE BY ECONOMISTS

The above parity equations are so simple, elegant and straightforward, ordinary mortals wonder why economists cannot accept or repose faith in it! The leaders of the economist pack are always beholden to the dominant economy or the political entity associated with the domineering economy for their acceptance, sustenance and recognition. The metamorphosis of the thought process of some famous economists is case in point. To my mind, the more apparent compromise on Defence spending issue (that defence spending is bad irrespective of the circumstances or the country) and on the virtues of (controlled/crony) democracy appears to be the biggest climb-down of this otherwise pro-proletariat (without Communist connotation) thinker. I shall have occasion to examine in greater details the significance of defence spending for economic growth, especially in creating job opportunities for the down and under. The established economists have virtually created a blockade against any consideration of economic parity issue. It seems to have never occurred to them that in interaction between developed and developing nations, the basic supply-demand curve is never smooth or continuous and it is hardly ever convex. They have no model to consider the situation where both the demand and supply parameters are controlled by the same party. The developing country can never pull themselves up by their boot-straps; if they are saddled with an exchange rate which is not parity based but is the one specified by currency speculators and manipulators.

Economists (especially the popular ones) keep forgetting that political class who are their Cheer-Leaders/Mentors/Sponsors/Patrons (all simultaneously) want quick-fix solutions to the complex economic problems and if, in the bargain, the political element can make some gains on the side, it is all the better! Sightlessness of the economists would not have been more pronounced if they were not prescribing devaluation of national currency to keep up export competitiveness. In case of India, its share of world trade continuously went down as it continuously devalued the currency since Independence. If we can be as limited in vision as the common-run economists, we could conclude that the basic reason for backwardness of the developing economics is their adverse Foreign Exchange rate. Kaushik Basu in his analysis of Chichilnsky or Prebisch theorems or paradoxes (Page 93 - 101 of his book)[17] did not dwell on the effect of intentional or mendacious adverse variation of the exchange rate. I am particularly pained at the non analytical approach in prematurely eulogizing the success of Taiwan or South Korea prior to their crash in the later part of the last century (Pages 100 - 101 of Kaushik Basu book).

DENIGRATION OF LABOUR

Over the ages, economists have identified various factors of production. Capital, as a factor of production was devised by early pre-modern man. Our concept (of course, conditioned by experience in Armed Forces) is that a factor *is critical or strategic* which can produce some economic goods or services without (or in the absence) of all or some of the remaining factors of production. On these criteria, labour turns out to be the only critical or strategic factor of production. No other factor of production by itself or in combination with other factors can produce any economic goods or services without the involvement, intermediation, intervention or supervision by labour. But, economists, over the centuries, have tried to project labour just as another replaceable factor of production and made sure that labour does not get its cardinal position.

Money evolved as a means of exchange of goods and services initially, but later, it was adopted as a factor of production and ultimately in modern economic dispensations, it has assumed a position of pre-eminence as a factor of production which has no economic validity but has all the trappings of greatness awarded to it by influential economists. Even modern economists, like Shri Kaushik Basu, can accept stereotyped production function, whose validity is untested ever. But, his line of argument to arrive at the output-capital relationship (Page 43 to 47 of his book)[18] completely ignores the contribution of labour, since labourers do not produce any economists. But no one needs to conclude that only lovers of 'Capital' have been guilty of neglect of labour; even eminent proletariats like Marx and Engels, Lenin, Stalin or Mao Zedong ultimately did not accept that labour can be its own master.

The above line of argument may appear as polemical and non-scholastic in approach. Hence, as advised by Bertrand Russell, instead of searching for pseudo-proof, let us start with some axioms, so that others may either accept the rational and valid conclusions derived from those axioms or start all over again with even totally opposite axioms and build up a set of conclusions and results after rational application of the revised axioms. Our axioms are:-

(a) Labour is the only important and strategic factor of production.

(b) All other factors of production only become economically relevant as a result of involvement, intervention, intermediation, and superintendence of labour.

(c) Labour can be replaced with only costlier labour.

(d) Colour of the skin has profound effect on the efficiency of labour - Fairer the skin/colour less efficient they are as producers of economic goods and services. Fairer the skin, more covetous they are.

(e) There is a regional basis of efficiency of labour. White continents i.e. Americas, Western Europe and Middle East, produce least efficient labour.

(f) Economy cannot operate without some non-economic supports or props.

(g) Military strength (i.e. proportion of population in military uniform) is the determinant of achievable economic strength.

(h) Whereas, labour has a limited supply and is more or less inflexible in use, in a given space and time, rest of the factors of production, especially capital, can be changed (increased or reduced) subject to limitations imposed by availability of labour.

PER CAPITA INCOME CONUNDRUM

The labour of highly developed countries has high per capita income. The reasonable corollary will be "to develop, increase per capita income". Also, the simple fact that labour of undeveloped countries are invariably paid less, not because they are less efficient or productive, but that fruit of their labour is priced at a low figure. World Bank, apparently, harbors economists who are committed to perpetuate the existing scheme of things and on the basis of their statistics one economist (Shri Kaushik Basu) without any qualms, also could make the astounding assertion that "per Capita Income in the United States is 100 times that of Bangladesh, and even if one makes purchasing power-parity adjustment it remains 20 times as high". The question remains, which purchasing-power-parity are we talking of? Rational purchasing power parity or World Bank's contrived/Elitist purchasing power parity? Also it begs the question, why is there shortage of capital in LDC's? Shouldn't the real parity for India be $ 1 = Re. 1. We wonder what will happen to Bangladesh if it also decides on a parity exchange rate of $ 1 = Bangladesh Taka 1?

Who can (and how to) convey to elite economists (like Shri Kaushik Basu) that the name they have given to theory (the so-called "O-Ring theory") is as fallacious and as accurate as the theory of O-ring failure causing the Challenger space craft explosion. Only the most gullible (or ardent followers of the proponent of "Profit-propelled Design Philosophy") Engineer/Scientist will ever accept that single 'O-ring' failure can give rise to a sequence of failures which can cause a multi-billion dollar/Hundreds of thousands of man-hours-worth Challenger to explode on ground or in Airspace. Apparently the Challenger could not withstand the challenges of the cussedness of the American system! Elementary design office manual dictates that there will never be fail-unsafe part or component and if failure of a component/part cannot be avoided, that will not cause other parts to fail seriatim or that critical component or part will not have redundancies. If an 'O-ring' can cause disaster, the design team would have identified it earlier. Our premier economists, like the rest of the gullible, have swallowed hook line and sinker, the canard put out by the NASA or some such agency that a small (poor) little 'O-ring' is the culprit. If anyone looks into the investigation reports of space-flight or air accidents of America, they will notice that American agencies always put out that a small insignificant part had failed and that caused the disaster. Their conclusion is that since a small little part did not behave, the mammoth agencies making the Challenger or such like devices, cannot be held to be blamed. Ordinary fellows (like me) would like to request the economists and similar erudite persons to ascertain from NASA and other agencies whether they just modified the 'O-ring' or tightened the quality control in manufacture and handling of that 'O-ring' only or make major modifications to the spacecraft similar to the ill-fated one.

The validity and authenticity of investigation of another disaster in America needs to be thoroughly examined. An Indian born astronaut, Kalpana Chawla, was one of the seven unsuspecting and unfortunate victims of the reusable spacecraft, Colombia. Within less than a minute after launch, it became (or ought to have been) apparent that the Colombia was doomed to burn up if it made an attempt at reentry into dense atmosphere of the earth. Some heat-shield panels of the Colombia fell off within a few seconds of the launch (an unpardonable crime of inappropriate design, manufacture/quality control!). The astronauts could have safely ejected while the spacecraft was still in dense atmosphere of the earth, if only they were alerted after the panels flew off. The spacecraft was allowed to complete its assignments during the next sixteen days of last sojourn in space, because some multibillion dollar experiments had to be carried out. All tell-tale signs of the impending calamity were underplayed to the astronauts so that they could not suspect any abnormality. In any case, American astronauts are always accustomed to fly in spacecraft, where every single manned flight had some serious problem or the other and the successful completion of all missions were always a matter of touch and go. In case of Colombia, NASA or relevant agencies made no efforts to save the astronauts. Their only concern was to hope that multibillion (or Trillion?) dollar experiments, the results thereof and if, possible, the spacecraft could be somehow saved. In American profit-propelled economy, value of human life is the economic value of his specialty and is determined by the replacement cost. Since the replacement cost of the spacecraft was many hundreds of thousand times more than the economic value of the life of seven astronauts, a conscious decision was taken to sacrifice the astronauts. There is an ethnic angle to this heartless decision - majority of the astronauts were non-white immigrants. The extent of damage to the heat shield could have been ascertained by an EVA (Extra Vehicular Activity) of Inspection. This EVA was not considered, (a) because EVA Kit was not carried and all onboard facilities for EVA were removed to reduce carried load, (b) any EVA activity would have alerted the astronauts and smooth conduct of planned experiments would have been endangered, which could not be economically justified. Since America did not have any suitable vehicle to dock with the stricken Colombia, they could have taken the help of the Russian Soyuz-series space vehicles to dock with Colombia to rescue the doomed astronauts. Another alternative was that the stricken Colombia could have been diverted to dock with the International Space Station and then Russian Soyuz spacecraft(s) could bring the American astronauts to earth. It is presumed that even American spacecraft have sufficient manoeuvrability and flexibility to change flight plans in space. All these options were rejected (a) because Colombia, possibly in this mission, was not capable of docking as docking equipment were not installed in it, (b) all other considerations depicted above in respect of avoidance of EVA played on the minds of the decision makers, (c) any attempt to involve the Russians would have necessitated giving lot of data about Colombia spacecraft, its technology, manufacture, quality control and management of space flights, which the Americans wanted to avoid under any circumstances. Further, any soliciting of Russian help would have punctured the synthetic aura of great superiority of American technology and invincibility. The whole world would have then known how phony the claims of American superiority in all fields are! Since in this case no small part or component could be immediately held out as the culprit, the powers that be sent out another set of cues. The electronic and print media in India suddenly started highlighting the great patriotism of Kalpana Chawla and scrupulously avoided any mention of mishandling of this mission by the ground handlers or the decision makers. Such a great cacophony of nationalist fervor was raised that more than hundred members of Indian Parliament demanded that Kalpana Chawla be conferred the highest award of the land 'Bharat Ratna' (Jewel of India). These MPs forgot that victims of terrorist killings do not often get any compensation even. Armed Forces Jawans (ordinary soldiers) killed while battling with terrorists are given a pension which is less than that of the lowest grade of civilian employee in the service of the government of India or the landed cost of the imported aluminium coffins, thoughtfully bought for carriage of the mortal remains, if terrorists leave some body parts to be retrieved! Kalpana Chawla's only act of patriotism that the Indian media could find out was that while she was an astronaut she had recommended some children from her Indian village to visit NASA installations for familiarization (indoctrination). She had forsaken her native land, culture, religion, native home/relations married a foreigner to achieve what she wanted and paid with her life in the bargain.

Contrast this with the quiet achievements of the USSR and even rump Russia. The USSR put a space station (MIR) in place more than two decades earlier (before America ventured into this field) and that carried out many path-breaking experiments which pushed forward the frontiers of knowledge. The space station with its visiting and resident spacecrafts (six space crafts could be docked and accommodated at any moment; how many spacecraft will be simultaneously docked in American International Space Station after it is completed, if ever?) had great manoeuvrability and many records in space application were broken. USSR/Russia forgot for six months, in the tumultuous period of break up of USSR under the able guidance of Gorbachev, that the crew was due for replacement. After six months the replacement could be sent. We wonder how long Colombia could hold on beyond the stipulated sixteen days of the mission. Our assessment is that very little time beyond the mission period was catered for. After all, additional stay in space means considerable amount of carried load which is a dead loss if mission is completed on schedule. Such luxury is not permitted in profit propelled economy. A most rational approach ought to have been to dock Colombia with a Russian Soyuz spacecraft or dock Columbia with the space station (provided, of course, the docking system was functional), rescue the crew members with Russian help, leave the Colombia parked in space station till a suitable repair scheme could be evolved. Russians would have been of great help, as they had earlier successfully repaired the MIR station in space after it was very seriously damaged by mishandling of a resident Soyuz spacecraft (laden with waste matter) while manoeuvring. Repairs to the Colombia would have been a simple matter compared to that carried out on MIR station, provided, of course, rational design philosophy was followed by USA. Might be it is too much to expect, knowing the state of profit-propelled US technology and management techniques. Have you wondered why America did not go for mammoth size rockets, missiles, engines or transport aircraft, nuclear or thermo-nuclear bombs etc. and yielded to USSR in all aeronautical and space records of size, speed, height attained or length of stay afloat? Not that they did not try or know their deficiencies, but their system critically depended on controlled and monitored immigrant labour (something more than 37 million in last count in 2007), whom they never fully trusted, because of their paranoia on national security, to deliver for big-sized projects. Their well-cultured siege mentality prevented any efficient use of resources. They had to go for miniaturization and sub-miniaturization so that the small bits and pieces could be forked out for design, fabrication, assembly to private parties and the subcontractors in captured and surrogate countries, without letting out anything about the end-use or the nature of final product. Computers came in very handy in this game of deception. Of course, deficiencies were touted around as great technological break-throughs by massive propaganda in captured media (which has been really the position in second and is continuing in 3rd millennium after Christ).

This diversion into discussion on high level technology was considered essential to put our ideas on economic issues in correct perspective as to what are the realities and how things are really presented. The type of canard, myths and falsehoods which are routinely purveyed in case of spacecraft high technologies are emulated with much vigour in case of economic theories and realities. We should never forget that economists are residents of fantastic world[19] to whom the realistic world appears as fantastic!

We can now authoritatively confirm that the plateau has been reached in costly, esoteric and absurd ways of technology development. Technologies are being synthesized in developed countries to keep growth within limits for control of its dissemination for ensuring continued profitability. Whenever a new technology or software programme is concocted, it is announced that it is the ultimate. The holder wants to foreclose further development. Why cars are still adorned with internal combustion engines only? Why micro-chips have not been adopted as extensively in cars as in say, aircraft or spacecraft or in communication systems or in nuclear bombs? When will non-polluting (e.g. without internal combustion engine for power) affordable individual locomotion systems be the preferred transportation in the world? When will storage of solar heat and light systems be evolved (at least for equatorial countries, which are having bounties of the Sun), say, with algae or some two/three parts aniline, bio-chemical, bio-electrical agents, paints--both inorganic and organic with some trigger, some even pure mechanical, etc. etc.? When will wind power propel the cars and buses? When will pure wind power stations (located on top of high-rise buildings without usurping agricultural lands) charge the complex spring systems of wind-power-driven vehicles instead of petrol/gasoline or that dangerously evil bio-fuel? Rational people ought to recognize now itself that bio-fuel and ethanol/alcohol based fuels are super costly, super-polluting and introduction of these fuels will mean the end of food security for Asia, Africa and Latin America and food-riots will be a constant occurrence in iniquitous undeveloped and underdeveloped countries like India. The field of alternative energy sources is really infinite, if only we can move out of profit propelled economic impulses for determining industrial choices! It is no use pretending that America does not determine the technology choices in the world. The status of management of technical equipment in America does not fill us with much hope for succour in the near future. Things will change provided Indian resurrection does come about soon enough!

These apart, now coming back to the "O-ring theory of low productivity". The venerable economist (Shri Basu) expresses the commonly known facts in mathematics and uses that to prove that developed countries are necessarily more productive and hence they deserve more income. There can be no greater example of the "circular Logic" as defined by Bertrand Russell! No wonder, developing countries can get no succor from the economists of the developed countries!

The parting gift of this author was in last Para of Section 2-4 (Page 39 Kaushik Basu *ibid*), proves once again that poor are ordained (by whom, God only knows) to remain poor and ill-equipped.

Analytical "Manifestations of unemployment" (Section 2.5 Kaushik Basu *ibid*) again glosses over the fact that enforced shortage of capital keeps employment of labour low in un/under-developed countries. Since most of the statistics in economic field are tendentious, doctored or fallacious, we can plead with the established economists to determine why employment of labour is so low (compared to developed countries) in education, basic services, food production and even in agriculture. Will someone, please, explain why number of soldiers per thousand population, or number of police men or number of judge's of High and Supreme Courts, number of public servants, number of Bank or railway ticket counters or square meters of covered accommodation or square meters of Railway Stations or Bus stations per thousand population should be so low in under and undeveloped countries as compared to developed countries? We are constantly being treated to the canard that India is a labour surplus country; then, pray do tell us, why Indian rice cultivators use less manpower per hectare than even the best rice (presumably most efficient) cultivators of Japan? Surely, enlightened economists will not tell us that for primary education, health care or production of basic food articles, imported technology, machinery, consultants or foreign exchange is required! The basic problem is that Indian economists do not have a national paradigm of development or even some relevant economic theories and Western (that is, so-called developed country) economists' theories or conclusions are totally irrelevant for a country like India.

Though economic theories of the developed world are irrelevant, on analytical considerations, but these have pernicious influence over the power and ruling elite of India. For example, the mathematics developed by economists[20] and conclusions drawn therefrom, might have prompted

Indian Government to invest and disinvest selectively, which, of course, increased the fiscal deficit and distress level of general populace.

EQUALITY AND EQUITY

Prof. Amartya Sen noted in his book[21] 'that 'the relation between inequality and rebellion is indeed a close one'. French revolution occurred due to perceived economic inequality. It is another matter that economic inequality or inequity did not get obliterated from France as a result of the cataclysmic events of the revolution. Manipulators, as always, captured the levers of power in every case. Historians may certify whether there is a single instance of a freedom movement or revolution giving lasting equality and equity to all the people of any country. Although Indian so-called freedom movement also was conducted, basically under the guidance of two stalwarts, Mahatma (a misnomer and a mistake by Rabindranath Tagore or is it that mahatmas do not come any better?) and Jawaharlal Nehru on the plank of perceived inequality vis-à-vis the colonizers, but India, in the morrow of independence, disavowed economic equity and equality as important for statecraft. They had a weird concept of equality, as Indian constitution only recognized racial or religious equality as fundamental right (to essentially legalize the partition of India on religious grounds and thereby gave constitutional sanctity to two/multi-nation state theory of the great Jinnah). Possibly, this delegalizing of equality, even though equality and equity have been nominally mentioned in the directive principles of state policy, prompted the Supreme Court of the country to even conclude that economic issues should not be brought to the court. We agree with Prof Sen that much of the modern welfare economics (to which Manmohanics pay obeisance) is concerned with precisely that set of questions which avoid judgments on income distribution altogether. Our politicians and judges are quite comfortable in avoiding the question of distributive justice and wax eloquent on having inclusive developments when the elite audience is receptive. The aberration of Manmohanics is buttressed by that captured organization going by the catchy name, World Bank. An[22] MD of the World Bank concluded on the basis of affluence of the upper crust of India, that India will become the world's third largest economy by 2030. Of course, this MD did not go through the annual WB reports as he would have noticed that India has one of the worst GINI index among large sized countries[23]. Of course, perverse economists can point out that the USA, the mighty super power, and Brazil, a massive country of South America, have some of the highest GINI indexes in the world, even though India is hankering for some technologies, as branded product, from USA and even imported aircraft for their VIP Squadron from a country like Brazil (2005, 2006 period)! How much blood and sweat of the natives of these countries are being shed for these technologies or aircraft! GINI index for India and other countries worsened with progress of economic reforms (see End Notes). Now Indian elite can go around telling that Indian future is 'Bright'[24], (like that of the donkey of the fables), as certified by a World Bank senior official! World Bank has given up on any semblance of equity, as will be evident from a newspaper report (*Hindustan Times*, New Delhi, 14 Dec 2006, *HT2 Business & World*, Page 27) Headlined

— BELL CURVE —

Developing nations in driver's seat:

Developing countries will grow at a higher rate than developed world. World Bank economist 'Hans Timmer' told reporters, "Developing countries are able to accelerate while high income countries are not doing that". In the next breath it reports "The gap between developing countries and high income countries is widening". Further ahead, the World Bank said globalization would spur faster growth in average incomes in the next 25 years. But unless managed carefully, that growth could spur growing inequality and potentially severe environmental pressures. Remedies suggested are, as ever, facile without any indication how inequality and ecological damages can be tackled. It seems, like our judges, WB also considers that equity cannot be made an issue in their courts!

Supreme Court of India has also put many limitations on exercise of the right to equality by their many judgments. We consider that equity being a single-dimension economic concept, equity can easily be ensured by sovereign exercise of power by a basically rational state. Assuming that the state has a stake in general welfare, we have incorporated our recommendations in the proposed amendments to the constitution. Before we discuss the validity of our recommendations, it is necessary to review the equity data furnished in World Bank Development Reports, e.g. report of 2000-2001. Some interesting data from this report is given hereunder:

GINI INDEX ANALYSIS

Serial No.	Country	GINI Index	INCOME DISTRIBUTION Lowest 10%	Highest 10%	Ratio of Highest 10%/ Lowest 10%
	FAILED STATES				
1	Sierra Leone	62.9	0.5	43.6	87 Totally failed
2	Guatemala	59.6	0.6	46.6	78
3	Central African Republic	61.3	0.7	47.3	68
4	Brazil	60	0.9	47.6	54
5	Lesotho	59.6	0.9	43.4	48
6	South Africa	59.3	1.1	45.9	42
7	Russian Federation	48.7	1.7	38.7	23 Least failed
	TERMINALLY SICK STATES				
1	USA (1997)	40.8	1.8	30.5	17 Totally sick
2	China	40.3	2.4	30.4	13

3	Germany	30	3.3	38.5	12
4	UK (1991)	36.1	2.6	27.3	11
5	India (1997)	37.8	3.5	33.5	10 Least sick
	SOMEWHAT CIVILIZED STATE				
1	Pakistan (96-97)	31.2	4.1	27.6	6.7 Worst
2	Japan	24.9	4.8	30.4	6.3
3	Rawanda (83-85)	28.8	4.2	24.2	5.8
4	Belgium	25	3.7	20.2	5.5
5	Sweden	25	3.7	20.1	5.4
6	Norway	25.8	4.1	21.8	5.3
7	Austria	23.1	4.4	19.3	4.4
8	Belarus	21.7	5.1	20	3.9 Best

The Extremely High GINI Index of America has a simple explanation. Of all the developed countries of the world, USA has the highest proportion of immigrant labour in its total labour force, which gets a fraction of the wages which white Americans get. Further, USA has a very high proportion of Negroes, Hispanics, Latin Americans, Mexicans and other people of Asian origin as its citizens, who get very unfair share of the national income. America has vast experience of handling slaves, and even though slavery was officially abolished long back, administrative, statutory and legal systems operate in such a way that virtual slavery is operating with full force even now. Leadership of every country knows it but they behave as if poor Americans cannot do any better than that under the circumstances (but what these circumstances are, is always kept a top secret from the natives of the respective countries). If any credence is to be given to World Bank data, the above mentioned depressed class of citizens of America is in overwhelming majority in the bottom 40% of American population!

Although, India has a better GINI Index than that of USA, the top most 10% of Indian population captures higher proportion of national income/consumption than USA. But bottom most 10% of Indians getting higher proportion of national income, (viz. it being dismal 3.3% for India as against 1.8 % for USA) indicates how fatuous and foreign is this question of equity in the citadel of Capitalism and Democracy, for which famous and powerful hearts of the Indian expatriates bleed![25]

Failed state like Brazil has got an improved GINI index compared to Sierra Leon by just having its lowest 10% earning 0.4% more than Sierra Leone, whereas, it's highest 10% had 4% more than the totally failed state. No wonder such a totally inadequate measure has been accepted by World Bank and IMF!

Our above analysis should open the eyes of the judges that market is not a leveler, whatever their great judicial minds might perceive otherwise.

The author was acutely aware that inequality data is rather several years old and has been looking out for more recent data to determine whether the downslide in Indian and world economy is continuing or has been reversed. The search was contra-indicated as the report in *The Hindustan Times*,[26] New Delhi, shows. GINI index and ratio of income of topmost 10% and lowest 10% of population have become worse for almost all countries. The mightiest super power, USA, and second world power, China, have joined the ranks of the failed states of Latin America, Africa and Middle East and Muslim-dominated Asia.

A few words on how and why some countries got selected for our review and conclusions. First of all, the best and worst countries got selected. Then some countries with special features or abnormalities, like, USA for its abnormally high GDP unsupported by correspondingly high productive efficiency, Pakistan without a properly functioning state organization or a representative government and also as a reference point for India; China for its large population whose governing philosophy is a heady cocktail of Communism and Capitalism. We selected countries wherein income distributions were absurdly skewed or highly desirable. The analysis gave us deep insight into how countries are being managed and why poverty is a constant companion of modern states. We have divided the selected countries into three categories, a) Failed States, b) Terminally Sick States, c) Somewhat Civilized States.

a) A state can be considered as failed, wherein the GINI Index is above 40% and/or the lowest 10% of the population get below 2% of the national income and/or highest 10% of the population get more than 40% of the national income and/or the ratio of the income of highest 10% of population to income of lowest 10% of population is more than 20.

b) A terminally sick state will have GINI Index above 30% and/or the lowest 10% of the population get below 4% of the national income and/or highest 10% of the population get more than 30% of the national income and/or the ratio of the income of highest 10% of population to income of lowest 10% of population is more than 10.

c) A civilized state will have GINI Index below 20% and/or the lowest 10% of the population get more than 6% of the national income and/or highest 10% of the population get less than 20% of the national income and/or the ratio of the income of highest 10% of population to income of lowest 10% of population will be less than 3, closer to 2 or less.

For mathematics-minded people the above conditions can be succinctly presented as below:

Category of Country	GINI Index	INCOME DISTRIBUTION Lowest 10%	Highest 10%	Ratio of Highest10%/ Lowest10%
FAILED	>40	<2	>40	>20

TERMINALLY SICK	>30	<4	>30	>10
CIVILIZED	<10-20	>6	<20	<2-3

After studying GINI Index data of the WB, we have also dared to classify the population of the countries into four categories:

a) Below Poverty Line (BPL) population are those who feature in the class who get lowest 20% share of national income as per WB. As per this criteria India has more than 200 million BPL personnel.

b) Poor are those whose income is above 20% but below 60% of income distribution as per WB. As per this criteria India in 2007 has more than 400 million poor people, excluding BPL people.

c) Middle Income are those whose income is above 60% but below 90% of income distribution as per WB; out of these, people earning income 80% to 90% of national income distribution of WB can be considered as Rich.

d) Affluent are those whose income is above 90% but below 99% of income distribution as per WB; Super Affluent pulls in income from 99% to top 100% of the national income distribution.

AGRICULTURE AND AGRICULTURISTS

Understanding Dr. Manmohan Singh's latest prescription (in mid-2007) for Indian agriculture needs Pavlovian reflexes of liberalized minds. Considering the fact that sickness of PSUs increased and agricultural growth rates have been steadily declining from the time he had something to do with the government - as RBI governor, Deputy Chairman of Planning Commission, central finance minister or Prime Minister - his sudden concern and allocation of Rs. 25000 crores to be spent on agricultural development in next four years tells a lot of untold stories. His 14 point action plan can, at best, be considered as an approach to understanding the problems and dimensions of agricultural crisis! As if, problems of Indian agriculture are not known since, at least, later part of nineteenth century! The whole intention of his scheme is to introduce and legalize contract farming and hand over farming control to profit-propelled private enterprises, so that all agriculturists can become contract or bonded labourers. Disabuse your mind that opposition parties will not join neo-Manmohanics! Portent is gloomy for India, provided agriculturists, artisans, workers and the poor do not make up their minds to 'deliver the order of the boot' to all overt and covert supporters of Manmohanics, i.e. everything evil perpetrated or being done under the slogans of economic reforms, liberalization or globalization.

We wonder what sort of mindset could conjure up a scheme for spending Rs. 25000 crores in four years for agriculture, whereas Tatas in one deal with Corus of UK could commit more than $12 Billion (i.e. about Rs. 60,000 crores) for taking nebulous control over a sick Steel company of UK. Apparently, saving UK based Corus is considered more important than ensuring Indian food security by our government and the Indian businessmen!

Absurdity of the scheme will be clear if we consider a simple arithmetic:

- Rs. 25000 crores to be spent in 4 years; hence yearly Rs 6250 crores to be spent.
- Assuming 30% of total population, i.e. 30 crores, i.e. 300 million agriculturists or agriculture dependent people,

Per capita yearly availability of fund will be = Rs. 62500 million/300 million = Rs. 208.33; or monthly Rs. 18.00!

We have assumed that all funds will reach agriculturists. That is a fond hope.

Congress Prime Minister Rajiv Gandhi, or someone as eminent, had said once that only 12 paisa per Rupee allocated actually reaches the target population.

You can now decide for yourself what revolution will occur in agricultural growth rate during the current tenure of this government.

Agriculturists constitute the bulk of the poor populace. If we have no intention of attacking perpetuated poverty, we cannot hope to tackle problems of agriculture. Ensuring SOCIAL SECURITY is the simplest and direct method of tackling problems of burgeoning poverty and those of agricultural sector.

SOCIAL SECURITY

There is no social security in India, as there is no money to spare for such luxury. The current theory of the elite is that social security can only be provided by rich countries – the corollary implied is that since India is an undeveloped country it has no call to provide social security, with the judiciary morosely agreeing with the power elite. If anyone argues that social security is more required in undeveloped countries, that person will be considered an aberrant specimen of humanity. Social security payments go in procuring the basic essentials of life and living, domestic consumption goes up thereby, more basic goods and services get produced and marketed. If income velocity shows trend towards decline that will be a notice that someone or entity is effecting supply-compression and supply-management for profiteering to improve the so-called 'bottom-line'. More GDP growth will necessarily result in more job creation, provided government policies do not permit job-compression by such diabolical devices as BPO (outbound Business Process Outsourcing by Indian or alien entities), acquiring of industries and businesses abroad by the wealthy Indians and excessive expenditures by the government and elite on luxury-goods.

We have recommended a simple social security measure. Every man/woman/child whose income level is low and male child upto age of 18, female child upto age of 20 and unemployed adult will automatically get (without any paper work) every month from central treasury or central bank (i.e. RBI) an amount equal to the 'Monthly Statutory Wages for Unskilled Labour', as social security payment. The requisite amount (indexed to inflation every quarter) can be credited monthly to debit/identity card issued to all Indians by Election Commission. It will be culpable crime of Election Commission if they fail to ensure provision of I-Card, interim if necessary, to all Indians entitled for social security payment from the treasury within first six months of the promulgation of social security scheme and provide regular I-card to them within first one year.

It is expected that there will be three strands of counter-actions from the power elite. First counter measure will be to ignore the issues raised here as absurd fulminations of unsound mind or those of marginalized political entities. Second counter measure will be to reduce statutory wages to absurd low levels. We have defined statutory wages to be equal to the average wages of bottom 50% of the employed unskilled worker and not less than average income of lowest 40% of all employed (skilled/unskilled) labour.

The third line of counter action by the elite might be in further distorting the remuneration policy. This line will not be available as we have recommended constitutional amendment to ensure equitable distribution of national income and that all remuneration will be linked to statutory minimum wages. They can go ahead and reduce statutory wages, then top bureaucrats, politicians, industrial and business tycoons will lose their cozy and costly life-styles. Prof. Amartya Sen has argued that comparative poverty is considered as most worrisome by the poor or dispossessed. It is also an established fact that production of high-cost luxury goods and super-complex technologies lead to excessive demands on the Biosphere – reprehensible actions by the super developed countries and super-rich segment of the nation.

COST OF ELEMENTARY SOCIAL SECURITY

Population of India – 1.1Billion (assumed in 2006)

People who will be entitled for social security:

a) Male children upto the age of 18 and girls upto the age of 20 (irrespective of whether employed or not) of the lowest earning 40% of population – say, 20% of population

b) Women and girls of lowest earning 50% of population - say 5% of population

c) Males of lowest earning 30% of population - say 5% of population

d) Unemployed adults – say 5% of population

e) Total percentage of population who will be entitled for social security payment – 35%.

Assuming minimum statutory wages as: [12 months × 365 days×8 hours per day×Rs. 6 per hour = Rs. 210240 or rounded to] Rs. 21000/- (for comfort of penny-wise pound-foolish economists) per year, the social security payment cost to the nation will be:

1.1 Billion×0.35×Rs. 21000 = Rs. 8085 Billion = approximated to Rs. 9 Trillion (to cater for the essential leak in administrative delivery system, i.e. pilfering by power elite). Judges, economists, administrators and politicians, 'Hold your heart, don't throw a fit'! This amount can easily be found by cutting back the requisite amount from the concessions of more than Rs. 35 Trillion now being given to big businesses, as reported by *India Today* weekly magazine published from New Delhi.

Above recommendations have sound economic rationale. Equity being a single-dimension economic concept, it can easily be ensured by sovereign exercise of power by a basically rational state. Assuming that the state has a stake in general welfare and it has still some residual powers in the privatized world, we recommended the desired constitutional amendment and for immediate enforcement.

Fulfilling all the elements of our recommendations pose theoretical and philosophical problems. We offer this as a problem to all developed country mathematicians (including Forbes Nash with a reminder that he has done enough damage to economic doctrines by applying his game theory for profit-maximization. He could consider applying Game theory for equity maximization/optimization also). Let's see if they come out with a solution acceptable to us. In the mean time we are happy to use the guide-lines developed above in this respect.

We consider that equity is easily attainable. The simplest way to bring about equity is adequate mobilization of the country. We presume doubting economists or theosophists like Prof Amartya Sen will not see red and comprehend the reason why we have so much impatience with the current liberalized economy and their supporters.

3

RELEVANCE OF WELFARE ECONOMICS FOR UNDEVELOPED COUNTRIES

Some partisans claim Economics to be a "Science", others acclaim it as an 'Art' and still others treat this as "Artistic Science". I personally consider this sort of organised study as "Voodoo Science" or "Alchemy". Like the last two pseudo sciences, economists do not believe in any set laws, rules or regulations universally valid or relevant for all circumstances or for all times and places. Economists often keep giving solutions to problems without knowing the problems or who are really affected or benefited. Economists do not have any need for a stable or significant relationship amongst various factors of the economy. They normally do not have or recognize any law like the "Charles' Law", "Boyles Law" "Avogadro's number", "Law of Gravitation", "Law of Mass Action", "Einstein's equation relating Mass and Energy" etc. etc. Some economists by ignoring the law of "Mass Action", eliminated the dominant factor (i.e. labour) from the production function to come to the astounding conclusion that capital is the determinant for growth[27]! Incidentally the law of 'mass action' stipulates that in chemical reactions, the relative masses of the reactants determine in which direction the reaction will proceed and the direction of the reaction can be changed by changing the relative masses at the time of reactions. In a similar vein, it can be expected that the so-called "Production Functions" of economics will nominally or notionally, if not rigorously, follow this law of mass action. Then, presence of large amount of labour (in a production function) can only mean more production. The whole basis of mainstream economics is on the principle that resources must go to the selected group in preference to some other group. The group is selected on the basis of some and other non-economic criteria if not by sheer application of superior force. Some contrived criteria are always used for such preferential allocation of resources, it is no one's concern that economic justification does not exist! The legal system does not also question the policies of bureaucrats, if these are not directly or indirectly hurting their or other bureaucratic interests.

LAWS OF ECONOMY

Study of the working of the existing economics and analysis of the behavioral patterns of the economy in international milieu, certain laws become apparent. The most fundamental Laws of International Economy are given below:-

1. **First Law of Economics :-** Wealth and Resources have natural anti-gravity characteristics. Higher the level, higher is the concentrations of the factors of production.

2. **Second Law of Economics :-** Resources flow or get allocated to non-productive sectors or elements in preference to productive sectors or elements.

3. **Third Law of Economics :-** Irrespective of philosophy of statecraft, controllers of economy prefer central allocation for distribution of Resources.

4. **Fourth Law of Economics :-** There is always an alien power/entity controlling the essential economic parameters of the 'controlled' country.

(a) ***Corollary*** : Economy of weak countries are controlled by economically strong country(s).

5. **Fifth Law of Economics :-** Military strength is the determinant of economic strength.

   (Note: A parodied version of the famous dictum of the great Mao Zedong succinctly expresses this law, viz: "Economic Growth Flows through the Barrel of the Gun". Of course, it is assumed that the gun is in the hand of the native and not in the hand of the alien!)

6. **Sixth Law of Economics:-** If Terrorism is not controlled, it leads to 'double capture' of Economy:-

   (a) Terrorism bleeds the economy directly.

   (b) Continued existence of terrorism indicates a weakened State. Foreigners get undue advantage, as helplessness generates dependence on imports for sustenance. These States are easily manipulated.

{Note: India is a classic example of the validity of this law. No one has made the common man wiser as to what is the cost of the standoff in the borders with Pakistan and continued display of India's strategic weakness. It is reported in mainstream media that Rs. 4000 crores (in 2003) are being spent per month for upkeep of military apparatus in ever lasting stand-off with Pakistan in J&K, with armed forces completely shackled and the economy lurching from one crisis to another. India, it seems, at super power insistence, cannot cross the Line of Control running within Indian Territory and punish the intruders, nor can it use the Indian Air force to cut off the cross-border terrorists or their logistics and training centres and weapons dumps. Apparently, what super power or Israel can do with a view to contain cross-border terrorism cannot be replicated by India! Pusillanimity, induced by fear of disapproval by super power, is ensuring that a new front will be added in erstwhile East Pakistan (now called Bangladesh) border with India in next 2 to 3 years. Everybody, including Indian judiciary, believes Indian variety of national sovereignty works here!}

ECONOMIC CONCEPTS AS BENUMBING NECTAR FOR PEOPLE

All learned economists, including my masters, instinctively believe that poor are actually responsible for their poverty. It seems, it cannot be academically justified that poverty and the "stable, quasi-stable equilibrium in poverty state[28] which poor country or the poverty-stricken face are not all ingrained in the system, or, imposed on the country. It has not occurred to the erudite persons that such arguments run counter to the explanations of the greatest man-made Bengal famine of 1943 during British regime and similar occurrences of acute scarcity of food in Africa and other continents given by Prof. Amartya Sen. It is astounding that it has not featured in analytical studies of the possibility of an external force or power giving that much (beneficial or inimical) inputs which keep the poverty state in a stable, quasi-stable or meta-stable state. My observation of Indian economy shows that left to themselves, government recognized economists will always ensure that bulk of the investment goes to those sectors where the Income Velocity of Money is lesser, with laws of economics operating fully!

Frederic Engels noted about two and quarter centuries earlier that at initial stages of pre-historic human kind, there was no exploitation of one individual by the other. Initially, both male and female were equally taking part in food gathering, especially hunting. Apart from some pilferage, one could not deny or deprive another individual for too long without meeting nemesis. As the individuals coalesced into convenient groups and families, exploitation of the weaker members of this group or family started off. In human beings, transition from savagery, barbarism, early modern and post modern civilizations, exploitation has grown in magnitude and complexity but camouflaged with well-meaning protestations.

Marx had correctly guessed that without annihilation of 'State' it will not be possible to free men/women from assorted controls and bondages but he also went wrong grievously by declaring that 'Dictatorship of the Proletariat' was the answer. In soteriology of the Semitic kind, one Lord or his representative (all the great people of the Semitic religions apparently had direct communion and communication with God and they apparently could pass on these rare powers to their successors like Popes, Bishops, Khalifas, Sultan's etc). These prophets and the chosen representatives of the god were supposed to be able to dictate what is right and wrong and issue edicts for conduct of humans and their affairs! If only Marx had acquainted himself with the Hindu doctrines of religion or statecraft, he would not have prescribed dictatorship for management of the state. The western and the rest of the world had at the same time legalized and justified exploitation of various forms in the name of propagation of religion, capitalism, market economy. Now a great build up is being given to oligarchic democracy. The western countries, with uncommon zeal, emphasized and enforced each of these instrumentalities on hapless countries of Asia, Africa and in South America. Even after some of these countries attained their so-called independence, European countries successfully used religion and captured market. The super/big powers found that international agreements, multinational institutions, elaborate treaties and conventions were very successful in keeping the people tied to developed country legal framework, so that unabashed exploitations could be continued. Of course, where such indirect control was not effective enough, these super countries did not flinch from waging direct military intervention without bothering about international reactions or sensitivities of that much-vaunted organization called the UN. Of course, the greatest of the super countries ensured that their foreign interventions were funded by virtually captured countries like Japan, Germany and India, with a P-5 country like China providing a big helping hand by maintaining massive international reserves and supplying abysmally cheap goods and services by starving the native population and by even risking heightened popular disenchantment with regard to management of the economy and social services.

The net result of all these has been burgeoning poverty. Here I will bow to Prof. Amartya Sen and accept his wider connotation of poverty. I ruefully note that Shri Kaushik Basu or Prof. Amartya Sen did not clearly recommend that the allocation of resource to be on the basis of Income-Velocity of money of that sector. Whereas, no one can contest the prescription for synchronized expansion in many sectors, but it is a fact of life that in a poor economy, synchronized expansion does not, or is not allowed to happen and poverty trap continues. That essential feature of Say's Law viz., "private interest"[29] is repulsive of Hindu concepts of equity or rationality and that this concept is suo moto absurd seems to be unthinkable amongst the mainstream economists. It is in this context that we have chosen to examine Malthus' ideas a little more critically hereunder.

MALTHUS AND SCIENCE/TECHNOLOGY

Malthus' conjecture on population and food growth rates is, possibly, the most puerile, most incoherent, most misused and most widely known economic concept in human history. Malthus, like other economists of his time and of later periods, could not find it convenient to accept that humans have two hands and one mouth only. Further, Malthus supporters are quite oblivious of the fact that labour always produces a surplus, as otherwise, capitalist or industrial production regimes would not have come into being. Malthus assumed that things will broadly remain the same as in his time. But advances in science and technologies may force economists to propagate the reverse of what Malthus did. Human beings need roughly 2 Kg of food per day 365 days in a year. If the available food could be distributed better and if systemic wastages could be reduced to some extent, there would be no shortages in the foreseeable future even at current rate. This is one aspect of political and economic game-playing with food security. The following developments may be noted.

Genetic Engineering of human body will ensure that the body can extract more energy from available food. Major portion of the ingested food is removed from the body in the form of excreta, urine, sweat, tear, mucous, gases, etc., etc. Already some Genetically Modified food is available in the market. This is only an elementary step. Future GM (hopefully, of course, not the mutants of the current variety, which have more deleterious effect than benefits) foods will be virtual energy packs, whereby small quantities of these will provide sufficient energy and roughage and medicines to the body. Notwithstanding facile protestations, cloned human beings will be produced rather in a short spell of time, say, in several decades or so (with the connivance and funds of the most righteous-sounding big powers). Cloned human can be made to need less food and that also infrequently. We apprehend that cloning will come under strict control and denial regimes!

Future GM modified body will need less energy for sustenance of life and living. Need and functionality of many organs of the body will change. Food might be demanded infrequently (say after a lapse of days, months or years like in many species of animals).

All these feasible and foreseeable developments will render current food economics redundant. The GM foods will make it possible to eliminate spectre of starvation and hunger, which is apparent in vast tracts of the world of today. Less food requirement will mean less dedicated land area for food production.

Food politics and economics is the main ingredient of power projection of the elite and exploitation of the less developed countries presently. As a consequence of these developments, the intra-national and international power equations will change a lot if individuals, communities and nations can be independent in respect of food.

We need not rejoice in a hurry, as all these developments will take place outside the sphere of influence of the developing and undeveloped countries. Once the developed countries comprehend the potentialities of such developments, they will move in with their denial, control and sanction regimes so that benefits of science and technology will not easily flow across the boundaries of the discriminating powers!

We cannot get Malthus to retract or make amends or change the mindset of the already developed countries, but our power elite needs to keep these factors in mind while formulating policies.

MANAGEMENT OF ECONOMY

The manner in which Indian government manages its economy reveals that the whole establishment has been convinced that sustaining poverty and keeping military debilitated is the only way that the economy can be satisfactorily managed. This comes out in stark reality when examine the great yearly ritual of national budgeting. Objectives of the budgets of the constituent states of the Indian republic are. worse.

BUDGET 2002-2003

Ordinary Indians can only gaze in wonder and disbelief how the Indian economy is being taken from one crisis to another year after year; as if, managers of the economy have nothing better to do than prescribe the same medicines in bigger doses which have been making the patient ever weaker! We had cautioned that privatization of Insurance business will increase fiscal deficit and lead to massive devaluation of the Rupee - these have come to pass - but managers of economy are not willing to take a detour or a turn - not to talk of a U-turn - in policy-thrust! We have been assiduously cautioning that privatization of PSUs and PSEs at this juncture, when the economy is in downswing, at below the asset-value (at throw away prices on the advice of consultant or Valuer, who are barely knowledgeable or who are barely competent for the job) is going to increase the distress levels in the economy and lead to increased fiscal deficit.

The reality check has also convinced all concerned that common man, in any case, is voiceless and helpless in the political milieu today. Otherwise, it cannot be rationally argued that items of mass and essential consumption must be taxed more and that different service sectors to be brought under tax net so that the burden can be passed on to the lower income groups. The concern for imported liquor, imported cosmetics and drugs and lowering of import duties to absurd low levels cannot be explained from economic perspective or logic. Of course, legion of economic and administrative advisers could not have made the ministers aware that India collects the least amount of 'Customs Duty Per Capita' in the world. If any of the advisors had cared to look up the US Budget of 2000, he would have found that America collected about $ 79 per capita, whereas India collected less than $ 5 per capita in Customs Duty as per the Indian Budget 2001. Who will tell these advisors that Customs Duty should be linked to share of world trade and linked to reasonable per capita collection?

Indian share of world trade has been precipitously going down since the liberalisation (i.e. westernization and impoverishment and derecognizing of the claim to equity by the common Indian) has been accepted as inevitable and internalized by the power-elite.

Further, who will convince them that artificially fixed Exchange Rate and constant devaluation of the Indian Rupee under the contrived REER (Real Effective Exchange Rate) and NEER (Net Effective Exchange Rate) of RBI is sapping the vitality of Indian Economy and debilitating Indian trade and business and making International Competitiveness a chimera? Who will convince them that India is duty bound to only support the Rupee-Dollar Exchange Rate fixed in 'Bretton Woods Agreement' and that USA has passed on its devaluation load (i.e. mis-management of American economy) to India by the mechanism of so-called 'Market Determined (actually speculator determined) Exchange Rate'? The power-elite know they can afford to ignore such issues as success as economy-manager is not dependent on welfare of or acceptance by the general populace of India. What will convince the managers that high price of imported goods and services in Indian market is due to absurdly low exchange rate of Rupee being maintained by the Government and RBI and this is the main cause of distress in the Indian economy? After Soros (that great American wizard of public finance, trade, economy etc.) publicly humiliated the Malaysian Prime Minister, the later abused back and did something more substantial. He ignored the advice of WB/IMF and other assorted foreign advisors and fixed the exchange rate of his currency, Ringit, to 3.5 Ringit to a Dollar, whereas, the so-called market rate was from 60 to 40 Ringit to a Dollar. In less than two years, the Malaysian economy came out of the woods!

How many Indians know that RBI and Ministry of Finance are mainly responsible for continuous devaluation of the Indian Rupee and for ensuring that India collect the least amount of Foreign Exchange for every unit of export and thereby ensuring continuously declining share of World Trade? The increased Dollar Reserve has been indicated as a justification for provision of full so-called 'Capital Account Convertibility' to NRIs and foreign entities. It can be authoritatively confirmed that this discriminatory 'Capital Account Convertibility' is economically unsound, violative of the RBI Act of 1934, and is fraught with dangers of Political/Social costs.

Almost every measure announced in the Budget 2002 can be faulted on considerations of economic prudence, political morality, political reality, international stability, Indian legality and propriety and, most important of all, national security. Take the cases of increase in prices of Kerosene and LPG or fertilizer. Which technically qualified Valuer, with IQ (Intelligence Quotient) and OLQ (Officer

Like Quality, as measured for Armed Forces Officers) equal to or above of average of top 10% Indians, will accept the contentions that these items of mass consumption by the people are really being subsidized or that it is not a canard propagated by interested parties? Will official economists/ administrators release the relevant data for comparison of retail prices in the supplying country, Import prices paid by India and actual Issue Price to Indian Consumers? Pray explain why prices of these mass consumption items must be so different in India in Indian Rupee as compared to what the American consumers pay in Dollars or Saudi Arabians in Dinars or Russians in Roubles? Some administrator/advisor/ economist must be responsible for ensuring continued import of these essential items. For example, some vested interests must have permitted the new Refineries (in Private and public sectors) not to produce or not sufficiently produce, kerosene for domestic use, LPG or feedstock for fertilizers, so that they could earn extra profit by manipulating import and export trade and raising the bogey of subsidy. Some oxymoron[30] or rank anti-national elements could permit import of technology or machinery for Oil Sector which permitted Billion/Trillion Dollars worth of Gas being 'flared' every year, instead of using this gas for domestic or commercial use!

In Indian scheme of things, National Security measures are not considered as a useful economic activity. Our power-elite need not know that "growth flows through the barrel of the gun" (of course, it is assumed that the gun is not in the hands of the terrorist). That defence expenditure should be met from normal budgetary receipts is not accepted Hence they have come out with a surcharge on Income Tax for meeting the cost of enhanced mobilization (for protracted periods) of the armed forces on the borders. Bulk of this economic burden will have to be borne by the low income tax payers as the Direct Tax regime is highly regressive in India and takes away the purchasing power of those in the lower rung of the economic *totem-pole*. The Budget 2002 could provide that this Surtax would only be applied to those with yearly income above one Million Rupees. The administrative cost for collecting this tax would have been then comparatively less. A little more money in the hands of the low-end Taxpayers would have been good for the health of the economy!

A study published in *Outlook* magazine dated 10th April 2001 shows that 99.5% Taxpayers with annual income below Rupees five lakhs pay 67% of the tax; whereas, 0.5% Taxpayers with yearly income of a million Rupees or more pay only 33% of the Direct Tax. An analysis will show that in India this Rich and Super-Rich segment of Taxpayers control 90% of the national income. Thus the top segment while controlling 90% of the economy/Income pays a pittance (33%) as tax. Successive Finance Ministers have been keen on reducing the Tax burden on this top and influential segment only. Thus the bulk of the burden of keeping the armed forces in alert in borders will have to be borne by the low and lowest income groups.

In the same study of *Outlook* magazine, it has been revealed that in no other developed or developing country are the low salary/income earners taxed so ruthlessly as in India. This unreasonable anxiousness to save the rich and super rich from the burden of direct and indirect taxes is at the root of India's economic stagnation and is continuation of the policies mandated by the British while they had the Indian sub-continent in their colonial control. If only the yearly income below Rupees five lakhs could be kept out of Direct Tax net and all the attention of the tax authorities could be directed to the ones with yearly incomes of Rupees one million or above, then the tax collection would have gone to International levels of 25% of GDP, even with the existing peak rate of taxation. Then purchasing power in the economy would have gone up and Indian economy could revive out of perennial stupor with the stagnation-deflation vanishing!

Although inflation has always been a bugbear of the Indian economy, there has been speculation in the media recently (around 2005) that the current low inflation rate (of around 2 - 3%) is not really good for India. No one has authoritatively clarified the links amongst the various indicators of the economy, viz.: low inflation rate, low employment growth rate, low interest rate, excess of liquidity in banking sector, low growth rates in manufacturing and other production and service or primary or secondary sectors, very low per capita availability of food, very high grain buffer stock (with high and fat rodent population), low off-take from public distribution system, very low rates of growth in almost all other sectors and high fiscal deficits. We believe this condition typically represents a classic **"Stagnation-Low Purchasing Power induced Deflation"** scenario, though not accepted as such.

The FCI could have used the stockpiled grains as a business venture and, with the massive yearly investment in it, could have easily converted itself into a Food Bank and Food-lending/Bonding agent for the cultivators. It was incumbent on the FCI to create vertical Silos of steel/stainless steel for storage of grains and thereby give a fillip to industrial growth, instead of creating sheds for stacking of grains in gunny or plastic bags. With their stocking arrangement, FIFO (First In First Out) cannot be ensured and only rodent, insects and intermediaries are the major beneficiaries. If only the FCI had gone in for building Silos of various capacities of, say, 5 tons to hundreds of thousands of tons and dispersed the storage to production areas with interconnection through underground pipelines for conveying grain and granulated products, lot of saving in storage, handling, transportation, quality assurance and nutrition support to the deserving could be ensured.

I am constrained to prognosticate that if this budget is passed without significant changes in approach and methodology, India is headed for increased social tensions aggravated by high inflation, further devaluation of the Rupee to anything, say, touching even Rs. 50/- per Dollar and occasional depleting FE reserves (to arrest the precipitous fall in Rupee value) and additional FDI and also, possibly, flight of capital, facilitated by preferential capital account convertibility. Only perceptive observers of Indian scene will admit that the riots in Gujarat are one manifestation of the peoples' frustration with the strategic pusillanimity of India with respect to Pakistan/Big powers, combined with economic stagnation and insensitiveness of the authorities to popular concerns. During British period, Bengal (particularly, East Bengal) was comparatively most favoured region and opposition to British (including armed intervention) was the most extensive in Bengal, particularly, in the Eastern part. In post-independent India, most of the heinous protests against the rulers took place in comparatively richer regions.

Conventional economists moan the lack of sufficient savings by Indians. Of course, a look at World Development Report of the World Bank reveals that India has one of the highest Savings Rate and lowest Consumption rate. Another significant feature of India's saving is that bulk of the saving is done by the unorganized Domestic sector. Savings by Corporate sector are very little and the saving by the Private Corporate Sector is more than offset by massive NPAs (non-performing assets) in Banks, FIs, NBFCs and Mutual Funds. In fact, public sector Banks and FIs, like IDBI, IFCI, ICICI and the great UTI have all been made non-viable by the NPA's run up by the private corporate sectors. And the doyen of private corporate sectors sit in the Governing Boards of RBI and of all these institutions and decide policies and rules of conduct! Of course, savings of the ordinary Indians go down the drain, albeit totally legally!

Small savings is a source of cheap capital. The interest payment for small savings is considered onerous, but not the additional fiscal deficit associated with fall in small savings!

The resilience of Indian economy is such that it does not need any shock-therapy of burdening the low-income earners further (as is often advised by foreign advisors and Indian advisors suitably 'educated' by the foreign entities) as was given by Gorbachov-Yeltsin duo to the Soviet Russian and Russian economy successively for crippling these for a long time to come. Some very simple and straightforward steps will kick-start the moribund Indian economy without increasing social costs or increasing burden on the poor/ middle class.

India has the least Per Capita Money Supply. Increase in money supply will enable monetization of the attainable GDP. Incidentally, no developed country holds back GDP growth for lack of local currency. Reserves required for additional money supply can be had by bringing the public-held gold in RBI/Banking Sector Reserves. India must have a proper "Purchasing Power Parity Exchange Rate". If Malaysia could get away with a fixed exchange rate, surely, India can take courage! India must leave reasonable purchasing power in the hands of the low/lower-income population. Direct Tax must start with annual incomes of Rupees five lakhs and above only. More of the high-end income earners and spenders must be brought under tax regime. Tax regime must be progressive instead of being regressive as at present. In order to reduce dependence on Indian labour, many Indian and all foreign entities spend capital disproportionately. In order to prevent extravagant expenditures for reducing local labour, certain amount of tax on expenditures in excess of the All-India-Average for different activities should be immediately introduced. Further, there should be an expenditure tax on capital expenditure in excess of all-India-average of "Capital-Labour Ratio".

Nothing done; this Minister got defeated in Lok Sabha elections in 2004 and got promptly selected for Rajya Sabha! Amen!

BUDGET 2003-2004

Budget 2003-2004 starkly manifested what Sharad Joshi used to say about the divide between 'Bharat' and 'India'. The most relevant comments made by some commentators were: "Heera will be cheap and Zeera will be costly", "we are Globalized, so we must destroy Indian enterprises so that high-cost import becomes the most natural thing", "we are such lovers of the country that we keep Excise duty three times or more than the corresponding Customs duty for same or similar items". Budget 03-04 is also silent on the need for or an outline of a rational policy for pricing of imported goods and services.

The FM has claimed that he is not an economist (as if we had any India-centric economist ever as FM!), but we do hope he will not remind us of 'Gujral Doctrine' ('of Helplessness and No Responsibility')! Since he is not an Indian economist (trained in Western universities and institutes for slave procurer/trader/driver) he need not have followed in the footsteps of so-called reformers, the succeeding FMs of the same ilk! Common Indians fail to see why there must be such massive Fiscal Deficit, when the Customs duties and taxes and charges on the Corporate and top 10% of the population were lowered, and simultaneously putting additional Service Tax and indirect tax loads which burden will mostly be carried by the bottom 80% of the population. Lowering of Interest Rates for small savings has been the most unnecessary and savage blow to the fixed wage-earners, pensioners and old, indigent and the low income earners. Shenanigans of the UTI, LIC, SBI, RBI, Banking sector, NBFC's, Bourses and Regulators have eroded the faith of the common man on sovereign guarantees and the instrumentalities of the State.

When Agriculture is languishing and retreating, fertilizer, diesel, electricity prices are increased to benefit the importers and corporate sector. When urban decay is almost complete due to badly planned and executed civic services, Flyovers, Over-ground MRTS and heartless dislocation of the poor from the central districts of the metropolises in the name of ecology, diesel, petrol and LPG prices are increased!

His Insurance scheme will also turn out to be a bad dream ultimately. If the poor really can first mobilize

Rs. 30,000/- for his treatment and hospitalization and then wait interminably for reimbursement from the Insurance agencies, why can't he pay even Re. 1/- per day, which is also proposed to be subsidized? We cannot imagine why finance ministry could not think of asking the Insurance companies to pay directly to the Hospital/ Nursing Home where the insured go for treatment/ hospitalization, instead of making the poor to run around to get his reimbursement? Why must all such schemes be so mindless or heartless? And which major illness/debility can be cured with Rs. 30, 000/- by a private nursing home or hospital?

After singing paeans for enhanced healthcare and medical facilities, mountain has produced a mouse! There is not a word about restoring or upgrading the facilities in the existing public hospitals, dispensaries or pharmacies which are in abominable state due to continued neglect, are filthy, without basic facilities and amenities and are in immediate need for attention of the powers that be! All facilities and concessions will only be available to private operators. Even Budget allocation for public medical and healthcare is only a miniscule percentage of the budget for one billion plus population and is much lower than so-called IT sector, for providing cheap goods and services to America/Europe at slave-rate of remuneration; infrastructure for ensuring continued import of dated technology products at exorbitant prices and at the cost of Indian labour, and other sectors which are comparatively less important for 'Bharat'!

Then the Antyodaya scheme! The politician in ***(name obliterated) ought to have understood that any partial coverage with token funds in India remains a prototype all the time and will never ever be allowed to cover the full target group by the bureaucracy. We cannot find any economic reasons for not covering all the people below poverty line with sufficient funds in one shot itself. The required funds could easily be found by cutting out some export subsidy (which is running anywhere between forty thousand to hundred thousand crores of Rupees) and ensuring that exporters do not sell goods and services below Indian or international market prices (once again the need for a rational pricing formula arises). The other alternative is to bring back some idle FE (international) reserves enriching the American Banking system and issuing more currency in the domestic market. WB report of 2000-2001 records that Industrial Sector in USA gets 170% of GDP from Banking Sector alone; the currency supply for the whole economy must be in excess of 400% of GDP. The MOF should direct RBI to immediately double the money supply and stop issuing public loans till the fiscal deficit is eliminated. The MOF could also pay more heed to the advice of Nobel Laureates of Economics like, Prof. Amartya Sen of Harvard/Cambridge and Joseph Stiglitz, ex-Chairman of Council of Economic Advisers of USA of Clinton era and Chief Economist of WB/IMF (before that Indian born economist Dr. Raghu Ram Rajan took over) in this regard. Keeping all our FE reserves abroad makes no economic sense and no developed country does that. We wonder when the politicians in our MOF will recognize that managing the Indian economy for the benefit of the Americans mainly may be good diplomacy but bad politics! However much praise and accolades the FM may gather from corporate magnates in India and abroad or in Davos or in other capitalist conclaves and conventions, he will not deliver the popular votes for his party/conglomerate or serve the basic interests of the country, if he does not orientate his budget objectives away from the present line.

This MP also lost his parliamentary seat in general elections in 2004 and promptly entered the Rajya Sabha, the sinecure of the invalids!

TAX MANAGEMENT

The aim of Indian Finance Ministers and other economy Managers and their methods of achieving their aims cannot be deciphered even by God, what to talk of mere mortals. The tax proposals of Finance Minister in the budget of 2005-2006 once again demonstrated why the Finance Minister must widen the tax-net to wider sections of disadvantaged people. This paper (*HT*, Delhi, March, 2001) in its front page gave the tax proposals and also gave examples of taxes and benefits of the new proposals for three levels of income earners:

Income Level	Tax		Tax Saving by Tax Payer and Revenue Loss to Government
	Previous	New	
Rs. 3 Lakhs	40,800	15,300	25,500
Rs. 6 Lakhs	1,50,960	1,02,000	48, 960
Rs. 12 Lakhs	3,68,016	3,14,160	53,860

Thus, for making up the revenue loss incurred on each income earner of Rs. 12 Lakhs, four additional persons earning income of Rs. 3 Lakh or below will have to be brought in the tax net; more such low earners will have to bear tax burden for comfort of high wage earners. This is the modern liberalized version of 'equity'!

Tax authorities are frittering their energies on chasing low income earners, so that they can leave the rich untouched. This sort of irrationality is abounding in all economic decisions of reformed and liberalized elite. One thing always stands out that our administrators and official and mainstream economists never ever think of carrying out a management game or war/paper game to determine to what extent the proposed measure or game/administrative/ economic plan will fulfill the desired aim or whether the desired goal (where it is articulated) will be reached in the specified time frame. The *E T*, New Delhi, 9th March, 2006, came out with a catchy front page headline "Did You Give P C (meaning P Chidambaram, the Finance Minister) Share of Money You spent" and depicted with lurid details how a little more than 17 lakh High Income Earners splurged more than Rs. 11 lakh (hundred thousand) crores – a third of Indian current GDP – of course without paying tax and legally at that! This sample data has been culled from the Annual Information Returns by banks, credit card companies and mutual funds. We are required to believe that such information was unknown (or ought to have been unknown) to the tax administration, revenue intelligence, plethora of government statistical organizations, economic think-tanks etc. or to the people who compile data on GDP, National Income, per capita GDP and other beautiful statistics, like GINI index, which the World Bank religiously publish in their annual reports and other statistics.

If any one thinks that the Government will take reasonable action to correct the existing state of affairs for the sake of equity, he will be sadly mistaken. With utmost concern we observed that even judiciary at the apex level hands down decisions/verdicts/edicts/*obiter dicta* on tax and other economic issues like privatization, disinvestment, market etc., with no demonstrated concern what collateral damages these might cause to the common men who cannot hope to seek clarification or special leave for review or reconsideration of the decisions etc. It can never be expected that some sort of paper game will be carried out by the registry of the apex court to bring out how grotesque and cruel some verdicts, obiter dicta, etc. might actually be to those people near and below the poverty line.

JUDICIAL INTERVENTION

Four communications were sent to judges of the *** court, one to the President of India and the so-called popular President of the republic was reminded several times, but there has been no response, even though the missives were rather provocative.

(Letter dated 19 July 2005)

I have the honour to refer to the news item in *The Economic Times*, New Delhi, Saturday 9 July 2005 (page 2) titled "— Judges deliberate on socio-economic changes". In the report it has been mentioned that '31 experts from diverse fields such as governance, economics, technology and science shared their knowledge with the people whose verdicts decide the fate of the people'. A photo copy of the news item is enclosed for ready reference.

We presume that the main theme of presentation of the experts was that the current course of changes being brought about in the socio-economics and cultural spheres are essentially beneficial to the people of India, and that these changes are inevitable, necessary and sufficient. We do not know if any alternative model of changes was also presented. I wish to most humbly enter a caveat that all the above said assumptions are wrong and are being foisted on the decision makers with ulterior motives with colourable and controlled exercise of judgment. All socio-economic parameters indicate that India has lost out in most spheres of human activities since independence and more critically in the last two decades. World Bank annual reports, annual Economic Surveys of government of India and annual budget documents of central government could be examined to get substantiation of my above submissions.

I am giving hereunder a few simple suggestions on economic reforms.

There is consensus amongst the leaders of all parties (left, right and centre – Hindutva or non-Hindutva) about economic reforms, and structural adjustments, as in the changed environment every public office has been converted into offices of profit!

There is, of course, a big disjoint between the leaders and the common men, as they do not see eye to eye on efficacy of economic reforms for improving the economy. Constant reports of privatization, wanton sale of public assets, even though these contribute massively to the national exchequer, unlike in the developed countries, lack of adequate money circulation in the economy, parking of hard earned FE abroad and constantly begging for help from abroad, and constant reports of collapse of social services and other overall distress signals in the economy and inability of the system to deliver the goods even after more than ten years of reforms have made the people quite skeptical. I dare say that Indian people perceive economic reforms as a Western mandated agenda to transfer wealth and resources from the poor to the affluent within the country and from the poorer to the richer nations. Many Nobel laureates and legions of other economists have made public the 'discontents of globalization'. We may not forget that "Indians Vote with their Tummies" and they are not unwilling to deliver the "Order of the Boot" even to their erstwhile favourites. It might not be coincidental that all governments after economic reforms were let loose had ignominious exit. This fact ought to have cautioned all involved in governance. This has not happened, apparently, because, gains in office more than offset the trauma of loss of office!

Further, leaders of main parties are convinced that the contrived election system will ensure that power and attendant perquisites will oscillate amongst them only.

The voting public is quite puzzled that Indian leaders always import external problems and helplessly allow the economy to go down. For example, the rise in prices of petro-products is due to problems inside the producing countries and there is no requirement for Indian economy to take a hit. This price-rise can easily be countered by allowing the Rupee to appreciate correspondingly vis-à-vis the Dollar.

IMMEDIATE STEPS NEEDED TO REJUVENATE THE ECONOMY

Some simple steps in economic management can lift Indian economy from the dumps by giving a push to people-sensitive simple measures, still being within the parameters of economic reforms:

a) Imposing of very adverse exchange rate on the country has been found to be an effective tool to keep the subject country under control. India has the worst FE exchange rate in the world. Hence, RBI be prevented from undertaking any market intervention till further instructions and it should be directed to attain 'Purchasing Power Parity exchange Rate of Rupee', as soon as possible.

b) Rupee and FE involved in private operations in market are to go back to RBI reserves after each transaction.

c) RBI and the Government to stop further transfer of FE to foreign Banks in foreign countries as Indian International Reserves.

d) RBI to hold all FE in India, except for maintenance of essential International Reserves (say, $ 5 to 6 billion) in foreign countries.

e) Indian consumers pay exorbitantly higher prices for goods and services. India exports at rock-bottom prices and pays very heavily for imports. Prices of goods and services in the country and for external trade to be regulated by income levels of respective countries. A simple ratio to be used for fixation of 'Rational criteria for Prices' in India and for external trade and for comparing prevailing prices in foreign countries. This rational ratio will be: prices in India and in foreign countries in their respective currencies divided by the 'Statutory Minimum Hourly Wages for Unskilled Labour' in the currency of the respective country. Prices to be determined on the basis of parity of the ratios.

f) In the context of Petro-product prices, government could consider and clarify why this simple policy change cannot be implemented. Also, there is some enigmatic mysticism in policy formulations by the Government, whereas, prices of Petro-products useful for common people are being raised, that of ATF has been lowered and the private airlines and tycoons might be celebrating.

g) India has the lowest per capita and absolute amount of currency in circulation in the world. The Government should aim for about 200% of GDP as currency circulation within one year for ensuring 15% GDP growth.

h) Further public borrowing to be stopped. Funds required to cover the fiscal deficits of centre and the states and shortfall in resources of Planning Commission and for increased spending in Social sector, Defence and Railways, underground mining etc., to be met by circulation of additional money without any restriction of 15% or so. Massive reserves are already available.

i) External Borrowings to be stopped. All FE requirements for trade, businesses and other essentials to be met from RBI Reserves.

j) To contain inflation, resource allocation to different sectors to be on the following criteria, (with differential interest rates for the inefficient sectors) :

   i) Income Velocity of Money in that sector (higher the income velocity, higher will be the allocation and lower the interest rate).

   ii) Capital-Output Ratio (lower the Ratio, higher the allocation; higher Capital-output Ratio will mean higher interest rate)

   iii) Labour-capital Ratio (higher the Ratio, higher the allocation and lower the interest rate)

   iv) Lowest allocation for Import-intensive, foreign-funded projects (highest interest rate).

k) Economic reforms have had negative impact on education. Education has gradually become unavailable for the common man. Cost of education should be on the basis of 'Rational Price Criteria', as explained above.

l) Any doubt about excess liquidity can be removed by increasing purchasing power of the common people. 01% Income Tax should be payable on income above Rs.5 lakhs onward only on a progressive rate of one percent for every additional block of Rs. one lakh or parts thereof upto a maximum top most rate of 40%.

No exemption of any type to be allowed for anyone. This will correct the current highly regressive Income Tax structures. 'Statutory Minimum Hourly Wages for Unskilled Labour' to be immediately increased to Rs. 15/- per hour and we should strive to provide minimum wages equal or slightly lower than average income of 67% of the working unskilled labour population.

These are non-intrusive, non-invasive, self-supporting India-centric essential steps, which will rejuvenate the economy, particularly, in the context of escalating crude prices. I like to believe that no economist concerned with the welfare needs of India would like to declare in writing that the above ad-interim and preliminary economic measures are: a) anti-national, b) un-necessary, c) impractical or d) unfeasible in Indian context.

It will be my privilege if you and your brother judges and others, as decided by you, wish to have presentation(s) on the above and related matters. I shall be always at your service to provide any clarification, amplification, elucidation.

(Letter dated 19 September, 2005)

I have the honour to refer to my letter dated 20 July, 2005, on the above subject.

While waiting for some response to this letter, another disturbing news item came to notice, which has considerable significance for the course that socio-economic changes will take place in India. The relevant news headlined "Scrap law or enforce CAS: HC" appeared in *HT Metro*, New Delhi, Friday, September 16, 2005. A photo copy of this news item is enclosed for your ready reference.

The court while hearing the case seems to have commended the 'Market' as the 'best leveler' and market forces as important mechanism for socio-economic distributive justice and equity. It can be said with certainty that there is no consensus on these issues. There is a massive body of evidence to show that perpetuation of poverty in India, large part of Asia, Africa, Latin America and now in Russia and CIS countries is due to operation of 'market forces', with the market regulators working for furthering the interests of the powerful entity(s). In India, market forces have always acted against the interests of the common man. The deleterious effect of privatization of Delhi electricity supply and allowing the DISCOMS (Distribution Companies) to determine prices and the actions of DERC stand out as prime examples of mismanagement of public utilities. Your Lordship might have noticed that virtues of the 'market' are always sold as a brand advertisement by those who want to capture the market of the targeted land. Since market forces cannot be unleashed without debilitating the public sector, the essentiality of privatization is also eulogized simultaneously, always fudging the issue that privatization has invariably reduced domestic job opportunities, denigrated labour, created gross inequality in distribution of income and consumption and transferred wealth, resources and opportunities from the poor to the comparatively more affluent and from poor regions and countries to richer regions and countries.

Even though Indian people pay the highest rate amongst all the developed and developing countries of the world for all the goods and services they consume, what is disturbing is that the comments in court might foreclose any debate on socio-economic consequences of a particular measure, particularly, on public interest, order or morality, by commending inappropriate devices, like market, as instrument of egalitarianism. I dread the situation of having no recourse, like Rosemary, in the book "Rosemary's baby".

I beg you to kindly consider the issues and measures mentioned in my earlier letter of 20th July, 2005, in order that you could suitably advise all concerned about the real socio-economic dimensions of economic, political and administrative decisions.

I will be honoured if I could get a response from you.

(Letter dated May 2006)

I have the honour to refer to my two letters dated 20th July, 2005, and 19 September, 2005, addressed to the then Hon'ble ***, on the above subject. Copies of the letters are enclosed for your ready reference.

*** might have been too busy prior to relinquishing his office to attend to this matter. You may kindly examine the important issues highlighted and do the needful.

I beg to once again submit that attacks on Indian interests and on livelihood of Indians are being mounted almost daily in ever newer ways with no recourse left for the victims. May I draw your kind attention to two news items in mainstream newspaper in this connection. The two enclosed newspaper cuttings – one dealing with concessions for setting up businesses in SEZ and the other on concessions to designated foreign countries through FTA - will demonstrate how easily unnecessary burdens are being imposed on the common man without any simulation study, management games or even paper-exercise! Unknown soldiers, like me, consider that actions of the government are malafide and vivid examples of colourable exercise of judgment violative of some or all of the Articles 14 (Equality), 15 (Prohibition of Discrimination), Article 16 (Equality of opportunity), 23 (Trafficking in Labour and forced Labour) and Articles 38, 39 (though not enforceable) of the 'Directive Principles of State Policy' of the Constitution.

Sir, you might have noticed that whereas, the national exchequer has no money for primary education, but there is always enough money for establishing and sustaining SEZs or FTAs of questionable values. It is considered that there is a need for closely examining the alternatives to current economic reform programmes.

I shall consider it a privilege if you seek any clarification, elucidation or amplification or wish me to interact with anyone detailed by you before taking desired action.

With deep regards and best wishes.

06th May, 2007

UNSETTLED ISSUES OF THE CONSTITUTION

Two news items in front page of *HT*, New Delhi, 8th Jan 2007, one from Nandigram, titled, "6 Killed in Bengal's violent land tussle. CPI(M) cadres, land acquisition protesters use guns and bombs in night long battle", and another from New Delhi, "Money sought for household expenses not dowry, says SC", set me wondering what is the difference between serial killers of Nithari village of Noida, UP, and Buddhadeb Bhattacharya of Bengal! It also induced the thought in us whether the apparent ambivalent attitude of courts with regard to forcible acquisition, before rehabilitation, of the only perpetual assets of the poor farmers for private profit of the affluent in spite of provisions of Article 300A of Constitution of India (earlier Article 31(f) of the fundamental rights), and apparent sympathy for the bride-killers (whether by burning or by forcing the bride into suicide), will embolden the killers in fields and homes. Many industries have been closed down or run down in West Bengal and the vacant sites are gold mines for the concerned industrial houses. We were wondering why Honourable Shri Buddhadeb Bhattacharya could not take over these sites before encroaching on farmers' land. Also, Shri Bhattacharya needs to explain why modern industry cannot be in high-rise buildings instead of low sheds or low height buildings, so that scarce ground space is saved. I only hope our elite are aware that 16% of world population is living in only 2% of world geographical area in India. The portent seems ominous. Although some SC judges had accepted briefings and indoctrinations from economic reformists, but they did not respond when we wanted to present the opposite viewpoints for balance. In this connection may I request you to kindly consider the three letters on immediate topical issues to your two immediate predecessors.

I would request your kind consideration and solicit your advice whether the following issues have been authoritatively determined or whether agitating these will be frivolous reiteration of the settled issues:

a) Is equity permissible and enforceable in Indian constitutional schemes?

b) Can Indians claim equity in distribution of wealth and property? (World Bank reports indicate unacceptable level of inequity in India and in some other super and big countries. Also, it has been noted that almost all economic decisions of the executive are loaded against the poor of the country).

c) Is the protection and augmentation of private property more important than the life of the poor? (Reference is made to police killings in Nandigram, West Bengal, in March 2007 and earlier in a tribal area in Orissa and still earlier in Hero Honda Plant in Haryana).

d) Is 'Profit' taking i.e. 'unauthorized extraction of labour and production surplus for private gains', constitutional or legal? Or, shouldn't profit devolve on the State?

e) If profit should devolve on the state, shouldn't profit be distributed equitably to the human elements of the production process, i.e. entrepreneur, labour and also to all Indians?

f) Who is the owner of fruits of labour- the labourer or hirer of labour?

g) Is labour entitled to withhold his labour, as and when he considers it essential? Is withholding of labour by the labourer repugnant to constitutional provisions?

h) Who is the owner of (that is, whose private property is) the deposits in banks and financial institutions? The depositors or borrowers of funds?

i) Can private entities be entrusted with sovereign state power of punishment or for restricting of other rights of common people of India?

j) Can economic reforms and market economy be permitted for ensuring concentration of wealth, which is prohibited in the Constitution of India.

My friends are aware that I am working for several years on a book connected with these issues. They advised me to solicit your personal views before going ahead and incorporating authors' interpretations on these issues. We believe that you represent what is the best in the judicial system and, hence, I am bothering you with such queries. Kindly advise.

With deep regards,

Will we be crossing the line, if we expect the apex court to take suo moto notice of the aberrations cited herein?

DELINKING ECONOMIC MANAGEMENT FROM GOVERNANCE

Our economic thinkers consider that governance is distinct from economic management. This line is necessary to keep private entities distanced from any responsibility for distress of the nationals. Thus a leader page article in a mainstream newspaper could proclaim "Falling governance, rising growth: In India: We face a paradox. By any measures, our governance is worsening, yet economic growth has averaged a record 8% for three years,[31] says Swaminathan S Ankeleswaria Aiyar". As instances of failure of governance, he cited some examples: more corrupt politicians, record black money spending in elections, rising crime, Naxalite attacks in 165 districts, proliferating Islamic terrorist attacks in vitals of the nation, entry of criminals in legislatures and cabinets en-masse, murderers with political clout escaping scot-free (*as in Jessica Lal murder case: author*), quality of services continues to be terrible. He further mentioned, "The latest development policy review of the World Bank says that a typical doctor at a primary health centre is less competent than in Tanzania, and the chances of his recommending harmful treatment are 50:50. Teacher absenteeism is rampant, and half the standard V children cannot read Class II texts. Water supply is just four hours a day in Delhi (*an exaggeration, as per our suffering experience - author*), 2.5 hours in Bangalore and 1.5 hours in Chennai, against round-the-clock supply in Jakarta or Colombo. Electricity supply is terrible, and 30% of it is stolen." The point which the author of this article was trying to convey was that even with these burdens the liberalized economy is galloping ahead.

To contrast the informative piece of *** another news item is quoted here. "Vidarbha tale: 102 dead in 32 days, PM's package fails to save", "Caught in debt trap"[32]. The newspaper reported, "Even the prime minister's economic package seems to have failed in stopping Vidarbha farmers from ending their debt ridden lives". The newspaper gave some data also (knowing full well that liberalized elite will not comprehend the significance): "704 Vidarbha farmers committed suicide in 2006; Rs. 35000/- is the average debt of farmers in banking sector" (to the miniscule few, who are well connected). Majority is filched by money lenders who charge usurious rates of interest. Even after six decades of independent existence, the liberalized government, and socialist to boot, could exercise no control over private money lenders!

Further, the author of the Article could not point out that stock markets are booming with the largesse of public funds in banks and Trusts, and hundreds and thousands of farmers are committing suicides every year, as money lenders, banks having abandoned them, are making it impossible for them to live and try another day! Liberalized/ globalized government of India cannot prohibit charging of usurious interest by private money lenders above prevailing Bank Rate. The Government could declare charging of excessive interest rates as criminal offence with burden of proof being on the accused money lender. Simultaneously, big businesses are never very concerned about returning their borrowed cache of money and banks are reeling under NPA (Non Performing assets) worth hundreds of thousand crores of rupees now (in 2006). Private parties (Indian and foreign) are causing run on Indian Public entities with borrowed funds usurped from helpless Indian depositors and public treasuries, not even caring to acknowledge that they are surreptitiously exploiting the helpless depositors and converting depositors' and public wealth into private property for perpetuating exploitation.

What can the (poor?) judiciary do if it is not brought on record? We are hereby bringing this in public record and solicit the indulgence of apex court to determine: 'Whose property is the deposits in the banks and other financial institutions? Is it of the original owner or of the borrower? Or, whether charging of usurious interest rates is constitutional?' While at it they could also determine if profit-taking is constitutional. I have a strong feeling that the courts will ignore these issues with the plea that they are not social, economic or even judicial reformers!

Further, author(s) of above or similar articles seem to be not aware that politicians and administrators get corrupted and get their share of the booty through and from businessmen. There is a close nexus amongst politician-administrator-business and they tango in unison (of course, unknown to the erudite author of the above piece of wisdom).

We wonder what this public spirited economist makes out of the news item in mainstream media:

"Overfed on hype, underfed on ground.[33]

THE GREAT Indian economic dream could falter if the most basic need of people, namely, food security, is not taken care of. A staggering 64 per cent Indians go to bed hungry and suffer from chronic malnutrition. While we may rejoice that spending on food as a percentage of income in both rural and urban areas is going down, the poor still have to fork out a disproportionately high percentage on food. For every 43 paise that the urban dweller spends on food, his rural counterpart's share is 55 paise. In addition, the food that the villager gets is of poor quality and contributes to nutritional deficiency. For those in the poorer states living below the poverty line, as much as 70 per cent of income goes on food. For India's 200 million people, who live on less than Rs 12 per day (again an average figure, as deprivation is much larger), this is bad news. And worse, the many schemes that the government has put in place to battle hunger and malnutrition don't seem to be working well enough. One major failure is in the area of child nutrition where, it now turns out, we are worse off than sub-Saharan Africa. The silver lining in the cloud is that instead of trying to obfuscate the issue, the Ministry of Women and Child Development has admitted that its showcase Integrated Child Development Scheme has failed to produce the desired results. The admission did not come easy, and only after both the Supreme Court and Nobel laureate Amartya Sen rapped it on the knuckles for this lapse. Malnutrition among children in the age group of 0-6 has declined a miserable 1 per cent even as the economy moves ahead at 8-plus. Why is this happening? No prizes for guessing. Nutritional intervention is not reaching the target children, thanks to the now familiar bureaucratic bungling and lack of political will. Even the content of the food appears inadequate.

And the Ministry has come up with what it obviously thinks is an innovative solution - restructure the whole scheme with the stress on more nutritious and balanced food. We may be pardoned for thinking that such considerations would have been taken into account in the first place. With 47 per cent children suffering from malnutrition, the Ministry had better find a way to get the scheme moving effectively. If not, economists say that there could be a 5 per cent loss in GDP due to malnutrition alone. The government should guard against the usual practice of setting up yet another scheme to cover up for one that has failed. The effort should be to take a look at existing schemes for food security and nutrition and streamline them. This is good news. Now let's see some results on the ground.

MARCH OF LIBERALIZED ECONOMY

"Centre may extend preferential treatment to Big firms at the expense of small players,

Large COs get better deal on coal" (*ET*, Delhi, 11 July, 2006)

Equity of liberalized government of India? Shall we say, return of the East India company logic?

"By the time your income doubles, your Directors pay zooms 10 times

Payparazzi masters put minions in shadow" (*ET*, Delhi, 19 Aug, 2005)

The newspaper reports:

Cumulative % Growth in last ten years (since 1995/96) (the great economic reformers, led by Dr. Manmohan Singh, were in action during this period.

	All	**Manufacturing**	**Software**
Net Profit	304.8	262.7	3132.2
Employee cost	249.3	126.4	4602.0
Directors' Pay	852.4	815.4	1889.8

Source of the newspaper: Capital Line Database

That concentration of wealth in a few hands is taking place in ever escalating rate is evident from a more recent study published in *ET*, New Delhi, 1st September, 2008, with the heading.

"Top honchos pip India Inc in 'profit' growth".

The newspaper reported, "Notwithstanding statements by Prime Minister Manmohan Singh and some business leaders such as Infosys chief mentor NR Narayan Murthy about excessive executive compensation, India Inc's top guns have given themselves handsome pay hikes. The total compensation of 25 top-paid corporate execs of public listed firms has risen by 69% in FY08, compared with the 54% profit growth recorded by their companies." The newspaper gave a graphic with the title,

"A FISTFUL OF RICHES"
Top ten corporate directors' compensation (in Rs. cr)

	FY08	FY07
1. Mukesh D Ambani	44.02	30.46
2. Anil Ambani	43.43	2.04
3. Kalanidhi Maran	32.41	23.26
4. Kavery Kalanidhi	32.41	23.26
5. PRR Rajha	32.04	24.78
6. Malvinder Singh	19.58	5.08
7. Sunil Bharti Mittal	19.55	14.95
8. Sajjan Jindal	16.73	13.25
9. Onkar S Kanwar	15.53	9.98
10. E Sudhir Reddy	15.07	9.85

Liberalized economist, Dr. Manmohan Singh, in his first stint as Finance Minister, had removed all restrictions on managerial and director level remunerations of private and privatized enterprises. Thus in some private organizations, the directors and top management often takes home bounty as pay many times that of the total take home pay of the total labour force! But this bonanza was not extended to public or government sectors with the plea, "where is the money?" Governments of the centre and the state have been regularly using their police forces for strike-breaking to allow the firms and their management to loot the national wealth without any hindrance! Retired S C judges appointed as Chairmen of Central Pay Commissions (particular mention can be made of retired Justice Sri Krishna, chairman of VIth CPC) also think, and get acclaimed for that, that they should consider that private sector is a holy cow, which cannot be touched and that private sector practices should be incorporated in CPC recommendations for enhancing inequity for increasing the disparities in favour of the pay and perquisites of the top management. Rebellion having gone out of fashion in liberalized economic scenario (notwithstanding what Prof. Amartya Sen thinks as the central cause of French Revolution), the VIth CPC could get away with their heinous recommendations, as the lower level functionaries of the state have got so disillusioned that they have lost heart for even registering effective protest! Armed forces personnel are so demoralized that serious attack on their economic well being effected by the VIth CPC did not elicit any public protest this time, even though comparatively less pernicious recommendations of the Vth CPC had evoked strong public protest from defence service personnel. We are convinced that the next (i.e.VIIth) CPC with a Supreme Court retired judge and with some thoroughly liberalized and reformed economists and bureaucrats will give worse iniquitous awards. Indians watch out!

Other illustrative select news items are given hereunder to show how much debilities are being heaped on common men by the liberalized power elite.

"Maharashtra No Match for RIL" (*ET*, New Delhi, 11 July, 2006)

Industry Net Sales/Revenues Rs. crores	States of Union Total Revenues (Budget estimate 2005-6) Rs. crores
81,211 Reliance Industries Ltd.	50,429 Maharashtra

20,602 Tata Motors	42,668 Uttar Pradesh
15,139 Tata Steel	35,976 Andhra Pradesh
14, 763 Larsen & Toubro	30,252 Tamil Nadu
13,784 ICICI Bank	29,218 Karnataka
12,052 Maruti Udyog	23,217 Gujarat
11,624 Reliance Comm.	21,234 West Bengal
11,349 Hindalco Ind.	20,538 Rajasthan
11,229 Bharti Airtel	19,848 Madhya Pradesh
11,215 TCS	18,719 Bihar
Grand total 202,976 **(69% of Top State Revenues)**	**292,099**

[Data and Graphics of the newspaper: (possibly) by Santan & Nadeem]

We have chosen to present this graphics with the data, as this brings out vividly what ails India today – totally iniquitous distribution of national wealth; earlier foreign colonizers were expropriating national wealth, now it is the indigenous exploiters with government and legal sanctions as in colonial periods. All relevant data has not been presented but even as depicted, RIL has as much wealth as two to four states of the Union of India.

Whither are the constitutional embargos on concentration of economic wealth and monopoly? We only hope our esteemed apex court will take note.

The most poignant part is that all the private industries get innumerable concessions from the public exchequer. *India Today*[34] carried a lead story about various tax exemptions and concessions which are being cadged by the private entrepreneurs cost the exchequer about Rs. 35000000000000/ - i.e. Rupees 35 Trillion. Incidentally this is more than three-fourths of Indian yearly budget. No wonder Indian social sector is so starved and impoverished. India is constantly trying to occupy the lowest position in all reports of social Indicators of the world bodies. When such reports come out Indian top leaders observe petulant silence or of injured innocence and take no action to correct this state of affairs.

Or take another example:

"GROWTH PRESSURES

As Cement prices rise, bulk buyers shop overseas"[35]

The newspaper reported that 'with cement prices rising and demand well ahead of supply, bulk buyers of cement have begun shopping overseas. Obviously, for big business, the world is a single market in liberalized economy of Dr. Manmohan Singh. The newsaper gave a graphic also to put the matter in correct perspective. As per this:

'Concrete facts

158.1 mt*	9.2mt
India's total annual capacity	Demand for export
141.8 mt	144.8 mt
Annual effective capacity	Total demand
135.6	3 mt
Demand in the domestic market	Total shortfall

*Metric tons

From the above data, it ought to be apparent to all leaders of people, notwithstanding the unauthorized praises heaped on the market as the great leveler by a judge of

Delhi High Court, who forced down the CAS (the so-called Conditional Access System for TV programmes, for unadulterated exploitation of the reluctant residents of South Delhi and some other unfortunate metros), that in reformed and liberalized economic dispensations private profiteering takes precedence over national interests. Should any prudent average individual allow export and import (squandering of FE) of cement at the same time without first meeting the domestic needs? Of course, the line of arguments offered by the judges (as reported in the *ET*, New Delhi, 15th November, 2006, page 11) in allowing export of pulses when the executive of the day had prohibited export of pulses due to scarcity in domestic market, go to show the flexible norms that the courts can follow in determining national interests.

So, Indian people are really at the mercy of the exploiters, like the villagers in dacoit–infested Chambal Valley. Or is it like the problem of Rosemary in 'Rosemary's Baby'?

This concentration of wealth in private enterprises is in violation of even the putrid Indian constitution, but the ruling elite and the apex court is totally unaware. All of them seem to have attained moksha and have forgotten about the mandates of the constitution of India, especially preamble and, particularly, Articles 37, 38, 39 of the constitution. There is a repugnant precedence of concentration of wealth in private hands (in Russian federation, after Gorbachev/Yeltsin duo had had a go at USSR/Russian economy) creating major political, social and economic problems. In case of Russian Federation, the incumbent President then (2006), (being an ex-KGB man and as per some reports, a double agent to boot), had no compunction in taking over the 'YUKOS' (or some such outfit) and send the ambitious entrepreneur to jail. We are convinced, our entrepreneurs will not consider it fit to read this book, but someone will caution them that unbridled concentration of power and wealth may not enable them to attain the final goal, as dialectics of opposing interests and forces will frustrate them in bizarre manners and the possibility of Tsunami of irrational public wrath is always lurking.

4

BIG NATIONS GET TO BE SOFT SUPER POWERS

We have noted that management of Indian economy has one guiding principle, viz. all advantages must first go to the already wealthy, then to the foreigners of advanced countries and the left-overs for the common Indians. Pursuant to this principle, whenever the foreigners conjure up some new technique of exploitation, the native leaders first strike a defensive ambivalent posture, then start conjuring up some pressures (but loudly proclaiming that they never can be expected to succumb to pressure, and, in fact, there is no pressure), and then start admitting some compulsions of this or that treaty, convention or understanding and/or any other convenient excuse (which are constantly made available by the foreign agents and lobbies). At this phase the mainstream media becomes mouthpieces of the potential exploiters and they constantly start haranguing how the foreign countries are badly suffering due to Indian recalcitrance and objections. All the arguments for toeing the foreigners' lines are laid out by marshalling all facts and figures (with massive sanitization) and then the ministers capitulate and sign on the dotted line. If any minister shows any spunk, he is either short-changed or sidelined to oblivion. After all, a politician comes to his current position of eminence as a minister or prime minister after many street fights and badly bruised, and they do not generally misread the cues and act out their assigned roles with uncommon loyalty and dedication. Country's interest is least of their concerns! President of the Republic is not involved and if his autograph is needed, he gives it with uncommon zeal. The judiciary cannot be bothered about economic or policy issues except for helping out big business, as we noted in case of pulses export case mentioned earlier or for administrative convenience.

PATENTS, FARMERS' RIGHTS, BIODIVERSITY

We saw this charade being played out for making our Patents Act to conform to TRIPS and TRIMS agreement (apparently signed by some compromised bureaucrats and ministers, without actively participating in the negotiations or understanding what are the issues involved). We participated in the farce enacted by a Parliamentary Select Committee. We had given a written submission and were invited to make oral presentation to the select committee on the 'Patents (Second Amendment) Bill'. There was animated discussion amongst the deaf and the dumb or as if it was an academic discussion between aliens of two different planets with two different sign languages.

We tried to impress on the committee that national interest must govern any amendment to the Patents Act, but that apparently was not the objective of government of the day, as contrary to propaganda by the interested parties, process patent protection and exclusive marketing right was available to Americans and other foreigners vide Article 48 of Indian Patents Act 1970. *What was not available was the right to deny manufacturing in India and uncontrolled import and price manipulation.* The Patent (Second Amendment) Bill gave freedom to foreigners to freely export to India whatever they want at whatever escalated and uncontrolled prices, and deny manufacture in India by quoting Indian Laws. We had hoped that pernicious aspects of the proposed bill have been noted by the Parliamentarians.

Further, the committee could not comprehend that genetic engineering etc. or application of other evolving sciences/ Technologies or advances to produce products/process etc. which will produce in subsequent regeneration's/ reproductions products that are in any way different from the patented items cannot be patented.

We insisted, but in vain, that provisions of this bill ought not be available for preventing competition or for facilitating growth or sustenance of monopoly or oligopoly; thwarting national endeavour for developing newer products or processes in any field; thwarting advancement of Science, Technology, and general well being of the people especially, indigenous population or for research in any spheres of human activity or imagination; or for developing harmful products, processes, mutants, derivatives by Bio/Genetic Engineering or by any other evolving science/technology.

Prices of products for which EMR is claimed cannot be more than average price of similar product in Indian market in the previous three years. For pricing of product for Indian market, the labour content and labour-denominated overhead costs will be calculated on the basis of Indian Standard Labour costs. Indian standard labour cost will be obtained from accredited agencies of the Government of India who will periodically notify standard labour rates. Price in Indian market cannot be higher than price charged in the parent country of the claimant for patent/EMR. The exchange rate for relevant currency will be the 'Purchasing Power Parity' exchange rate to be ascertained from the accredited Indian agencies that will notify the Purchasing Power parity exchange rates periodically.

The claimant of Patent/ EMR will have to disclose the documentary proof of cost of original Research/ Development/Production in support of price to be charged and for IPR to determine reasonability of price charged and to ensure there is no excessive profiteering.

Assessment of sales or profit will be made by the Government of India and can be contested only in Indian courts. Also Patent/EMR application will not normally be entertained or approved for companies/organizations which have participated or collaborated in any unfair trade-practices or have been charged with violation or abuse of Patent or Intellectual property right in any country of the world or have participated/supported/collaborated in any manner in imposition or continuance of trade/economic or any other sanctions/restrictions against the Union of India or any part of it or any of its organizations (private or public) or instrumentality's.

Any country or official entity of the foreign country, which imposes any sanction or practices any denial/control regime against India, cannot be treated as a convention country till the sanctions and denial regimes have been removed and Parliament approves afresh according of status of 'Convention country' to such countries. Where a country has already been declared as a convention country, and that country or its official entity imposes any sanction etc. subsequently, that country will automatically cease to be a convention country from the date of imposition of sanction etc. and remain so till Parliament decides otherwise

We want to assure our readers that the committee of thirty Lok Sabha and Rajya Sabha members, possibly, forgot about our submissions and long presentation/cross-examinations as soon as that day's grueling session was over. When stalemate was reached, we suggested to the Chairman of the committee that instead of making piece-meal amendments, we should adopt full American Patent Acts. We also cautioned the Chairman that Americans will never permit that. The Chairman only nodded his head, signifying nothing. This is how public consultation goes on in India! Incidentally, only a few committee members attended the session where we made our presentations. Most of the comments were made and most of the questions and clarifications were sought by officials and lobbyists' (we suspect), who attended in strength. Most of the members were fidgeting and some had shut-eye. A few questions were asked by the chairman and by a communist member, who seemed to be intrigued by our pricing norm. We submitted that written script evolved about two millennia before North America had tryst with western variety of civilization. All of them guffawed when we mentioned that Indians should not be required to present printed document for all their claims for or against a patent, as all our traditional and folk knowledge developed long before printing was discovered, and our country is famous for SHRUTI (Listen and memorize)!

Our efforts to bring some sanity in competition bill may be seen from the narration below.

The Bill is silent on the definition of "Competition", presumably on the assumption that the normal definition contained in Dictionaries is enough. We begged the Committee to kindly accept that 'Competition' per se has no intrinsic value without being vested with some social, political or economic significance. The value of competition manifests when it furthers some desired social, political or economic values.

To our belief, the purpose of and necessity for competition is to serve national interest, national security interests, public order and public morality. Competition Bill 2001 does not recognize that there might be necessity for some Anti-Trust prevention provisions for furthering competition. The Committee was advised to note the comprehensive definition of anti-trust activities in American statutes. But the Committee had other objectives.

The preamble of the bill under consideration did mention that consumer interest will be protected; we advised that the Bill must acknowledge suitably that apart from 'consumer interest', the bill must protect national, security interests, public order and public morality!

The Committee was requested to note that two principal Democratic countries have very strong Anti-Trust and Competition Laws and their Acts are quite elaborate and do not leave matters concerning national interest or procedures for reporting to the elected bodies to be left to be surmised or to be later devised by the ubiquitous bureaucracy. The UK Bill has clear provisions and channel of reporting to their Parliament.

The USA is, of course, the leader in Anti-Trust and Competition Laws and they are merrily operating with laws as old as 1890 or earlier. Committee's attention was drawn to the fact that USA has four major Basic statutes as follows:

The Sherman Antitrust Act

Clayton Act (Commerce and Trade)

Statutes enforced by Federal Trade Commission

Federal Trade Commission Act

We pleaded for amendment to the Preamble as follows:

"A Bill to provide for establishment of a Commission to prevent practices having adverse effect on competition to enhance public and consumer interests, national security interests, public order and public morality, to prevent monopoly or oligopoly and to ensure freedom of trade by all participants in markets in India and to prevent lack of competitiveness in markets outside India."

As regards price, we mentioned to the Committee to kindly accept that price manipulation by various stratagems is the major source of profit by the foreign entities, the major component of which is Exchange Rate management (continuous devaluation of currencies of underdeveloped countries), whereby, the undeveloped countries are made to pay heavily. First, the production price is kept exceptionally high on the plea that the developed countries have high standards of living and their production cost is necessarily higher! Secondly, these developed countries through International organizations, rating and other consulting agencies and think-tanks inure and co-opt the local economists and power-elite for exploitation of the undeveloped countries like India. This foreign or co-opted

Indian intelligentsia will never accept any rational basis for price fixation.

"Reasonable Price in International Trade" - The price in the importing country will bear the same ratio in local currency as the price in the exporting country bears with respect to the "Statutory Hourly Minimum wages for Unskilled Labour" in the exporting Country's currency.

Example: For an item imported/exported by India from/ to USA, 'Reasonable Price, will be as follows:

"(Wholesale or Retail Price in USA in Dollar) / (Statutory Hourly Minimum Wages for Unskilled Labour in USA in Dollar) = (Wholesale or Retail Price in India in Rupee) / (Statutory Hourly Minimum Wage for Unskilled Labour in India in Rupee)".

Such a pricing formula may be considered (by Indian elite) as giving too much advantage to India and other undeveloped countries; hence, we suggested another pricing norm for consideration and acceptance by the Committee. The Importer and (or) exporter will have to declare the labour content (Direct and Support labour, Executives/ Management, Design, Marketing/public relations, Advisers/ consultants and such labour content of all intermediate stages of production and implements and where with all of production in the manufacturing/producing country). The cost in the importing country will be the cost of such labour content in Indian Rupee (Importing country's currency) with Standard Indian (or Importing country's) Rates of Payment for such various types of labour. So far as India is concerned, designated Indian agencies will announce the Standard Indian Rates of Payment for all such classes of labour from time to time. Only difficulty in accepting such a scheme is that the canard propagated so far about lack of competitiveness of Indian labour will get nailed then! We warned the Committee that unless a 'Rational Pricing Formula' is evolved, India will continue to be trailing in the race for development and no amount of competition law will be of any avail for India!

One cardinal fact that we impressed on the Committee was that national security interests, national interests should over-ride all other concerns or obligations of the state or its entities. We submitted that in most of their legislations, the American legislative wing ensure that national interests, national security interests or jobs for Americans are not compromised or diluted in any way. Hence, there was a need to incorporate in the draft Bill the requirements of the Armed Forces of Union of India, Indian Atomic Energy Commission, Indian Space Research Organization or by Intelligence and Counter-intelligence and Enforcement agencies when so authorized by appropriate Ministers of the Union of India'.

The MRTP Bill should subsist to the extent it prevents the growth of Monopolies and Restrictive Trade Practices. If MRTP Act at any time prevents competition, obviously it will be decided by appropriate agencies which act will prevail in given circumstances; the determining factor will be which law sub serve better national/national security/consumer interests. The move to delete MRTP Act is ill-timed when Indian economy is under great stress. The 'Statement of Objects and Reasons' betrays a lack of understanding of Indian situation and requirements. Can the Government really certify that Monopolies and Restrictive Trade Practices are no longer a perceivable threat to Indian economy, particularly in the face of Control/Denial/Sanctions Regimes erected by developed countries against India and its entities? As we have pointed out earlier, America operates with a host of Statutes in the Monopolies/Restrictive Trade Practices/ Anti-Trust Activities/Competition areas and India should try and learn to operate in complex legislative environment.

We wish to report to the readers that, unlike the chairman of the Patents Amendment bill select committee, the chairman of this Standing Committee was a well-seasoned politician and a veteran, who successfully negotiated many treacherous rapids without getting wet and he knew that it is better to ignore a problem than confront it, particularly, if there is no chance of stinging of the own skin in the process. Hence this committee took the time-tested bureaucratic procedures of procrastination and sepulchral silence.

Unquestioning surrender of Indian national interests continued in incorporating a Bio-diversity Act. If any Indian considers that political affiliation has any impact in sacrificing of Indian interests then we can disabuse their minds and confirm that all parties in political firmament currently are equally responsible or culpable. The Chairman for this Committee was a BJP member.

The preamble to the statute was considered unsuitable for a sovereign state dedicated to protection of its national interests. It was pointed out that harmonious constructions of the provisions of WTO agreement do not call for any sacrifice of basic national interests. It also needs to be kept in mind that, unlike NPT and CTBT, WTO agreement do not recognize any preferred state, nor any state has been given any veto powers over the national Acts.

Who will convince these people that plant breeders' and farmers' rights and obligations should follow from and be in consonance with the national interests. This bill has succeeded in giving freedom to foreigners to freely export to India whatever they want at whatever escalated and uncontrolled prices, and deny manufacture in India by quoting Indian Laws.

Our reworded preamble ought to have been: "To protect indigenous Plant Varieties, Germ-plasm, Gene-pool from unauthorized exploitation, prevent degradation of ecology and threat to the Biosphere by application of Genetic Engineering and/or other evolving sciences and technologies, protect national interests against exploitative uses of the indigenous Plant Varieties, especially, unauthorized exploitation or use of traditional knowledge, folklores, geographical or regional appellations of the tropics".

Draft bill did not define Terminator Technology. Hence we provided one, viz: "Terminator technology - Bio/Genetic engineering etc. or application of other evolving sciences / Technologies or advances to produce products/processes etc. which will produce in subsequent regeneration's/ reproductions products that are in any way different from the registered variety. Developing harmful products, processes, mutants, derivatives by Bio/Genetic Engineering or by any other evolving science/technology. Development of harmful, undesired or undeclared by-products or progeny/products (in subsequent reproductions/ regeneration's) or which, in any way, acts in an unnatural or undeclared way in the biosphere." Terminator technology ought to be prohibited for any alien entity.

In India rules and regulations take effect by default. There should be a positive determination by Parliament of the rules/regulations framed.

Only abbreviated summary of our objections to the three bills are given here in. Copy of the detailed comments will be sent by the author if any reader is interested in reviewing the elaborate comments.

We consider that the PATENTS, FARMERS' RIGHTS, BIODIVERSITY measures were introduced in India at persuasions of foreign power in spite of our strenuous objections, as the Indian elite had the basic intent to perpetuate inequity. Above comments, recommendations and objections were for opposing the legal and enabling provisions intended to make India a dependent surrogate country of the super power. But attacks on the low income-earners are being mounted in multiple fronts as will be seen from the narrations given hereunder:

ABANDONMENT OF THE TOILERS

We have noted that the burden of the economy ultimately falls on the toiling people and the actual position comes out in economic data, sooner or later. The denouement of Manmohanics (Dr. Manmohan Singh variety of economic management) has been succinctly highlighted in the following report:

"Real Manufacturing wages drop 22% in India, says ILO (*ET*, New Delhi, 30 Aug 2006). The newspaper reported that the ILO has zeroed in on the bleak side of robust growth in trade, investment, output in India and China. The ILO report, 'Realizing decent work in Asia', prepared for the 14th regional meeting held in Busan (South Korea) between 29 Aug and 01 Sep 06, has maintained that all the action on the economic growth front has failed to keep pace with growth of the labour force. Among the key decent work challenges identified by ILO is wage growth lagging behind productivity gains. Both India and Pakistan have experienced a decline in real manufacturing wages since 1990 (when Manmohanics determined the economic choices in India); a significant drop of 22% in India and a drop of 8.5% in Pakistan. Apparently, Pakistan was fortunate in not having a vigorous Manmohanics (working for big business and foreign interests) operating in their country. India's wage decline, the report holds, occurred despite an increase in manufacturing labour productivity of over 84% over the same period, indicating deterioration in workers livelihood despite the increasing efficiency of labour. However, the most worrying aspect of the report is the job deficit among young people, who comprise a sizable chunk of the current population of India and are expected to dominate the demography by 2020. What's more, unemployment rates have increased over those prevailing five to seven years ago in much of Asian region where labour force is growing by at least 14%".

This situation of depriving labour of its dues could arise as; in recent years, socialists, communists or nationalists, who were hyper-active in labour movement, have abandoned labour of both organised and unorganized sectors to pursue their individual private profit inclinations in line with Say's Law of 'private interests'! If the situation is so bad in organised sector, the position in unorganized, agricultural and farming sectors must be worse. Might be that is intended also by the economy managers to facilitate introduction of contract farming, SEZ, big business in retail and debilitate agriculture and rural sector legally, so that import and foreign dependence can be accepted as a national necessity. This brings us to the next important issue.

EXCHANGE RATE AND STATE OF ECONOMY

Economists, although, professing concern with resource transfers from the poor to the rich inside the country and from the poor regions to the rich regions in the external side, have always ignored or obfuscated the economic issues and facts to ensure capture of disproportionately higher percentage of the national Income by the affluent in the country and abroad. We have recompiled the World Bank data (in World Development report 2000-2001) in a more coherent way to present facets of the mechanism of resource transfers.

HIGH INTERNATIONAL RESERVES ENSURE POVERTY OF INDIGENOUS POPULATION BY EMPHASIS ON IMPORTS

Country	IMPORTS Million $ 1998 (a)	GROSS INTERN-ATIONAL RESERVES Million $ 1999 (b)	RATIO OF RESERVES/ IMPORTS (b/a)	NO. OF DAYS OF IMPORTS MAINTAINED AS GIR
Belgium	180,998	10,937	0.060	22 Days
Brazil	74,415	34,796	0.47	170 Days
China	165,894	157,728	0.95	347 Days (FDI & Surrogate production/ Export, without national capital/fund)

Denmark	59,501	22,287	0.37	137 Days (Dependence on FDI)
France	342,244	39,701	0.12	42 days
Germany	587,353	61,039	0.10	37 days
India	59,138	32,667	0.55	201 Days (Even without much FDI)
Italy	270,320	22,425	0.08	30 Days
Japan	363,488	286,916	0.79	288 Days Legacy of Allied Occupation & their large outward FDI abroad)
Malaysia	60,200	30,568	0.51	185 Days (Surrogate Production/ Exports)
Pakistan	12,819	1,511	0.17	61 days
Sweden	89,268	15.015	0.17	61 Days
Switzerland	108,277	36,321	0.34	122 Days (American pressures & Investment of Secret Funds)
U. K.	386,259	29,834	0.07	28 Days
USA	1098,181	60,500	0.05	20 Days

We have noted that there is a direct relationship amongst adverse Foreign Exchange Rate, adverse distribution of National Income/Consumption and GINI Index. Adverse exchange rate is one of the most critical factors for impoverishment of India and such other un/underdeveloped countries of Asia, Africa and Latin America. Thus countries, whose currencies are over-valued (GNP at PPP/GNP ratio is less than one) with respect to the US Dollar, have low GINI Index (signifying more equitable distribution of national income/consumption) and top 10% of their population have command over lesser proportion of national income/consumption and they, invariably, have high per capita income!

Amplification is required of the fact that although GINI Index for India is better than that of USA, the top 10% of Indian population captures higher proportion of national income/consumption. RBI is continuously devaluing the Rupee to preserve the so-called 'Price advantage'. The net result has been that India's share of Foreign Trade has been continuously going down (precipitously down since 1990) and India has been gradually withdrawing from 'Manufacturing' and concentrating on supply of 'Primary Goods' and 'Low-Value Goods and Services'. This fact is vividly documented in Table 20 (Global Trade) in above mentioned World Bank Report: "Manufacturing %age of total Merchandise Exports 1998: it is 94% for Japan, 90% for Philippines (of course, major portion surrogate production), 87% for China (partly surrogate production), 85% for UK, 84% for Pakistan, 82% for USA, 79% for Malaysia (surrogate production) and only 74% for India and declining as per Newspaper reports.

The dismal state of manufacturing in India is also evidenced from the fact that employment in manufacturing is less than 25% amongst urban workers (*ET*, New Delhi, 23 Oct 06, Page 16, under the heading "Employment in manufacturing rises to 246 per 1000 urban workers). This record also shows that there has been a decline in employment in Public administration and Education from 19.5% in 1999 to 18.7% in 2004-05, notwithstanding that India is readying to plunge in an educational black-hole! Of course Indian leaders are not cognizant of this!

Indian exports (Import-intensive) do not fetch enough foreign currency and the exported items fetch only a small fraction of the 'Market Price' of the item in the foreign country! Most of the major exported items are priced at such low prices (compared to the Indian market price) that most often they face "Dumping Duty" in the importing country. India tries to maintain the profitability of the Indian Exporters by Devaluing the Rupee (i.e. lowering the external purchasing power of) the Rupee and by all sorts of subsidy. Thus, most often the cost to India for its exports often exceeds the export-earnings (IT sector, for example)! India pays out exorbitantly for its imports and the burden is carried by those who do not benefit from imports!

There is an urgent need to Up-Value the Rupee and gradually bring it in line with Purchasing Power Parity.

PURCHASING POWER PARITY EXCHANGE RATE

Modern or liberated economists do sometimes mention PPP exchange rate in the passing. These economists never take rational PPP exchange Rate for comparative study of economics of different countries or regions. The reluctance of the economists to use parity exchange rate is rooted in the conviction that much of the successful theories and elaborate economic edifice created (by sacrifices of the undeveloped and under-developed countries) will fall through then. After all, economics is art or science of making political decisions to conform to the economic interests of the dominant country or political entity. It is a historical fact that over the centuries, the dominant economic country provided maximum number of more popular economic theories. If we look at the growth and decline of the wealth of the nations and the growth and declines of the economic theories developed in that country or region and the distribution of Nobel prizes, the correctness of this hypothesis will be established. Economists, somehow, find Parity exchange rate as a cumbersome, awesome, unethical and imperfect tool to work with. Economists have also designed many abstract (and sometimes absurd) definition of parity exchange rate. Majority of these measures depends on the Ratio of Ratios. For example, Reserve Bank of India uses the ratio of Inflation Rates in respective country to calculate the "NEER" and "REER" (The Net Effective Exchange Rate and Real Effective Exchange Rate respectively). RBI has been able to effectively Devalue the Rupee continuously by using these REER/NEER and they have been appreciated by the media, Importers, Exporters and economists of repute in India/or abroad.

RATIONAL FOREIGN EXCHANGE RATE

In 2007-2008, when Indian FE rate climbed vis-à-vis Dollar, there was all-round gloom in Indian government, political parties/conglomerates (cutting across party lines), business, economic and academic circles, as if a disaster had struck India. Erudite pronouncements were made by the (ignorant) finance minister and his staff, scholarly persons, economists of repute. Common man like me considers that people condemning the rise in value of Indian rupee vis-à-vis dollar are untouched by Indian reality.

For the sake of rationality in economics, it is necessary that the exchange rate between countries be found on the basis of the "Statutory Minimum Wages per hour for unskilled labour". If more rationality is needed, then instead of per hourly rate any other time-dependent rate can be utilized, if reliable and continuously updated data are available. Statutory Minimum wages for unskilled labour (SMWHUL) is not changed easily and only in a few countries is it indexed to inflation. SMHWUL is a significant parameter which is common to all countries.

People also wonder what makes economists so sure of their analytical study and their conclusions when most of their operating data are conjectural unrelated to foreseen reality. Economists while carrying out analysis do not seem to acknowledge, what mathematicians treat as Basic criteria of any analysis, viz, the two questions, a) is it necessary? b) is it sufficient?

It is considered that aim should be to use some direct measure and not use the technique of "Ratio of Ratios" to determine the rational exchange rate. Ultimately it has been concluded that the best measure of Parity Exchange Rate will be the comparison or the Ratio of "Statutory Minimum Wages Per Hour for Unskilled Labour" for all countries.

I want to define PPP exchange rate by equating the SMHWUL of two countries under consideration. For example, for India and USA, the PPP exchange rate will be

SMHWUL of Indian labour = SMHWUL of American labour, i.e., Rs. 6/- = $ 6/-.

Thus, Indian one Rupee should be equal to one US Dollar in the worst case scenario. But under Indian Finance Ministry and RBI dispensations, the exchange rate is something like Rs. 46 or more is equated to 1 $. That is, Indian Rupee is under-valued by 46 or more times. No wonder, Indian economy will not ever rise above the subsistence level, and India will never get a good share of international trade.

This issue is fudged with lot of economic jargon-mongering. Economists have always pretended that exchange rate management has nothing to do with resource transfers! But the data presented by World Bank in "World development report 2000-2001 (Attacking Poverty)" vividly brings out that adverse FE exchange rate is always associated with extremes of poverty, iniquitous distribution of national income/consumption and enables the rich to corner all economic benefits and resource transfer to powerful countries take place, as we have already pointed out.

FE RESERVES AND FDI

We consider that FDI is only paper investment so far as Indian national interest is concerned and that FDI into India actually benefits foreigners mainly. Powerful (militarily), and consequently developed, countries get all the benefits of FDI at the cost of un/under-developed countries, like India. Whereas FDI coming into India is covered multiple times by its 'International Reserves', the developed countries utilize the International Reserves of less fortunate countries. It will be apparent from the following table:

HIGH INTERNATIONAL RESERVES & LOW FDI ENSURES POVERTY OF INDIGENOUS POPULATION

Country	GROSS INTERNATIONAL RESERVES Million $ 1999 (b)	FDI Million $ 1998	FDI As %age of International Reserves
India	32,667	2,635	8.06
Italy	22,425	2,635	11.07
Japan	286,916	3,268	1.14 (Still paying War reparations?)
Malaysia	30,568	5,000	16.36
Pakistan	1,511	500	33.09
Sweden	15.015	19,413	129.03
Switzerland	36,321	5,488	15.11
UK	29,834	67,481	227.71
USA	60,500	193,373	319.62

Solution for India is simple - maintain 'International Reserves' in the same proportion as in super developed countries without eternal dependence for imports and exports and thereby on foreign market and be subject to all manners of manipulation.

It is always made out that Asian countries must maintain massive external reserves. America has always been consuming Asian reserves for its economy. It is no wonder that World Bank has reported that industrial sector alone in USA gets 170% of GDP whereas in all Asian countries this particular sector gets only a small fraction of their GDP as advances from the banks and F.I.s. America seems to be able to absorb any amount of F.E. without significantly increasing its international reserves but Indian RBI administrators and economists go crazy if the Indian F.E. asset increases and that is promptly declared a liability by the Indian experts. In the late 90s and early 2000 Asian economies were passing through the bad phase but that has not curbed their sentiment for building up huge external reserves. An interesting headline came out (*Economic Times*, Sat 06 Dec 2003) "Asian Foreign Exchange Reserves 29% to Record 1.85 Trillion - global markets fear Asia may start diversifying reserves as dollar weakens").

Indian economy managers have not been seeing the obvious but have been looking for reasons abroad for explaining the perilous state of Indian economy! Some thinkers consider this situation as self-created, akin to "Self-inflicted Injury" or "Malingering" in Armed Forces vocabulary. The basic macro-economic factors responsible for continuing poverty of India are: a) Low external purchasing power of the Rupee, i.e. the grossly undervalued Rupee compared to all foreign currencies of the world, as per World Bank data; b) Indian financial assets are sent out of the country without a quid pro quo, i.e. by maintenance of unnecessary massive "International Reserves" in foreign Banks; c) Low inward FDI vis-à-vis international reserves maintained by India d) High outward FDI by Indian private businesses; e) No price parity with foreign markets for Indian imports and exports, i.e. Indian consumers pay out exorbitantly for imported items and collect very very low prices for its exports (it is, of course, another matter that the Indian importers and exporters make huge gains); f) Iniquitous distribution of national income combined with extremely regressive system of taxes and duties.

INSTRUMENTS OF EXPLOITATION

FCCB: Leaders and economists always moan the lack of funds, but power elite never seems to tire of conceiving newer techniques of reducing the stake of the general populace in the economy. FCCB (Foreign Currency Convertible Bonds) is one such diabolical instrument of torture conjured up by the RBI/Government of India. FCCBs are bonds issued by Indian companies and subscribed to by a non-resident in foreign currency and convertible into ordinary shares of the issuing company in any manner, either in whole, or in part, on the basis of any equity related warrants attached to debt instruments. The scheme for issue of foreign currency convertible bonds and ordinary shares was notified by the Government in 1993 (when Finance Ministry was headed by the Father of Reforms) to allow companies easier access to foreign capital markets. Under the scheme existing for some time, bonds upto $50 million are cleared automatically, those up to $100 million by the RBI, and those above that by the Finance Ministry. These bonds have been thoroughly misused for profiteering by private entities, and, possibly, by accommodating the power elite.

Gradually matters became so scandalous that even government could not tolerate it further. But, as is usual, the contemplated move got disclosed to the concerned parties and that became a source for money laundering. I quote from a news item in a mainstream newspaper.

"Amidst rumors of North Block's (in Lutyen's Delhi, which houses the Finance Ministry of Government of India) plans to tighten the norms for FCCBs - coming close on the similar strictures on ECBs - bond holders are celebrating as all these stocks have appreciated substantially, up to 200% in some case, since the bond issue date. The Finance Ministry has now sought details of the net outstanding position of FCCBs from the Reserve Bank of India. The ministry is currently studying the impact on foreign exchange reserves if corporates are given a free hand to issue such bonds. During November 2003, bondholders of ** have approached the respective companies for conversion of their holdings. Sources said FCCB holders of ** have already converted more than 22% of the $100 million bonds into equity shares. The company had raised $100m (including a green shoe option of $10m) through FCCBs in July 2003, with a conversion price of Rs. 250.75. On Friday November 28) the scrip closed at Rs. 409, which meant that the conversion was at 63% discount. In one of the largest off-the-market deals, two foreign institutional investors - Capital International and Government of Singapore Investment Corporation - picked up a 9.8 % stake on the **. The power utility allotted 5 million GDRs, representing 1.5 crore shares, to them. With the stock market booming (of course, with largesse of public funds), foreign investors, who subscribed to foreign currency convertible bonds (FCCBs) in the past, are making a killing by simply converting them to ordinary, equity shares. The conversion price of all these bonds is usually at a huge discount to the market price, with the discounts ranging from 25-90%. This is obviously paving the way for an increase in the equity base of these corporate, and a substantial reduction in their respective promoters' stakes. FCCB holders of ** , for instance, have now come forward to convert their bonds in record time. While ** issued the bonds 3-4 months ago ** raised foreign funds just a month ago"

EXTERNAL COMMERCIAL BORROWING

ECB has been used to siphon away Indian wealth for benefiting the foreigners especially the super-developed countries. The ECB which came into fashion after the international lending agencies like World Bank, IMF, Asian Development Bank (ADB) and the other external funding agencies curtailed the concessional lending and after India was forced to build up big foreign exchange assets with the banks and FIs' in foreign countries. The ECB game is rather innocent looking and projected as big benefit for the Indians. The Ministry of Finance and RBI quietly buried the inconvenient provisions of the RBI Act of 1934 to permit borrowings by commercial entities abroad and parking the borrowings also abroad either directly by themselves or the RBI. Although initially the External Commercial Borrowing permit was being given for specific manufacturing needs in India but gradually that concept was given up and the borrowings could be parked and used outside the country for buying of foreign assets or for strengthening the manufacturing base of the foreigners in their own country. Of course, it is not expected that ministry of Finance or the RBI or the businessman concerned are to understand the detrimental consequences of any strengthening of manufacturing base in a foreign land for which either a large demand or huge production capacity exists in India. The ECB route is being allowed for hurting India's basic interests in various ways, especially, by reducing the Indian capacity to manufacture and by denying enough jobs to Indian labour. We have explained in another chapter how the Indian economy is kept tied to a tight monetary policy for production facilities within the country and how Indian wealth is being utilized for strengthening the production capacity of the foreigners. The ECB is acting as another tool to keep India poor and militarily weak.

It is always made out as if the ECB is cost-less for India. In fact, it involves massive repatriation of Indian wealth as commitment, holding, disbursement, consultancy and other assorted charges, but the money or funds never reach Indian shores. No prudent man will understand why Indian entities must borrow abroad with instruments like the ECB when the RBI is overburdened with FE and various stratagems are being devised to check the inflow of Foreign Exchange into India. It is not ever clear to average man as to why the Indian entities cannot borrow F.E. from RBI or government of India reserves or the F.E. holdings of the Indian banking system.

That ECB as a means to increase and perpetuate import dependence of Indian manufacturing facilities is never highlighted anywhere. The implications are always conveyed that infrastructure projects cannot be funded by rupee by spending rupee for obtaining the equipment in Indian market. It is always made out that import of equipment is essential for growth of Indian infrastructure and Indian economy as such. Although Indian agriculture is the mainstay of the Indian economy and the state of the agriculture determines the state of growth of the Indian economy but agriculture has never been considered as an infrastructure.

FCEB

The Economic Times, New Delhi, Saturday 16 February 2008 reported on page 11 (page title being ECONOMY):

India Inc gets to issue FCEBs to unlock value in group cos

"The Government on Friday allowed firms to issue foreign currency exchangeable bonds to unlock the value of their holding in group companies. In the case of FCCBs, bonds can be converted to equity of the issuing firm. In the case of FCEBs, bonds can be converted into equity of a group company. As a result, payment of interest on FCEBs would be subject to payment withholding tax." Do you agree that this measure will weaken India and strengthen foreign entities? Of course, the businessmen concerned will be benefited.

"The new instrument would provide corporate groups more flexibility to raise funds abroad as they can leverage value of a holding company; etc."

It seems Dr. Manmohan Singh's government has given up all pretensions of a national government and is working overtime to serve his foreign masters for strengthening foreign companies. Simultaneously, Indian national security and economy is languishing due to lack of funds. Can you imagine any worse situation for a country, other than in a captured country paying reparations? India is working overtime to become a de-mobilized soft super power.

5

MANAGEMENT OF NATIONAL SECURITY

ARMED FORCES

Indian national security seems to be of no concern to the power elite in India. This is apparent from the conduct in public space of the president of the republic, prime ministers, defence ministers, cabinet ministers, MPs, supreme court advocates, journalists, Chairman, Kargil Review committee, Tehelka commission, central pay commissions, supreme leaders of some parties and sundry others. We harboured a faint hope that some individual or organization will be public spirited enough to follow up on critical national issues. The Government and bureaucracy conjure up one scheme or another to put the armed forces in the back-foot. One such diabolical scheme is 'DEEP SELECTION' for promotion, whereby a junior can and most often does supersede a senior of many courses. This scheme shattered the morale, fighting quality, loyalty, integrity, spirit of self-sacrifice and brotherhood of servicemen in India. Pay commissions have been acting as hired agents to denigrate the military in all possible ways.

Our efforts to persuade the power elite to review the induction of a British AJT for Indian air force reproduced here will reveal how concerned the nation is about keeping the armed forces adequately equipped for all contingencies. Letters were sent to high constitutional authorities, but they were least bothered.

In any country, defence procurement is an integral part of national policies, but in India, under the overall guidance of the British-indoctrinated bureaucracy, this can only serve faithfully the interests of the "Central Authority" (earlier it was the UK and now it is the USA). A complete weapon system is never procured from one source! Can the Government clarify why SU-30 aircraft was not fully operational in India (after almost a decade) and why there were major slippages in supply of equipment from Indian side as revealed in C&AG Reports? Much vaunted Indigenization of DRDO (defence research and development organization) is really a smoke screen for westernization of Russian designs and thereby make national security subservient to western (read profit-propelled capitalists) manipulations.

Our observation is that the Finance Ministry always makes sure that only that much fund is made available to Defence Ministry which keeps the military services going for internal policing duties and the armed forces remain incapable of any strategic power projection! The bogey of lack of Rupee funds is touted around by the Finance Ministry to obfuscate the economic fact that "power and growth flows through the barrel of the gun".

Defence procurement is always tailored to the strategic requirements of the western powers! The Defence and Finance Ministries always make sure that the armed forces never have strategic weapons or capabilities. Thus available funds and resources are deployed in such a way that the Air Force is never be allowed to obtain strategic weapon systems like, say, indigenous Refueling Aircraft, AWACS, Cruise Missiles, Long Range Ground to Air Missiles, Operational Nuclear weapons or massive number of indigenous combat aircraft or even adequate WWR (war wastage reserves). Navy is not provided with nuclear powered surface or under water vehicles or nuclear power Sea-launched Cruise missiles, Sea-skimming missiles etc. or adequate number of indigenous ships. Armed Forces Jawans are provided with pay, pension, perquisites and facilities worse than that of the slaves in medieval periods. They are always kept equipped for fighting the last lost battle!

The CVC (a bureaucratic outfit called 'central vigilance commission' manned with traditionally low IQ/OLQ personnel) was assigned the responsibility to investigate the old defence deals, but in the meantime Air Force went ahead to procure western (British) AJT (Advanced Jet Trainer), when the Air Force, (whose 80% to 90% aircraft are of Soviet origin), over the years, have reduced drastically the use of Basic and Intermediate Training Aircraft and Simulators; more Mirage–2000 aircraft at highly inflated price when the same aircraft was rejected in favour of the SU-30 aircraft earlier.

What the specialists had apprehended has happened in that procurement of the western AJT for the Air Force has adversely affected the overall national security. It might have been noticed how procurement of SU-30 (a sterilized version of the formidable SU-27 without its full-range of conventional, nuclear and other special Russian weapons) by India solved one strategic problem of America by destroying or emasculating the MIG Design bureau of Russia, the bug-bear of American military aircraft. Procurement of AJT has solved, for a very long time, another strategic irritant for America, as then Indian Air Force has no money left for a strategic nuclear bomber like TU-22M, appropriate Refueling aircraft, AWACS, Cruise missiles, long (of approx. 5000KM) range ground to ground missiles, operational nuclear weapons etc. or even WWR (war requirements). Everyone must be aware how Indian Air Force played the part of a By-stander during Kargil operations.

Love for Western equipment is endemic in the Defence Establishment. Even though British authorities had imposed sanctions on India at the behest of the Americans and have crippled Indian security environment, India went for an antique AJT from Britain. Evidence of greater naiveté or unconcern for national interest or strategic interest of India cannot be easily found. British had impounded critically required aircraft and helicopters of the Indian Navy on the specious plea that some installed equipment to be procured from USA are being denied on the basis of illegal sanctions regimes of US Government, Indian authorities have again gone to the same British sources for the Training Aircraft.

Since after signing of the so-called strategic agreement of 2000 with Russia during visit of President Putin to India, Russia has no special defence-relationship with India and this important relationship has degenerated into commercial terms. It seems Russia has been made aware that the defence budget will be more or less equally divided between West and the East and so long as Russia gets its share, they need not bother about the overall strategic requirements of India! It would appear that defence budget is being mortgaged for some transient diplomatic gains, of course, at the cost of national interests.

ADVANCED JET TRAINER

We always considered that procurement of western AJT is a serious blow to national security, as this type of aircraft is totally unsuited for Indian Air Force requirements. No one cared to confirm or refute the following facts:

a) 80% to 90% aircraft and weapon systems of Indian Air Force are of erstwhile Soviet origin. Design philosophy, cockpit layout, training, safety and simulation philosophies, control response, safety features etc., etc. are much different in Soviet aircraft as compared to Western designed aircraft. Whereas, Soviet aircraft and equipment/system designs are Technology-driven and most modern, those of the western world are Profit-propelled and Sales-driven dated-technology devices. A western AJT can only be used as a poor simulation device for training the pilots.

b) Indian Air Force, after cutting back, over the years gradually, on the extent of flying training on Basic and intermediate training aircraft and doing minimal use of Training Flight Simulators (as reported in C&AG reports), concentrated all its efforts on procurement of an AJT at the cost of even other essential armament (when WWR requirement is even not met), not to talk of requirement of other strategic weapon systems.

c) No other big or developed country of the world USES imported AJT in their Air Force except supplicant Indians in spite of massive indigenous resources always put to generate profit for private businesses and government of the day coming out with complementary policies and inviolable administrative decisions.

d) Every time Indian Air Force loses an aircraft in an accident, it is claimed that the accident was due to Technical Defect or due to Natural Causes or Normal Operational Risks. It is a fact that Indian Air Force first ascribes the accidents to technical defect and then claims that loss of aircraft is due to non-availability of Advanced Jet Trainer, although Soviet air forces could very well attain the status of super power with global reach without a so-called AJT?

e) Western AJT's are of vintage designs with old technologies unsuited for Indian Air Force. Pilots have to be made to unlearn what they learn on western aircraft before they can be effective on Soviet/Russian aircraft.

f) The agents who were the kingpins in Bofors gun deal were hyperactive for pushing the AJT deal also.

g) The AJT and associated equipment have been bought at a price much inflated than the initial "offer" price, for some very special undisclosed reasons! The western suppliers were being given double benefits of: a) Price escalation, b) Market determined Exchange Rate variations.

The Government did not agree to a pre-contract audit by CVC or by a Parliamentary Commission about:

a) The Air Force requirement for a **western** AJT for training pilots for operation on **Soviet origin** aircraft.

b) Why Air Force failed to provide adequate flying Hours on Basic and Intermediate Training aircraft and why Air Force either did not procure or adequately maintain the Flight Simulators.

c) In spite of the fact that large number of pilots are employed, why is it that only inexperienced and inadequately trained pilots are put up for flying high-tech supersonic aircraft for not only for peace time exercises but for actual active operational sorties in times of emergencies.

d) Air Force had to cut back drastically, over the years, on flying training to keep the aviation fuel Bill within control to keep overall expenditure within the budgeted amount. Share of the Air Force in the aviation fuel consumption of the nation has drastically gone down, over the years. Shouldn't the funds to be spent on an AJT of doubtful utility, be more profitably spent on providing adequate flying hours to the existing pilots?

e) In spite of Air Crew Examination Boards being in existence in Indian Air Force for very long, we can confirm that there are serious gaps in knowledge and awareness of pilots (senior/junior alike) about Basic and Specific to Type airmanship, combat techniques and procedures, weapon selection/

delivery limitations and techniques in different terrains. The Government never carried out independent assessment of the motivation, awareness of the pilots about essential knowledge of the aircraft they operate by organizations like DIPAS of Defence Ministry, NCERT or other relevant organization(s) of HRD ministry. Such a review before procurement of AJT would have shown where the scarce resources should be applied.

FORCE MULTIPLIERS

The Government considered procurement of AJT as more important than other force-multipliers or offensive-capability-augmentation facilities.

KARGIL (VIJAY) OPERATIONS AND SIDELINING OF IAF

We considered that the sudden interest in an antiquated British aircraft as AJT immediately after the Kargil operations was related to the effort of neutralization of Indian Air Force as an effective combat arm! Kargil (VIJAY) operations were conducted with enormous sacrifices in life, limbs and livelihood of large number of families. Perusal of the 'Executive Summary' of the Kargil Review Report left me with serious doubts and queries.

It is not clear whether the committee could comprehensively query Shri ***, who became governor of Sikkim immediately on relinquishing charge as Chief of RAW. Since acts of omissions and commissions of RAW was the main reason for India (as usual) to be caught off-guard/unprepared and surprised, thorough examinations of chief of RAW was called for.

It is not clear whether our intelligence agencies did convey to the President (the so-called Supreme Commander of the armed forces), PM, Defence Minister the full implications of visit to Pakistan of General 'Zinni' and one 'Ames' (or someone like that, a rather lower rank functionary of US state department) during currency of Kargil operations. Visit of an American delegation headed by the Chief of

'CENTCOM', when Operations Vijay was already underway, ought to have put our intelligence agencies on overdrive.

Everyone in power expressed unconcern that General Zinni's visit was demanded by Pakistan. They ought to have been aware that Pakistan has a subsisting treaty with America/CENTCOM whereby CENTCOM is required to immediately get into consultation with Pakistan when Pakistan's security is threatened and take steps to get the threat vacated.

It seems that General Zinni and Pakistan agreed that Pakistan would not be able to fight India in conventional war. That is the time Pakistan made simple demands. Since Pak Air Force will not be able to prevail over Indian Air Force and since Pak ground forces will not be able to hold on without air superiority,

a) India should be prevented from effectively using 'Air Power',

b) In case that is not possible, America should prevent Indian nuclear retaliation after Pakistan has preemptively attacked Delhi and Mumbai with nuclear weapons.

Although General Zinni was briefed by US authorities that India does not have adequate operational/deliverable nuclear weapons, fail-safe delivery vehicles and Indian armed forces have not exercised with nuclear weapons or even dummies, but he, it seems, succeeded in convincing Pakistan that although USA and its Allies will be able to pulverize India from off-shore bases, USA cannot prevent destruction of major population centers of Pakistan without positioning American troops and weapons in Pakistan territory. Since any induction of American troops and offensive/defensive weapons may act as a trigger for Indian preemptive action, Pakistan should not consider the nuclear option as viable, although belligerent posturing should be all right.

It is in this background that Ames (or whoever he was)

visited India and conveyed that Pakistan will use nuclear weapons if India uses the Air Force or crosses the line of control. It is conjectured that Indian Government, knowing the awful state of IAF and other arms and knowing fully the state of nuclear un-preparedness, in spite of the tall claims of the scientist/engineer duo, had to, per force, put Indian Air Force on 'training' and uncommitted 'observation' roles and allowed Army to slog their way up the hills at enormous cost to their lives and limbs, albeit unnecessarily. Power elite ought to have known the actual state of affairs.

It is apparent that Indian Air Force was happy to be sidelined during Kargil Operations. As per reports, Air Force carried out 1200 combat aircraft sorties in the 71-day conflict apart from some helicopter sorties for communications etc. Contrast this with what America and other supporting countries did during 41 days of war in Iraq I. The developed countries had assembled 2100 aircraft in the war zone and mounted more than 1,96,800 sorties in 41days, i.e. about 4800 sorties per day. As per foreign publications like that of the Institute of Defence and Strategic Studies of London, India had more than 1200 combat aircraft on strength at the relevant times. If only Air Force could mount one sortie per day per available aircraft, it could have solved the cross-border insurgency and terrorism problems forever!

VIOLATION OF OATH OF OFFICE

It is for consideration of the readers whether Indian Air Force and the Government of India should take credit for not crossing the LOC, when the LOC falls within Indian Territory as defined in First Schedule, Article 1 of the Indian Constitution. The chairman of Kargil review committee (a self-appointed and elite-anointed strategic specialist) did not acknowledge that failure to protect territorial integrity and sovereignty make the Chief of IAF and Air Force Commanders, all MPs and all Ministers culpable and guilty of violation of oath of office as per the constitution! Tehelka

Commission chairman also apparently considered this as a minor lapse and sidelined this issue while clearing the then Defence Minister of any lapse in conduct of Kargil operations!

INDO-SOVIET/RUSSIAN TREATIES

Knowledgeable people ought to be aware that significant provisions of the Indo-Soviet treaty of 1971 was that the two high contracting parties would get into consultation whenever the security of India was threatened and take necessary steps. This was interpreted as a 'nuclear shield' by USA and China and had checkmated these powers in military matters vis-à-vis India. We are not sure whether the readers are aware of the pernicious provisions of the so-called Indo-Russian Strategic Partnership Treaty of 2000, which absolved Russia from any liability in Indian defence matters. This has made India totally defenseless, as

a) The strategic force, the Indian Air Force, has been made totally incapable of protecting India's interests,

b) Indigenous Nuclear Deterrence capability is non-existent, as evidenced by the fact of succumbing to Pakistani threat and American persuasions during Kargil operations,

c) Informal 'nuclear shield' provided by Russia having been withdrawn,

d) Pakistan's military alliances and 'Nuclear Shield' is subsisting even though they exploded, with impunity, American bombs supplied through China.

We hope all concerned, especially, powerful people will review the matter in light of above perspectives and confirm that India's security interests, in fact, are not being compromised on subjective gung-ho feelings generated by friendly noises from American sides, even while they are maintaining full rigours of the Economic Sanctions and other Denial and Control Regimes.

INACTION OF DIFFERENT AGENCIES DURING KARGIL OPERATIONS

We had suggested that the authorities consider and clarify the following queries, but they, as usual, refused to oblige:

a) Why Indian Earth Observation Satellite imageries and many hundreds of Millions of Dollars of imageries being bought yearly from abroad by Indian agencies were not used for observation of Kargil and other Borders?

b) What was super-high tech (Strategic and Tactical) Photo-Reconnaissance/Signal Intelligence aircraft of Air Force, RAW, Survey of India and other agencies doing in 1997 or 1998 that they found no evidence of infiltration?

c) Why Indian Air Force was not used during Kargil operations as America or Israel use their Air Forces? Why the Air Force was not sent in first before sending the Army Jawans and officers to sure death?

d) In which other conflict in any other part of the world was the Army left to do "Opposed Mountain Conquering" without first strategic and tactical destruction by Air Force of the target areas and the support bases of the enemy?

e) Which other Nuclear Power would have allowed 500 or so of its army men to be killed and thousands maimed and injured in an undeclared war with the neighbour?

f) Which Nuclear Power allows its territory to be violated and its civilians and military men killed repeatedly at random from safe sanctuaries across the border and still take no punitive action across the border?

g) Is it probable that the crux of the matter is, after the tall claims, India has had no operationally deployable nuclear weapons and yielded to Pakistani threat and American persuasions?

I was wondering whether there is any truth in the assertions made by Shri K Subramanian, Chairman, Kargil Review Committee (or some such thing) in a discussion with me that Indian Air Force did not have any plans or training to fight in the hilly terrains or that they hardly carried out any war-gaming or paper or simulation exercises for such contingencies. He also made the astounding assertion that Indian Air Force or other military forces do not have any standing instruction to suo moto protect Indian sovereignty or territorial integrity. That is the reason why Air Force had virtually to be cajoled by the Army to join the fight. Is it a fact that every single action or move of the armed forces has to be sanctioned by the bureaucracy fronting for the Defence Minister and sometimes low level bureaucrats intimate the Government sanctions or non-sanctions of major operations?

SIDELINING OF ARMED FORCES IN NATIONAL SECURITY MATTERS

Further, we observed that although Task Forces were constituted as a follow-up to Subramanian Committee Report for recommending measures to strengthen national security, not a single Task Force was headed by a military man. Also the newspaper reports on the labours and recommendations of the Task Forces filled us with apprehensions (which proved to be reality later), as the military has been made more thoroughly subservient to the bureaucracy to make the military even more non-effective as an instrument of assertion of national will!

CORRUPTION IN DEFENCE HIERARCHY[36]

Corruption is all pervading in Defence Ministry (possibly, like in all other ministries, especially, in Finance, Economic, trade and industry related) and invariably starts at and is sustained by the topmost Minister and secretary. To my experience, there are two classes of ministers and bureaucrats: *Type (a)* Do-gooder, weak and non-effective time-servers who believes in somewhat laid-back approach and ever ready to condone wrong-doings by subordinates and seniors, so long their own skin is not scalded; *Type (b)* Go-getters, who are activists and believe in pulling in as much moolah as quickly as possible. These are the earthy, rational and totally balanced individuals with rather high worldly intellects. (They hardly ever fail)!

Every Defence deal involves pay-offs to agents and bureaucrats and in deals above Rs. 20 crores to ministers as well. It is left to the agents - Indian, NRI and Foreign - to subvert the system and buy up the key personnel at all levels of service cadres. The agents and their think- tanks, mostly retired administrative branch civil officers from vigilance and enforcement agencies with some key personnel from the retired IAS cadre and some retired servicemen (to run around as errand boys) arrange for the services of key serving officers.

Retired Service officers can easily be recruited as they are given pay and benefits, which they never enjoyed in service before they were retired out at comparatively young age.

Serving bureaucracy also make sure that difficult (for the agent) service personnel are dealt with appropriately through time-tested service disciplinary techniques.

Here again there are *type (a)* and *type (b)* defence force personnel. The agents ignore the type (a) personnel and concentrate their efforts on type (b). Service officers normally get a fractional percentage to max. 1% of the deal, whereas, the bureaucrats/ministers get anything from 3 to 10% of the deal. The agents get anything from 5 to 15-20 % of the deal.

So-called secrecy in the name of national security is actually exploited to the hilt by the bureaucracy, particularly, in Defence procurements from abroad. Great secrecy is maintained in the country for all procurements from abroad, even though the required items are often procured from countries that are all set to keep India militarily weak or crippled by all means. Indian Defence establishment and bureaucracy could never be made to appreciate that defence requirements per se' is not secret, it is the timing, quantum, or equipping of a particular force and its probable area of operation is only secret. Our security conscious bureaucrats could never understand that procurement of Defence equipment abroad on behalf of the armed forces never remain a secret from the powerful or strategic powers of the world. The Defence bureaucracy will be incredulous if informed that every single procurement from western countries are routinely and clandestinely reported to America and in any case all dollar payments are noted as a matter of routine in USA and they particularly monitor Defence payments. Only procurements from erstwhile USSR was secure in this respect and now even that security has vanished after liberalization and the newly evolved practice of paying in US dollars for supplies from Russia and other CIS countries. Secrecy in national security is a big source of lucre to the bureaucracy.

The Defence bureaucracy is oblivious of the fact that only vintage weapon platforms and not the specially designed weapons are allowed to be procured by India by the Americans.

After the Bofors fiasco, great show was made about excluding agents from Defence deals. At present the agents are hyper active. Important agents, their main functionaries and operatives are well known to the secretaries to Government of India and most of the serving ministers. Agency business is so lucrative that important people are now in it and their activities are multi-level and multi-disciplinary and invariably encompasses industry and import and export business. All agents have in their, direct and indirect, employment people from all enforcement agencies and all important departments of the Government

The list of important agents active in defence deals (in later part of 20th century CE and beginning of 21st century CE) is a veritable list of who's who of India. An unedited list prepared for a top political leader was handed over to the TEHELKA Commission, possession of which is now with the CBI after the Justice Pathak Commission was sent packing by the UPA.

— is very active in Navy deals. His various front companies get a cut in most of the overhaul and refurbishing of Navy ships, their engines, and other major equipment. Had a share in HDW Submarine deal and German diesel engines for Army Tanks. Could successfully scuttle many navy projects and is instrumental in massive escalation in price of the Aircraft carrier 'Admiral Gorshkov'. Man suspected to be the mastermind behind sacking of Admiral Bhagwat, serving Chief of Navy and Chairman, Joint Chiefs of Staff Committee. Has his links with Israel and has been able to sell to Army, Navy and Air Force much so-called high-tech (but really American rejects) electronic warfare equipment fabricated in Israel. He and other agents have been assiduously building up the case for pseudo-American equipment through Israel and fully exploited the weakness for Israel of some of our political masters (e.g. sugar barons). He ostensibly does a thriving export business, especially, with African countries. Have had his business premises and houses raided many times by the ham-handed and thoroughly compromised investigating and enforcement agencies but he is none the worse for that.

———, is very active in Russian deals and in other deals with British companies. Is very successful in pulling off some major deals for Israel. He is one agent whose services are highly valued by competitors. Thus, he has been representing competing Firms of Israel and Russian Federation. For Russian organizations, his technique is simple and straightforward – he buys up the top bosses of these organizations with some attractive down payment and monthly retainer in US dollars, which are huge amounts in Roubles terms and his patrons are happy and do his bidding. Of course, the net result is MIG-design bureau has been disbanded and merged with SU-design bureau and other organizations are languishing; though the bosses have been adequately provided for. He has, unwittingly or might be willingly, fulfilled the American strategic plan of demolishing the most successful and the most formidable MIG-Design bureau, dealt a death blow to truncated Russia's strategic pretensions. He was the main sub-agent for the SU–30 aircraft which IAF never wanted (at least, till mid-1994). Pay-off in this SU–30 deal has surpassed all previous records by orders of magnitudes and leaders of three successive governments are the beneficiaries.

——, are very active in French and American deals. They had facilitated the initial Mirage deal and many French and American equipment deals for Hindustan Aeronautics Limited. They, like all other agents, have many businesses as front and for 'whitening' the massive agency commissions. They have captured many evacuee properties and have many firm houses, like all other agents and bureaucrats. Whereas, PM —— used his trusted ministers and aides to deal with suppliers, ____used his brother and trusted —— to cut out the intermediaries for at least the Mirage, SU-30, AJT deals of Air Force but without much notable success as the UF Governments fell unceremoniously. —— and has put forward his party secretaries to handle the suppliers. Outcome is still uncertain but prognosis is that again India will be saddled with some weapon Platforms without weapons. (That is what ultimately happened after a few years).

There are many small operators who are doing well for themselves without offering much competition to the big guys; these entities, all in their small and big ways, are hurting India's interests and perpetuating Indian decadence.

Who will cut the Gordian knot and how? No one in India cares!

You can rest assured Indian government, under the thrall of Indian and foreign businessmen, will land India into more trouble in exercise of strategic options in years to come by their unquestioning subservience to super power dictates. A sample of Indian surrender is in nuclear option:

Sept 2008

CRY, MY BELOVED COUNTRY, CRY

PRIME MINISTER (DR. MANMOHAN SINGH) TRYING TO CLOSE THE LAST WINDOW OF FREEDOM

NUCLEAR CO-OPERATION TREATY WITH USA IS A MEASURE TO DESTROY INDIAN MILITARY, PERPETUATE INDIAN POVERTY AND DEPENDENCE ON AMERICA AND FINISH INDIAN INDEPENDENCE

The civilian nuclear cooperation deal with USA is signed and delivered behind the back of the people of India (It is no consolation that the totally counter-national British mandated constitution does not require any reference to Parliament) by the UPA or a successor government with the communists raising their pro-forma protests to hoodwink the people of India by organizing some token Bandhs and strikes, mostly in West Bengal earlier; socialists of different hues were already behaving as if this matter was of no significance and the so-called Hindutva-mouthing BJP was striking a posture of injured innocence! We had suggested to some BJP leaders that they should declare in and outside Parliament that if this deal is signed without the concurrence of two-thirds majority of Parliament, the BJP-led government will treat the treaty not binding on them. Only that Indian people and Indian nation will lose all claims for independence of action in national security, national wellbeing and national sovereignty issues; in fact in all matters of national interest. The day this deal will have been surreptitiously finalized will mark the day when India will be formally re-colonized by the western nations! There could not be anything more heinous (the other being partition of India) criminal act against Indian nation than this pernicious deal; only that the perpetrators of the crime against humanity will go unpunished! The communists half-heartedly demanded ratification of the deal by Parliament but not done. BJP, under the present leadership cannot effectively protest, as

Vajpayee government only made UPA government so bold as to go for such a totally anti-national deal. How Indian interests have all along been sacrificed will be clear when we recount the Pokhran II and subsequent shameful acts of the governments of the day.

"11th May 1998!" "What a day!" Instantly an average Indian started walking 20 feet taller and an average Indian chest was 100 inches wide. We felt India has ultimately arrived and joined the coveted nuclear club! But as always happened with Indian leadership (whether in pre-British days or during and after the British rule, whether Kings or Maharajas or so-called popular leaders) their courage left them completely on the first sign of displeasure by inimical powers! I had personally hailed Shri Atal Behari Vajpayee as the "Greatest Son and Sun of India"! What a misplaced euphoria!

Only an Indian Prime Minister, like Vajpayee, could write an apologetic letter to the American President and similar letters to some other nuclear powers after doing a rightful job after long delays! By 14th May 1998, the capitulation was complete and India declared an unconditional Moratorium on further nuclear tests, although it was quite clear by then that Pakistan was getting ready to set off some nuclear devices obtained from USA/China and that USA and its collaborating countries were going to impose unspecified amounts of sanctions on India. India never articulated strongly that Pakistani devices were ready-made bombs supplied clandestinely by USA/China, as Pakistan still does not have the infrastructure to manufacture the nuclear devices. Fear of American censure is overwhelming in Indian administrative psyche, there was no retaliation of any sort from India. Indian bureaucracy and leadership shudder at the very thought of imposing any sanctions on offending countries. Indian media and leadership never condemned America and Russia for exploding six nuclear devices up to March 1999 after Indian experiments with explosive nuclear devices in May 1998, even though these countries were swearing by CTBT. How many Indian intelligentsia know that the Mayor of Hiroshima (one of the Japanese cities destroyed by America by Nuclear Bomb) invariably write similar letter immediately to the Head of Government which explode a nuclear device. The famous holocaust museum in Hiroshima displays these letters. There were six letters to USA/Russia (out of which four to USA) after May 1998 till March 1999, but, not a whimper from any of the peaceniks or Indian Government or Indian intelligentsia. The current (2005) Defence Minister of India visited the Holocaust museum some time in the above period but he was unmoved. It is now clear that 1998 nuclear tests were a command performance to legalize Pakistan status as a nuclear power and get India crippled economically, as a bonus. The government of the day and all subsequent governments are accessory to the fact and are culpable.

India proved once again to the foreigners that it is an overgrown, overweight and overvalued international harmless busybody! Indian political and business leadership is literally crawling seeking some sort of accommodation from a few highly developed countries.

We have noted all the arguments given by the pro-treaty camp (obviously composed of those who benefit, or likely to benefit, by American domination over India). All arguments are pre-supposed on Indian permanent dependence on a few highly developed countries. The arguments in favour of signature is so facile and frivolous that these can be rationalized only if it is pre-supposed that India is destined to remain an undeveloped, militarily insignificant, economically impoverished country without any chance of ever securing its rightful place in the comity of Nations. India has a strategic co-operation agreement with Russia. What attempts did India make to get the 'Bomb', enriched Uranium and nuclear technology, which were given away to all and sundry during and after 1990, the period of break-up of USSR under the able leadership of Gorbachov and Yeltsin?

There was no justification in the world for India to ever sign the treaty in its present form. This treaty was also intended to subject India to 'legal' espionage against India and perpetuate the discriminations enshrined in NPT. The NPT is being used by the P-5 for coercion of the threshold states and will be stringently applied against India. After overt nuclearization in May 1998, the military asymmetry between USA and India, particularly, in Southern region of Asia and Australia, had been obliterated and India could not be tied down without getting its commitment to a treaty, which no one wants. (Other western powers do not matter, as they have no independent stance and they leave military and diplomatic issues to be decided by the USA).

The objective condition before signature on such a treaty was that India's security interests would not be compromised. It was an acknowledged fact that signature on this treaty will finish off India's independent security status and it will turn itself into a surrogate or dependent state of America (like Saudi Arabia, Iraq, Pakistan and Afghanistan etc.). If India is so afraid of conducting Zero-yield and laboratory grade nuclear explosions for fear of American disapproval even before signature on (unsigned) CTBT, who can claim that India will not 'voluntarily (?)' abstain (the posture made famous by Congress party and of which the Communists were the great admirers then!) from all nuclear related explosion experiments after signature on the co-operation agreement? Incidentally, the unsigned CTBT permits Zero-yield and low yield nuclear explosions and America (and even Russia) conducted many nuclear explosions after heaping praise on CTBT. Someone may ask Indian government, Dr. Abdul Kalam and Dr. (scientist) Chidambaram, how come India did not feel need for any further nuclear, at least, low yield, tests, when India has a lot of catching up to do! India really produces some official genius! Actual fact of the matter is that these official scientists/engineers are operating on the firm belief that political leadership or administration will never ask them to live up to their claims (or bluffs) and their claims can never be tested by the average Indians.

Another canard is assiduously propagated by interested intellectuals and non-scientific/non-engineering official elite that India has no escape but to make all sorts of compromises for so-called "Dual-Use Technology" from America. These elite clean overlook that no country develops by begging for foreign technology. Our observation is that after licence-Production of innumerable aircraft and aero-engines, India is nowhere near having an indigenous Military or Civil aircraft production capability. The myth of necessity of dual-use technology is to perpetuate Indian dependence on America. America is not the fountainhead of Technology. They have caught up a lot by surreptitiously getting all talented scientists, engineers, technologies, and nuclear materials by wholesale plunder of USSR materials, scientific and technological resources at the time of break up of USSR under the able guidance of Gorbachev-Yeltsin. Incidentally, the technique of starving Indian Public enterprises of financial resources (for creating artificial scarcity and debilitating all national facilities) has been successfully used in USSR to cripple first USSR and now Russian Federation and all other splinters of USSR.

It must be understood that USA is the only strategic military power and it does not consider itself bound by any external limitations of any nature and it feels completely free to reject any international treaty, obligation, understanding if it suits its national strategic interests of the moment. It can be ruthless in getting other countries to obey treaty etc., if it suits them. America also has convinced itself that massive military and thereby domination of technological edge is at the root of their strategic power. If India is rooting for such technologies, God can only help India! USA is quite happy to cohabitate with four other declared nuclear powers and three other close confidantes as nuclear powers, like Israel, white South Africa (prior to Nelson Mandela) and Pakistan, and they would have in time accepted India's nuclear power status. But violent reaction of America is due to the fact that tall claims of the Indian scientists unnerved them (or posing as if they are so disturbed), as they cannot permit any country to make or claim any technological breakthroughs. They will try and stop India and India's intelligentsia, peaceniks and Communists have come quite handy.

Prior to signing on this co-operation treaty, the government must have authoritatively declared whether Sanctions, Technology Denials, Control Regimes had hurt India's interests, particularly security interests, or not? And if India's interests have in fact been affected, they are duty bound to explain why the offending countries were not dragged to the WTO and why no sanctions were imposed by India against these countries and why they are not demanding dismantling of the restrictive regimes before co-operating.

These specialists would like everyone to believe that nuclear explosions have to, necessarily, be for development of a 'Bomb'. They cannot believe or they have not articulated that nuclear explosion is an extension of the research in nuclear sciences. They would want us to believe, with tongue in the cheek suggestions, that nuclear explosions are essentially a weapon-related activity. We wonder whether these scientists/specialists have really pondered whether highly developed countries like USA need about 1200 and Russia about 700, UK about 250, France about 350 and China about 60 explosions to refine their weapon technologies! All these tests could not have been for development of the bomb alone as then China could not be considered to be a nuclear weapon state. Then, also, on the "number of tests" criteria, India cannot claim to be nuclear weapon state. The Indian Government and intellectuals must accept that, barring a few, majority of the tests are for development of technologies.

The truth may be that naiveté has not permitted the Indian scientists and thinkers to consider that such large number of explosions is not really meant for development of weapons at all but to push hard at the doors of frontiers of knowledge. The naiveté that underground nuclear explosions are cleaner than atmospheric or space explosions need to be rejected. Underground explosions are pernicious in more than one way. In fact, the underground test cell is a fully instrumented laboratory designed to conduct short and long duration tests. Scientists are talking of many kilometer diameter particle accelerators for studying quarks and gluons but they do not mention publicly that such experiments can be simulated in the core of the nuclear explosion. Most of the parameters of modern Particle Physics, Chemistry and a large variety of metallurgy can only be studied with the range of energies, temperatures, pressures and flux densities available close to a nuclear explosion. Again, high intensity photon experiments can only be conducted close to a nuclear explosion. How many Indian scientists have thought of conducting "Pulsed", "Flattened Peak" or "Throttlable" explosions? Have we thought of "Tunnel", "Directed" or "Polarized" energy explosions? When shall we be talking of 'Plasma Lasers' (Pasers)? Indian scientists need to consider that most of the super-conductivity experiments can be carried out in the arena of nuclear explosions. These explosions may give whole range of semi-conductors and VVLSI circuits and Bio-engineered mutants, etc. etc., once properly arrayed in the test cells of underground explosion chambers. How many Indian Universities or laboratories or research institutes have carried out 'Pinhead' or laboratory scale nuclear explosions?

Again, an essential component of star-wars programme is a variety of nuclear explosions for energy and high-powered particles, because the order of magnitude of the energies required in star wars programme cannot be obtained by any other means.

That nuclear explosions have moved far away from weapon development regime can be surmised from the way USA and USSR/Russia are co-operating in nuclear testing. They are carrying out tests in each other's test-sites. This set of agreement or understanding would not have been possible if the tests were primarily for weapons development. In case of India, American objective is just to cage India in. Where is the question of co-operation between a donor and a recipient or an alms-giver and a beggar or between the lamb and the lion?

India's steadfast adherence to 'No-Test' declarations can only mean that India has opted for the second and third rate power status not only in military matters but, more specifically, in scientific matters. India's decision not to carry out nuclear further explosions till Pakistan so does it or her security concerns is seriously questioned cannot be supported from the point of view of advancement of science. Nuclear explosions are so vital an ingredient of a large field of sciences that the decision of not carrying out nuclear explosions can only be considered as a part of big Indian naiveté. Prime Ministers of India did not exhibit vision, moral calibre or courage of conviction to do long term good for the country.

We had hoped (but he failed us) that Vajpayee (because of his RSS background) would be rational and realist enough to comprehend that opportunity for exercising nuclear option is already over-due and more time will not ease pressures on India. In fact, the liberalization and market forces unleashed by VP Singh-Narsimha Rao-Manmohan Singh-(non-scientist) Chidambaram have reduced and are reducing continuously room for manoeuvring by Indian Government Pressures of globalization (read American) will become more sophisticated, diverse, divisive, intense, and internecine in the times to come. Indian leaders seem to keep forgetting that 'bullies always threaten and attack the weak-willed ones'.

India is a big country and has a big population and needs to display big will-power also. There will never be a better time for exercising the nuclear / missile options. The skeptics could take courage from the fact that when China exercised independent nuclear, missile or military options, that country was more vulnerable than India is today.

India will have to carry out minimum of 100 nuclear tests in the first phase, in which first 60 to 70 or so will be mainly weapon-related and the rest mainly Scientific/ Engineering/Technology demonstrators. Fortunately, foreign funds will not be available or required for this and since all these engineering and scientific work will lead to growth in GDP, enough Rupee funds can be made available as 'Income Velocity of Money' is still above one. Even liberalized economists cannot dispute this. The government's promise to improve labour employment situation (or concern for 'Aam Admi') can be given a significant impetus by the simple act of overt nuclearization of Indian State.

However, there is one positive aspect to naiveté in India and also in Pakistan. The father of nuclear/missile activity in Pakistan, i.e. A.Q. Khan (the greatest innovator and organizer the world has ever seen and compared to whom Edward Teller, or the like, are no match) knows very well that if Pakistan bombs Delhi with nuclear weapon, he (i.e. Quadeer) will not have much to celebrate as the fall-out of his bomb(s) will be carried back to his soil by the winds (in some seasons, at least). Similarly, he cannot bomb Bombay without being ready to sacrifice Karachi also in the bargain. On the other side, India cannot get away by bombing Lahore, Islamabad or Peshawar, as the wind will blow it right back over Punjab, Delhi and other places close to Pakistan. .

We consider that the window of opportunity provided by Pakistani's declaration of its possession of nuclear bombs and its test-firing of 'Ghauri' missile and promise of test-firing still better and longer range missiles, should be fully utilized by India for its nuclearization and militarization. India should not forget that: "Growth flows from the Barrel of the Gun". But the fast pace in which this government is picking up 'Americanization', it is apparent that it is resorting to *time-tested naiveté or duplicity of keeping nuclear option* firmly CLOSED *while claiming it as 'Open'!*

Moratorium on nuclear explosions is a political and diplomatic tool and it must be used as such. India declared unilateral and unconditional moratorium on testing but that did not deter America and others from imposing sanctions which are badly affecting the Indian general public but hardly affecting American interests. India should declare that it will be forced to resume nuclear testing if attacks on Indian economy continue with economic sanctions and hardening of interest rates on foreign loans and debts and motivated down-grading of India's credit-ratings by American or Western-country-based rating agencies like (moody?) 'Moody's' or (sub-standard?) 'Standard and Poor' etc. Further, Indian leaders may also declare that number of tests for upgrading technology will be graded as per the amount of technology denial (in any field) practised by the developed countries. We may also declare that India will go for long-term moratorium only if America and the other P-5 countries agree to share with India all the data collected so far on all their underground, space and, particularly, atmospheric explosions. This is a tall, but scientifically, technologically and logically a totally tenable demand and lot of discussions (and many times acrimonious) will ensue. People will forget about co-operation.

We are convinced this government has been behaving defensively and has almost lost steam on nuclear issue in the face of the concerted move of the so-claimed "Secularist" parties and the western powers. The position is so bad that only those intellectuals, ex-bureaucrats, ex-military leaders or even think-tanks (considerably funded by the Government) and Government-owned and private media is projecting elaborately and mischievously only the bad implications of the nuclear issue without any prominence being given to the nationalist main-stream interests. Positive steam on nuclear issue must be built up, if the party(s) in power wishes to capture and maintain pre-eminent position in the centre-stage of Indian-psyche! This can only be done by stressing on India's *inalienable right* to develop and share in development of technologies in All (R) All fields without any hindrance or let up! And if resumption of testing is necessary for the P-5 to see reason, India must do that!

First national blunder was committed by Pandit Nehru by declining permanent membership of UN (for fear of Chinese might)[37] and another gigantic blunder of national dimensions has been committed by another Congress prime minister, in this case to sabotage all Indian fledgling national security measures to keep India beholden to USA. Of course, we expect this treaty to hold till Congress or BJP rule prevails and a truly national Indian government does not take office! Indian official philanthropists may stand cautioned that once India signed on the dotted lines on the nuclear co-operation treaty, then its claim for a permanent and equal seat with the P-5 in the Security Council will be just thrown out of the window, without even a cursory nod at India. You cannot beg your way to power or to a seat in the Security Council (with Veto power)! You cannot have power without wanting to project your power! India must start believing in international fundamental diplomatic truth: "If you really want to get in, just bomb your way in"! Stark evidences daily being thrown up in India of the failure of globalization and economic reforms under capitalist production and distribution methods, for furtherance of privatized profits, points to dismal trends of breakdown of social harmony, essential for progress in the chosen line. Regular reports of starvation deaths and suicide of farmers in the country, alongside the stories of the charging 'Bulls' in the bourses, show the great divide, which could be legally created for 'development' in western models. Competitive politics of 'inclusion' of the deprived humanity is preparing the ground for a revolution, compared to which French or Bolshevik revolutions may appear as picnics in the garden! No historian or philosopher can dare to contemplate the dimensions of the Tsunami of roused passions of billion plus super-cultured, super-productive people contained within 2% of world geographical area subjected to constant contempt of much less endowed minorities and their servants. Our prime ministers like to pretend that they are not gold fish in a glass bowl. The current (circa 2008) ruling gold fish could avoid retribution in his earlier incarnation as the finance minister; that time the poor Narasimha Rao, as the PM, took the kicks while he walked away with the kudos. The prime minister might like to remember, after signing on the nuclear deal, that the flashlight is on the ruling gold fish in the bowl and it will be advisable for him to not forget that the Italian Mafioso or Colombian drug lord or American warlord cannot shield him for ever from disaster of Sudarshan Chakra of public wrath, as the limit of his permissible mistakes is fast approaching!

This deal is so beneficial for USA and Western powers that America will give some American-reject technologies after dilly-dallying to make India accept some more restrictions in the confidence that Father of economic Reforms is beholden to west and his foreign leader is only too eager to accept many additional restrictions ultimately, because India has already closed all other options by signing the co-operation agreement with USA.

Hence, fellow Indians, 'Don't lose heart! You can do whatever you like, if you are militarily, and consequently, economically strong!

THE RECALCITRANTS

Type of efforts made by us to bring some rationality in security management and the response of the power that be may be discerned from our letters to various high authorities. For example, in March, 2002, we wrote to Venkatswamy Commission on defence deals (Tehelka), titled "Corruption in defence deals - impact on sovereignty, territorial integrity and national security". We learnt from media that the commission had exonerated the then defence minister of all wrong doings. The succeeding UPA government after considerable deliberations terminated (or discontinued, disbanded or whatever legal term) the commission and handed over the investigation to CBI. CBI, as per standard operating procedures, went into active hibernation. Outcome can be easily foreseen – the job is just too big for CBI (they have invariably failed to resolve any cases involving big-ticket deals or those involving surviving VVIPs or big businessmen – Indian, NRI or foreign)!

"We have the honour to refer to ***** letters to the Commission dated 18 April 2001, 10 May 2001 and 25 January, 2002.

In the above referred letters and depositions by our representative, *****on $10^{th}/11^{th}$ December 2001, India Defence Foundation had stressed on the intimate relationship, adverse effect and negative impact that corruption in defence deals have on sovereignty, territorial integrity and national security of India. We had expressed our conviction that endemic and institutionalized corruption has systematically neutralized the national security apparatus, so much so that, the armed forces of India do not now take even direct attack on them or their commanders with seriousness befitting an armed force! The latest instance of strategic and tactical inability of the armed forces to protect their own interests or honour is demonstrated by the attack on C-in-C of an Air Force command, while he was flying in Kargil Sector. As per media reports, his AN-32 aircraft was being escorted by two Mirage 2000 aircraft. But, apparently, these so-called most modern combat aircraft did not fire back at the attackers or try and neutralize the enemy fire, even when the enemy had directly attacked their own commander! Demoralization or politicization or subservience of armed forces to the diplomatic niceties, could not have been demonstrated more vividly than in this instance! Even conceding that C-in-C had inadvertently strayed into POK, still the enemy had no right to fire on the aircraft of the AOC-in-C without fear of massive retribution, especially, as POK is Indian territory as per First Schedule of the Indian Constitution and no one is entitled to cede any Indian territory as per the constitution of India (kindly recall Berubari enclave transfer case). We are convinced that the armed forces have been unauthorizedly prevented from acting in national interests. The Commission would recognize that any one restraining the unhindered movement and operation of the armed forces in the territory of India is culpable for crimes of violation of oath of office, amongst other crimes.

The Commission will recall that in our submissions on the shenanigans in procurement of combat aircraft, we had laid great emphasis on the issue of debilitating the capabilities of the armed forces of India and that the scarce resources are being applied for procurement of inappropriate weapon systems. We have submitted to all concerned, including Your Lordship, that procurement of the western AJT (Advanced Jet Trainer) will be a gross attack on Indian national interests, as it will debilitate Indian Air Force further. Moreover, in spite of the fact that agents in defence deals add no value, the Government has gone ahead, during currency of the deliberations of this Commission, to give legal status to the agents, so that they can have official access to defence organizations and subvert these legally!

We are constrained to submit that, although we had raised the above important issues in our submissions and depositions, the Commission had only summoned us to depose on SU-30 aircraft procurement. We beg the Commission to kindly accord priority to consideration of all issues raised by us in respect of SU-30 aircraft, and also the question of procurement of western AJT for Indian Air Force. Incidentally, in spite of the continuation of the deliberations of this Commission, it is reported in media that Government is all set to procure the British HAWK -100 aircraft as AJT. If the pattern established earlier is any guide, the Government will give some (a few hundreds of crores of Rupees) advance, so that a fait accompli could be presented (as in SU-30 deal). The intention of giving legal status to defence agents is to remove one 'limiting factor' for conveniently clinching such a deal!

We beg the Commission to kindly issue directions to the Government that the following be kept in abeyance till the Commission submits its Report and Parliament has considered the report:

a) Procurement of western origin AJT for Indian Air Force

b) Induction/Recognition of Agents in defence procurement."

No action by the venerable Commission

We did not relent. We pursued the matter with heads of state, government, defence minister or other cabinet ministers (who deceived us by their public utterances), political leaders, and media leaders of all hues, socio-cultural and other assorted leaders. An excerpt of typical letter sent in January 2001 to the then defence minister (on procurement of Western AJT and other weapon systems for Indian Air Force) has been reproduced in earlier pages for posterity. We also tried to drive sense (in Sept 2000) to Sri Arun Singh, Chairman of Task Force on Management of Defence. An edited summary of the letter is given hereunder containing issues not agitated in earlier part of the book.

ELIMINATION OF GROSS AND PERSISTENT DISCRIMINATIONS AGAINST DEFENCE SERVICE PERSONNEL

There are gross and persistent discriminations against the service personnel. It is in national interest to have a contented armed force. The Task Force was implored to note that attack on pay, privileges, perquisites of the armed forces started in the morrow of Independence, after the British-indoctrinated bureaucracy could instill the fear of "Coup" in the psyche of the political class. It was never articulated that there has never been a coup in a country with a large military (above one million strong) force which is integrated in the national political-cum-administrative set up. In no other developed country does the military deal with the political masters, even on important matters, through the intermediation of the civil bureaucracy! In no other developed country is the military kept completely isolated from administrative and legislative arms of the state! The civil bureaucracy started lowering the armed forces personnel in Warrant of Precedence first and then scuttled all their claims for appropriate pay/allowances/ perquisites and privileges. The entire working of the Armed Forces got warped and other than announcing of some sops during War or war-like operations, such as Kargil, armed forces remained neglected by the political class. It was in this psychological milieu created by the vested bureaucracy that the armed forces could be kept sidelined even in the event of national crises. The way the different arms of the armed forces were used during Kargil operations or not used at all during hijacking of Indian Airlines flight IC814, goes to show how national interests can be sacrificed for administrative convenience or comfort.

In spite of the fact that all advanced nations have used defence outlay as an engine of their technological and economic growth by directing the expenditure into the right channels, Indian economists are loathe to accept this. Split thinking at the national level is indicated by the fact that while we want the integrity of the country properly defended but we see a strong, motivated armed force as inimical to the interests of the political leadership. Another facet of our immature thinking concerns the defence expenditure. Indigenous defence expenditure always turns in 'Income Velocity of Money' more than one, i.e. one Rupee spent on defence produces more than one Rupee worth of GDP. Further, beneficial cascading and multiplier effect of defence expenditure has been accepted by all economists in highly developed countries (after all, it needs 20 civilians to support one man in arms). No wonder that India, with its lowly 2.3% of GDP expenditure on defence, occupies almost the bottom rung in economic advancement, and the state of our technology fares no better.

When Soviet Union disintegrated, their nuclear weapons, cruise missiles, long range ground to ground missiles, very advanced technologies and top-flight scientists/engineers were available for pittance, but Government of India practised abstinence (actually for fear of disapproval of the

USA). America, Israel, Germany and other western powers, big and small, had a field day in procuring the super-high-tech equipment and technologies from Russia and CIS countries. India, without signing the NPT, was overly concerned about not violating any provisions of this treaty, when the super and other developed countries obtained the nuclear weapons, nuclear materials and other super-high technologies freely from erstwhile Soviet Union or the CIS countries.

WOP (Warrant Of Precedence) is vitally important for the services and we can confirm that bureaucracy also considers it vitally important to assign to themselves all the higher precedence! Rank differentiation is integral to service structure (even PLA of China could not successfully abolish it). And even civilian bureaucracy is mimicking rank structures of the services. No worthwhile recommendation in respect of career advancement or operational planning in defence can be made without restoring the pre-1948 WOP. The defence Task Force was requested to consider and recommend the following changes in WOP:

Army Rank and Equivalent for Navy and Air Force	WOP or equivalent
Chief of Army Staff/ General	Cabinet Minister of Government of India
Army Commanders/ Principal Staff Officers in Army Hq.	Minister of State of Government of India
Lt. General	Deputy Minister of Government of India
Major General	Cabinet Secretary of Government of India
Brigadier	Secretary of Government of India
Colonel	Additional Secretary of Government of India

Lt. Colonel/Major	Joint Secretary of Government of India
Captain of Army	Deputy Secretary of Government of India
Lieutenant/ 2nd Lieutenant	Under Secretary of Government of India

Warrant Ranks in defence forces ought to be senior and superior to Class II Gazetted Officers of Government of India.

The Constitution of India needs to be amended immediately to bring some rationality in statecraft.

Successive Central Pay Commissions have failed or refused to recognize the need for a wage/remuneration/compensation policy for different classes of personnel. They refused to recognize talent or academic achievements and IQ (Intelligence Quotient) as determining factors for remuneration packages. Generalist bureaucrats, with requirements of very average academic achievements (55 per centers) and intellectual capabilities and with just about with average IQ, has gradually dominated all spheres of national activity and have got complete control, so much so that low calibre mediocres are ruling the roost now and has got complete control over all talent manpower, especially technical, scientific and high skilled professionals. The result is that in the comity of nations, India is treated as an overgrown, ignorant, unsophisticated, cowardly busybody ever willing to compromise with national interests and dignity.

We have repeatedly mentioned that armed forces personnel are neglected and despised by the administration. These personnel have been reposing trust in Central Pay Commissions headed invariably by a judge of Supreme Court, but every time the central pay commissions failed them – the worst award having been delivered by the sixth central pay commission in 2008. We felt particularly galled as the VI CPC seemed to have the script to hurt defence forces immeasurably and brought the private sector practices in the government sector also without caring to read our memorandum and confirmed our worst apprehensions. Copy of our memorandum is given hereunder to demonstrate how superannuated judges and their supporting bureaucracy mete out justice to the servicemen.

SHENENIGANS OF THE CPCs

July, 2007

VIth CENTRAL PAY COMMISSION : REQUEST FOR ELIMINATTION OF DISCRIMINATION AGAINST DEFENCE SERVICE PERSONNEL

Respected Justice ***,

We, the servicemen, especially ex-servicemen, are happy (a misplaced wish; subsequent events showed that servicemen had reasons to be most unhappy) that you are the Chairman of VIth Central Pay Commission. You are aware that Vth Central Pay Commission Report was so loaded against the servicemen that serving airmen, officers and personnel of the sister services had publicly demonstrated (1997-1998) their angst against the heightened discriminations mandated by the Vth Pay Commission. Of course, government of the day, with the Home minister being an acclaimed Communist and the Defence Minister with the background of an active member of the erstwhile Socialist International, ruthlessly suppressed the agitation, with the judiciary, NHRC and other constitutional authorities discharging the roles of uninvolved on-lookers! The composition and terrns of reference of the VIth CPC does not inspire any confidence in us that your commission will be able to do justice to the public servants, especially, the defence force personnel. One of your members, became quite famous as the 'last samurai' battling for the imploding capitalism and perpetuation of inequity. His contribution is no mean in ensuring that IIMs (and such other management institutes teaching or indoctrinating the youth from the affluent class) charge massive amounts of tuition fees and other charges from their students, so that students from poor or average income families are automatically debarred from access to the portals of management institutes. Shri Dholakia did not care to recognize the existing standard of living in India and that even the apex court determined minimum charges were almost two and half times more than charges of Chicago (USA) Business School, which has faculty with quite a few Nobel Laureates and candidates for the award. Since capitalism and inequity are synonymous, we cannot expect rational recommendations from the Commission whose one member, at least, does not believe in equity. (Our apprehensions turned out to be totally well founded. The VIth CPC turned in the most disgraceful and iniquitous award!)

We agree with Prof Amartya Sen that much of the modern welfare economics (to which incumbent government pays obeisance) is concerned with precisely that set of questions which avoid judgments on income distribution altogether. Our politicians and judges are quite comfortable in avoiding the question of distributive justice and wax eloquent on having inclusive developments when the elite audience is receptive.

The terms of reference and its allusion to the economic conditions in India is an attempt to circumscribe the commission so that public employees can be kept in comparative disadvantage vis-à-vis private sector counterparts. The Commission must be aware that the PM has recently declared that he has no intention of putting any restraint on remunerations of CEOs of private sector. This government had earlier removed all limits on managerial remunerations of private sector. This government seems to believe that the monetary and other resources of the nation are for the use of the big businesses only and that the government and public sectors are really interlopers. Before finalizing your report, you may wish to ascertain the correct position from the PM regarding these and related important issues.

You may wish to query the PM on the following, as otherwise your Commission will be labouring in vacuum of unreality (which subsequent events show they have been doing):

a) Does the private sector carry out more nationally-relevant activities than the government/public sector so that private sector operators are entitled for more remuneration and compensation?

b) Does private sector get their resources from a separate national stock?

c) Which sector has or should have first claim on national resources?

d) Private sector is highly iniquitous: whereas labour gets less than 4% of his annual produce, managers and CEOs take home anything from 50% to 80% of the value of annual production. How such inequity could be tolerated by the incumbent democratic government?

e) Is the government relaxed on this matter, as the courts are ambivalent on constitutionality of enforcing equity?

   Note for Chairman VIth CPC: Incidentally, letters written to the Chief Justices of India, including the incumbent, by an ex-servicemen remain un-responded.

f) Pay commission cannot determine pay structures of the public servants in the vacuum or in the absence of a rational policy. What is the national policy on remuneration, wages and compensation or on distribution of national income? Is the policy different for government and private sectors, if so, why?

g) Is 'Profit' taking, i.e. extraction of labour and production surplus for private gains, constitutional or legal? Or, shouldn't profit devolve on the State?

h) If profit should devolve on the state, shouldn't profit be distributed equitably to the two human elements of the production process, i.e. entrepreneur and labour?

i) Who is owner of fruits of labour - the labourer or hirer of labour?

j) Is labour entitled to withhold his labour, as and when he considers it essential? Is withholding of labour repugnant to constitutional provisions?

k) Can private entities be entrusted with sovereign state power of punishment or for restricting of other rights? If so, under which constitutional provisions?

l) Who is the owner of the deposits in banks and financial institutions? The depositors or borrowers of funds?

m) Some ex-servicemen have estimated that a simple and easily administrable Social Security System will cost Rs. 9 Trillion. Can such a Social Security System be introduced by cutting back on subsidies (costing about Rs. 35 Trillion, as mentioned above) to big businesses, or by bringing in some national reserves held in foreign, especially, American Banks in America?

n) If government has no funds to pay equitable remuneration to public servants, why is the government giving away subsidy to big businesses and affluent to the tune of Rs. 35 Trillion (about 1/3rd of yearly budget estimates)? Why subsidies, tax and other concessions are mounting every day with astronomical profit margins of the private sectors, by denuding the central and state treasuries? Why is the government sending out FE to foreign banks as so-called National (actually, International reserves of India, for use by international operators) Reserves (much in excess of the practice of developed countries)? Why government is permitting FE investment abroad by private parties for stashing away Indian wealth and thereby compressing Indian job market and perpetuating destitution of vast number of Indians?

o) Why there has been a spurt of FE investment abroad by Indian big businesses, much in excess of inward FE investments by foreigners, from the time that an Icon of big business (Shri Ratan Tata) was employed by the Indian Government as the Chairman of Investment Commission?

p) Why is the government maintaining highly adverse FE exchange rate of Rupee, ignoring the fact that the realistic FE exchange rate is Re.1= US$1?

q) Must the government administered FE rate always remain highly adverse for India, as otherwise there will be squeeze on the astronomical profit margins of the exporters and Importers?

r) After the FE rate started becoming favourable to India recently due to market (i.e. manipulator) forces, the exporters raised hue and cry. Unlike the PM and FM of the developed western countries, our PM and FM do not consider that favourable exchange rate denotes the rising strength of the economy; it would seem that they have no free choice, might be their big business handlers from India and abroad decide the broad parameters of Indian economy.

THE ECONOMIC TIMES, New Delhi Saturday 30 June 2007

Reported on Page 11 (ECONOMY section)

**** Help on way for Exporters: FM

The newspaper reported (by Sudeshna Sen from London): The finance ministry may finally accede to the clamour of exporters against rising rupee. "We may take measures to 'help those who are being hurt," P. Chidambaram said in London, "but in the long run, the rate is market determined and I believe we have to learn to manage capital flows," he added. With the rupee rising, he said: "exporters are feeling the pinch, importers are happy. ...". "The issue is not that the money cannot be found. We have persuaded the RBI to lend $ 5 billion from the forex reserves for infrastructure...." ****

Questions which arise are: "Is RBI still a branch of Bank of England? Why it needed to be persuaded? Are forex reserves not a part of national reserves or that these reserves cannot be used as and when needed for the economy? Why can't the reserves be monetized into rupee for funding the social security expenditures? What is the amount of FE reserves we must maintain abroad? How does USA an UK get away by maintaining miniscule international reserves vis-à-vis their import trade?

Special Note for Chairman, VIth CPC: You will notice how blatantly Indian wealth is being squandered to tell the judiciary and the retired judges that India is passing through financial straits and the defence services and the public servants must suffer for comfort of big businesses. Even Lord Clive could not be as blatant, without facing the Privy Council!

We consider that proper answer to the above queries and proper evaluation of the answers will enable the VIth Pay Commission to do justice to their assignments. A short list of wanton (illegal and unconstitutional) discriminations against service personnel is placed at Appendix 'A'. If VIth CPC also fails to understand and correct the discriminations, we apprehend a Tsunami of public disgust.

World Development Report 2000-2001 and Human Development Report 2006 indicate that both in respect of 'GINI Index' and in respect of the 'Ratio of the income of Richest 10% to that of poorest 10% of population', our country is 'Terminally Sick', so far as equity is concerned. It is not much of a consolation that the Role Models of the constituents and supporters of present government, viz. USA, China and Russia, are all adorning the ranks of the 'Failed States', giving company to the Latin American, African, Middle East and Muslim dominated Asian countries.

We shall provide sufficient supplementary data and information, as and when desired by you. If you so wish, we can give presentation(s) to the Commission members and others, as decided by you.

Your commission, by virtue of your experience in public life, must be knowing that in terms of IQ (Intelligent quotient), OLQ (Officer Like Qualities, viz. all-round perspective; leadership; spirit of self sacrifice for the country, compatriots, subordinates and superiors; commitment; love for the country and its value systems; devotion to duty in the most challenging situations; loyalty; integrity and all other noble qualities, which distinguishes the servicemen from others), in terms of social awareness and other academic and job-related qualifications, servicemen surpass their civilian counterparts in government and private sectors by orders of magnitudes. But political leadership and British-tradition-indoctrinated bureaucracy have, since Independence, typecast the military men as dispensable unnecessary drag on the economy or potential mutineers. These classes of people clean forgot that an effective and powerful massive military is essential for ensuring national sovereignty, territorial integrity and freedom of action in national interests. We are seeing all round compromise by the power elite in India in all such matters. Power elite and big businesses treat the armed forces as conveniences and are unconcerned that servicemen and their families suffer extreme hardships, loss of freedom, frequent disturbances and dislocations, privations, deprivations with constant possibility of loss of life or limbs of the near and dear ones.

If this Commission is alive to Indian and international realities, it will recognize that the military and servicemen (both serving and retired) must have first claim on national resources and wealth. This Commission should specify that military men will get, at least, 10% more pay, allowances, promotions and perquisites than the corresponding civilians in government, public, private sectors for each year of service. Career advancement of military men must be better than their civilian counterparts. [Explanation: Military Commissioned officers will get better terms than Class I Gazetted Grade 'A' civilian officers (who command nothing more than the table in their offices) of All India Services; Warrant Ranks, Non-Commissioned officers, ordinary Jawans and equivalent will get better terms than Class II Gazetted officers and other non-gazetted civilian employees in government, public or private sectors. Same equation should be extended to ex-servicemen also]. The commission will have to ensure that its secretariat and member-secretary do not nullify its recommendations by bureaucratic manipulations.

But we are worried that this pay commission may follow the path travelled by their illustrious predecessors and bring untold misery to servicemen and civilians not blessed with hereditary or ill-gotten wealth of current operators and ancestors. They may also turn in grotesque recommendations like the previous CPCs and push the public servants, particularly, the servicemen, to despair and to barely-suppressed anger. We wish to remind the Commission that only serviceman (which no other instrumentality of the State can) ensure the viability of the Constitution. Suppressed discontent or anger of this most important instrumentality of the state does not augur well for the country. We hope you also will not tread the 'Via Dolorosa' bearing the 'Cross' of public curse with the hope of attaining the pinnacle of success!

We are looking forward to your response. If you do not wish to dirty your hands and conscience by asking the Prime Minister these questions yourself, you may wish to forward our letter or parts thereof, as deemed fit by you, to the Prime Minister and inform him that the Commission will only proceed further after full and final satisfactory answers are received and the Commission is so convinced. In order to contain the discontents of the public servants, the Commission may give an interim recommendation to the government, staying strictly within the natural meanings of the terms of reference, to double the pay/allowances of public servants immediately and simultaneously reduce by 50% the remunerations of CEOs and top level managers of Private Sector enterprises/corporations/entities to balance the extra expenditure, without prejudice to final determination by the Commission. Necessary changes in laws, statutes and rules may be effected expeditiously by central and state governments, as necessary.

Kindly acknowledge and advise.

With deep regards

FACTS (forwarded to Vth CPC and repeated to VIth CPC) ABOUT GROSS DISCRIMINATION AND NEGLECT OF INTEREST OF DEFENCE PERSONNEL

Most political leaders do not care to take into account the quality of life that the defence personnel enjoy during their service and thereafter in India since independence and the extent of uncalled for discrimination and indignity suffered by them solely because they take the vow to defend India even at the cost of their life. Incidentally, such a vow is not taken by even highest level civilian bureaucrat or others. You may kindly take note of the following facts when working out the revised pay.

COMPARISON OF TREATMENT TO CIVILIANS AND ARMED FORCES PERSONNEL

CIVILIANS	ARMED FORCES
1. No downward revision of Pension	1. Pension rate reduced substantially w.e.f. 1.6.1953.
2. Upward revision of Pension scale w.e.f. 1.7.59	2. Pension rates revised only w.e.f. 1.4.1961
3. DCRG scheme introduced w.e.f. 17.4.1950.	3.DCRG scheme introduced w.e.f. 10.9.70 and existing rates of pension were depressed by 16% for officers and 11% for PBOR.
4. Family Pension scheme introduced	4. JCOs/Ors made eligible
5. No depression of actual service for civilian.	5. From 1.5.1953 onwards JCO'S/OR's actual service was reduced by 2 years, if the total service was less than 23 years. It was only rectified wef 1.3.68.
6. Full DA admissible, full DA was merged with pay in 1959 and civilians draw pension as per full amount.	6. JCOs/ORs were granted DA at 50% initially and at 80% later. In 1961 this reduced DA was merged with pay. Pension entitlement therefore remained lower for Defence Personnel. This injustice was removed by Kamat Committee on 1.3.68. It was only on 31.12.69 that full DA was admitted for merger.
7. Minimum pension applicable for civilian.	7. Minimum pension denied to defence recruits till 1.6.1984.

Contd...

8. Qualifying service for pension 10 yrs. For officers and other ranks.	8. Minimum qualifying service 20 yrs for officers; 15 yrs for Personnel below Officers Ranks (PBORs)
9. Leave encashment upto 300 days plus 10 days earned leave without restriction.	9. Restricted to ;_ i) Less than 17 yr Service: 113 days ii) Less than 20 yrs service: 132 days iii) Less than 22 yrs service: 265 days.
9A. HRA increased with effect from 1.8.97.	9A. HRA increased w.e.f. March 99
10. 13 months pay for RPF, CISF, CBI, also extended as per recommendation of 5th CPC to BSF, CRPF, Assam Rifle, ITBP, Para Military Forces.	10. Not available to Defence Personnel. One month pay as Bonus.
11. Residential Telephone recommended by Vth CPC for under secretaries (attained in 5th yrs of service including training period)	11. Residential Telephone recommended for Lt Col's (Attained in 18-20 yrs service, if selected).
12. Discriminations as at para 11 in respect of travel concession, daily allowance, Hotel Stay etc.	
13. As per figures provided by the 5th CPC in respect of Total Employees and total amount spent on their Pay and Allowance it is seen that the Government spends : Per Civil Employee (other than Def civilians) : Rs. 44600 Per armed Force Employee : Rs. 38,600	

Pay, allowances, perquisites and status is so low that **Military** is the **last choice of our youth** as a career.

During the last over **2 decades** even **graduate engineers** from **second rung institutions are not deeming it fit to join the IAF** which has the technically most sophisticated equipment. The graduates of IITs do not join IAF Technical branch any more.

Government per capita expenditure on Pay & Allowances alone **on a civilian is 20% more than a defence employee.**

Defence retirees were the **only** class of Central Government employees who were not entitled to full Medicare on retirement.

The Government was spending 150% **more per civilian retiree than a Defence retiree on Medicare** without taking into account heavy subsidy on CGHS, this has since been corrected partially. Lot still remains to be done.

On an average a **Defence employee is a loser by about Rs. 18 lakhs compared** to his civil counterpart (calculated in 1995) due to truncated nature of his career. This hiatus must have increased after the awards since then.

Almost all benefits are first given to the civil employees and only later, sometimes much later, made applicable to Defence employees, take the cases of DCRG (Death Cum Retirement Gratuity) or implementation of award of the Vth CPC.

In 1947 as per the Warrant of Precedence (WOP), the ARMY COMMANDER WAS PLACED 16TH AND A SECRETARY TO THE GOVT OF INDIA WAS PLACED at 26TH in WOP. Today Army Commanders have been equated at 23rd place. All manners of posts (occupied by serving/ retired civil bureaucrats) have been created and given higher WOP.

That today when a serving General rank officer walks into a Police Station the SHO may not even get up. In pre-independence days, even if a Lt. Col. walked in, the THANA in-charge would present him a Guard of Honour.

Technical staff, constituting an overwhelming majority in IAF resorted to UNPRECEDENTED PUBLIC AIRING OF THEIR SERIOUS GRIEVANCES DUE TO YEARS OF NEGLECT.

Armed Forces Personnel constitute one-third of ALL central Government employees. Yet: -

1. The Vth CPC visited 72 establishments. It did not include a single Air Force establishment, instead it found time to attend the "Fire-power demonstration". There was only one visit to infantry Div in J&K and it attended an "exercise" in desert.
2. 14 working Groups were formed by the Commission to study work on various topics/subjects. Only 2 related to the Armed Forces out of which one pertained to review of "Ration Scales" to reduce the scales as much as possible!
3. The CPC took oral evidence of 547 Associations/ unions, consulted 70 Judicial/Government functionaries and 25 prominent persons. Negligible percentage belonged to Services.
4. The Defence Services have never been a part of the Pay Commission. As always the IAS dominated the deliberations of CPCs and got whatever they wanted.

The Vth central pay commission report sent serious shock waves in the Armed Forces, including Ex-Servicemen and has eroded their Pride, Self Esteem. Morale in armed forces is a part of history now.

The pay scales of our gallant Jawans are lower than their metric entry civilian counter parts and Assured Career Progression (ACP) given to the civilian elude most of the NCOS and JCOS. Not only that: their Leave encashment and Education allowance are severely restricted, they have been denied 13 months pay in a year recommended for BSF, CRPF, ITBP etc.

Like the Jawans, the officers have also been treated most shabbily. 'Guaranteed Financial Upgradations' even to higher posts (which do not exist in most of the services), have been assured to all civilian Group "A' cadres, but have been diluted for Service Officers. Similarly, 'Model Cadre Structure' authorizing upto 17% and 3% posts equivalent to JT. Secy. And Addl. Secretaries, respectively (and one post of Special Secretary even to the smallest cadre) have been totally denied to Armed Forces, who are having only 0.6% and 0.2% of comparable ranks.

Lt Colonels to Brigadiers ought to have been classified as 'Senior Executives' in accordance with pre-revised pay method followed by the Commission. This has not been done for armed forces. However, it is shocking that a DIG Police with much lesser service than a Lt. Col. has been classified as Senior Executive.

The anomalies regarding class of travel for Jawans and officers are examples of shameful act of the Vth CPC, which remained to be rectified. Similar is the fact for discriminations in respect of Daily allowance, Hotel stay and residential telephone for officers etc.

The project allowance in addition to NE and Sikkim 2.5% has been introduced for civilians, not for armed forces allowances.

An average civilian has pay and allowances 20% more than a man in uniform.

During the period 1979-1989 the civilian employees strength increased by 12.4% but their Pay & Allowances grew by 13.28%. During the same period Defence strength grew by 14.6% but their Pay & Allowances grew by 11.56%.

VIth CPC crossed all limits of irrationality and turned in venal recommendations (in 2008) detrimental to national interests. Bad recommendations were made worst by deliberations of COS (Committee of Secretaries) and GOM (Group of Ministers) comprised of consummate politicians with undefined scruples

Common Indians are now convinced that expecting justice from retired judges is impractical. Jury is out still so far as the serving judges are concerned.

6

SOLUTION TO SECURITY AND ECONOMICS RELATED ISSUES: NATIONAL MOBILIZATION

National Power manifests in its expression through national security measures. All countries conscious of their responsibilities of power know the value of military and national willingness for exercise of military option for justified and unjustified causes. All powerful countries accept as gospel truth Clausewitz's formulation, "War is an extension of diplomacy". Big powers understand this scenario and *modus vivendi* on the basis of dynamically variable pecking order amongst the powers get established. WWI established USA as the centre piece of western world and WWII gave total powers to USA to establish order in the international interactions on earth. During WWII, after the capitulation of all countries in main land Europe to German onslaught, only USSR and Britain remained to be conquered. The great Churchill handed over all initiatives to USA during WWII. People who succeeded Churchill were much lesser men and they handed over all their colonies and subjugated all their foreign interests to American convenience. But America did not follow the traditional colonial practices of sending their armed forces to conquer or capture the foreign land except when considered essential or more profitable to be directly involved. American brain-children like UNO, World Bank, IMF and hosts of other organizations like FAO, WHO, IAEA etc. were created or others (like International Red Cross or similar charitable institutions) were bludgeoned into conformance to tie up all the people outside USA with all sorts of financial and non-financial regulations, controls and denial regimes maintaining a façade of democracy, debate and consensus, with ultimate controlling strings being in American hands always.

USSR and China, for a short while, tried to be alternative power centres. It failed, as basic doctrines of Marxism were faulty as it encouraged Semitic inequity and irrationality through dictatorship[38]. In proclaimed communist states the change-agents like Gorbachev/Yeltsin sold their country (USSR and then Russian Republic) cheaply, for a few million dollars apiece, if we are to believe the market rumour relayed to us by the taxi-drivers in Moscow.[39] We do not know for sure what price was set for Deng Hsiao Ping by his foreign handlers for selling China. Might be pathogenic hatred for Mao Zedong and a general dislike for China and its value systems prompted him, like Dr. Manmohan Singh, who has congenital contempt for anything of Hindu India and its value systems and has unquestioning love for the colonial British rulers and Americans, to sell their respective countries.

The concept of a 'Soft Super Power' conquering the world with their un-interrupted services to the super and big western powers and to their surrogates, like Japan, China[40], at the cost of native population, has captured the imagination of the business class and elite in India. This concept was evolved by Deng and his committed successors for China; China-observers now ascribe the increasing financial and diplomatic clout of China to their adherence to the status of a soft super power and increasing convergence of interests with USA. Glory of this demilitarized powerless model of statecraft so impressed the father of Indian economic reforms

(Dr. Manmohan Singh) that he threw all other considerations out of the window and tried to emulate the Chinese model, come what may! Indian mainstream media is full of conjectures when will India catch up or overtake the currently acknowledged soft super power, China.

We have examined the fundamental differences between the conventional super power and the soft variety. Now we can examine the significance and essentiality of national mobilization for national glory with equity.

NATIONAL MOBILIZATION

The degree or extent of national mobilization has been defined by me as under:-

$$\text{Degree of Active Mobilization} = \frac{\text{Total Population of the country}}{\text{Total no. of personnel in Active Service}}$$

Similarly,

$$\text{Degree of overall Mobilization} = \frac{\text{Total Population of the country}}{\text{Total no. of personnel in Active Service + Reserve + Para-military forces}}$$

Both these are expressed as one soldier per .... Population.

I initially called this as "Militarization" in a presentation in National Defence College to a class of service, civilian and service officers of India and of foreign friendly countries, but almost all were feeling acutely embarrassed or dismayed by the term. Hence the change to 'Mobilization'.

I queried quite a few of the course members in NDC, in 1987 when I first calculated the figures for Active and overall mobilization. The first reaction of almost all was that China was the most mobilized state. The truth is quite different as you will see from the statistics given overleaf.

Active Mobilization

Sr No	State	Population	No of personnel in Active Service	Degree of Active mobilization (1 soldier per ..... population)	Rank
1.	Israel	4,400,000	149,000	30	2
2.	Iraq	15,400,000	845,000	18	1
3.	USSR	279,500,000	5,130,000	54	3
4.	Iran	45,200,000	704,500	64	4
5.	Hungary	10,789,000	105,000	103	5
6.	France	55,502,000	557,493	100	6
7.	Egypt	49,500,000	445,000	111	7
8.	USA	240,900,000	2,143,955	112	8
9.	West Germany	61,134,000	485,800	126	9
10.	Britain	56,132,000	323,800	174	10
11.	Pakistan	98,125,000	480,600	204	11
12.	China	1,052,700,000	2,950,000	357	12
13.	India	778,000,000	1,260,000	617	13

Note: All data taken from "The Military Balance 1986-87", published by The International Institute for Strategic Studies, 23 Tavistock Street, London WC 2E7NQ"

Overall Mobilization

Sr No	State	Total No of active Service + Reserve +Para	Overall mobilization (1 soldier per ..... population)	Rank	
				Overall	Active
1.	Israel	707,500	6	1	2
2.	Iraq	1,499,800	10	3	1
3.	USSR	30,700,000	9	2	3
4.	Iran	1,124,500	40	6	4
5.	Hungary	316,000	34	5	5
6.	France	1,034,201	54	10	6
7.	Egypt	1,488,000	33	4	7
8.	USA	4,533,708	53	9	8
9.	West Germany	1,275,800	50	7	9
10.	Britain	628,830	89	12	10
11.	Pakistan	1,157,600	85	11	11
12.	China	20,327,000	51	8	12
13.	India	1,755,000	443	13(Last)	13(Last)

Note: All data from "The Military Balance, 1986-87", London.

'One Soldier per — population' has been taken as the 'National Mobilization' status, although the more conventional way of expressing 'Militarization of a country' is No. of soldiers per million population. But those figures are so large that worthwhile comparison is not possible. But our chosen parameter of national mobilization figures succinctly brings out the state of mobilization, i.e. 'Lesser' the figure, 'More' mobilized is that state, viz. there is inverse correlation between the figures and national mobilization. Our definition also neutralizes the scale effect and is neutral to population strength. Thus, Iraq and Iran (two comparatively small states, population-wise or geographical area wise) were then the two most mobilized states of the world, third position being taken by erstwhile USSR. India was and continues to be the least mobilized state.

The position for Russian Federation and India must have worsened since 1997. We are aware that the armed forces of India are facing acute shortage of manpower, especially, officer cadre, for various reasons – both national policy stance and realities of the international compulsions. But it is an empirical fact that mobilization state determines the outcome of any war-like engagement of national significance. India-China conflict of 1962 was unsatisfactory for India, as Chinese mobilization was higher than that of India, although authentic data for China was not readily available. China-North Vietnam conflict (during concluding phases of American defeat in Vietnam) resulted in rout of China as well. Visiting North Vietnamese Generals boasted that they massacred 30,000 Chinese in one valley of Vietnam when Chinese fool-hardily entered there to punish the recalcitrant Vietnamese. (When some of us visited North Vietnam in 1987 as part of National Defence College delegation, the Vietnamese Generals showed us marked on the map and also took us on a visit to the area where this rout of Chinese took place). This was possible because of much higher comparative mobilization state of Vietnam, whereas total population of N. Vietnam was only a small fraction of that of China. In Middle East, prior to Iraq I, Iran (with almost 3 times the population of Iraq) could not prevail over Iraq in spite of bitter blood-letting over many years, as both countries had comparable mobilization status. The results of Indian engagements with Pakistan have not been propitious for India so far. We surmise that poor mobilization state of India is the root cause of Indian inability to control matters vis-à-vis Pakistan. There has been spill-over effect in that discontents, dissent against national policies have mounted and in some cases crossed the acceptable limits. This can be corrected and that also on most cost-effective basis.

India boasts of housing the second largest population of the world (16% in 2% of world geographical area, thereby indicating high density of population) A study by Rice

Research Centre, Bhubaneshwar, found that even rice cultivators of a labour-short country like Japan uses many times more labour per hectare for rice cultivation than Indian agriculturists, notwithstanding the fact that Japanese use something like ten to 100 times more organic and inorganic plant nutrients and other inputs in their agriculture.

There are other factors which are militating in effective utilization of even the available manpower. For example, squadron/flight level aircrew and engineers constitute the real cutting teeth of the Indian air force, but these officers have to carry out so much of house-keeping and administrative work that they can devote only a small fraction of their time in actual professional work they are required to discharge.

This forcible (but essential in Indian reality) diversion from essential main activities have created other problems. An experimental study on 'Awareness of essential technical, functional, administrative powers and responsibilities of airmen, NCO, SNCO, Warrant and Master Warrant ranks' carried out in an operational command in IAF in 1989 showed serious gaps in essential and routine information even. A sample study of a small batch of available technical and logistic officers showed that they also did not fare much better than the men under them. State of awareness amongst aircrew was also found wanting. After it was suspected that the 'Relight procedure' was mismanaged by the pilot of a MIG 21 aircraft involved in a fatal accident, some pilots were asked to do the relight procedure in a MIG 21 Simulator. Only one pilot out of six pilots, selected at random, could do the procedure correctly. This study also showed that the personnel in the Base operating the latest aircraft of IAF had the best awareness. This indicated that best men and officers have gathered in the Base operating the latest acquisition, which had necessitated denuding other bases and facilities handling older equipment. This was necessary as the pool of personnel for selection was very small.

Although India has highest overall density of population in the world, man power-intensity of major equipment like aircraft is very poor. A study by the author in Air HQ showed that "Number of men/officers per aircraft" was lowest in Indian Air Force compared to all the major air forces of the world. It was found that countries operating mostly indigenous aircraft and weapon systems needed lesser man-power per aircraft compared to countries (like India) which operated mostly imported aircraft and weapon systems. Rate of air accidents in countries operating indigenous aircraft was lower than those operating imported aircraft. India has unenviable record of highest air accident rates, mainly because engineers are kept busy on non-engineering jobs away from their actual work place. 'Officer to Men' ratio is also very poor in engineering branches in Indian Air Force. Whereas, work on aircraft needs 100% supervision and cross-checks over and above that but all supervisions are carried out by personnel below officers' rank. Incidentally, when the study was made in 1988 and 1989 on the basis of data pertaining to 1985-1986, it was revealed that US Air Force had almost as many officers (more than one hundred thousand) as total men/officers in IAF. Qualification status of USAF officers was much better than in IAF, as USAF had many post graduates and doctorates in officers' cadre. IAF had a miniscule percentage of such degree holders. Sample details are given here under.

COMPARISON BETWEEN USAF AND IAF

		USAF	IAF	Remarks (USAF to IAF Ratio)
1.	No. OF AIRCRAFT (1988)			
	Regular Air Force	$ 6724	$ 1961	3.4 times.
	National Guard plus AF Reserve	2235	Nil	
	Total	8959	1961	4.6 times

2.	No. OF MEN (1989)			
(a)	Military	5,35,200$	1,14,000+	4.7 times
(b)	Civilian	2,48,875$	30,760 +	8.1 times
	Total	7, 84, 075	1,44,760	5.4 times
3.	No. OF OFFICERS			
(a)	General	13*	1 =	13 times
(b)	Lt Gen & below	1, 03, 684 *	10,007 +	10.3 times
4.	DEFENCE BUDGET PERCENTAGES			
		(1991) $	(1990-91) ++	
(a)	Army	26.5%	56.1%	
(b)	Navy	33.8%	12.7%	
(c)	Air Force	30.3%	24.9%	
(d)	Defence Agencies	8.5%	7.2%	
		USAF	**IAF**	**Remarks**
5.	AIR FORCE BUDGET	(1990)	(1989-90)	
(a)	Budget as a percentage of GNP	1.7% *	0.92% Y	
(b)	Operating Budget	(1990) (Billion of Dollars)	(1989-90)	
	(i) Operation & Maintenance	21.75 *	0.446++	
	(ii) Personnel	20.03	0.191	
	(iii) Procurement	30.20	0.510	
	(iv) Other heads	27.62	0.803	
	Total	99.60	1.230	81 times
6.	CAREERWISE DISTRIBUTION OF OFFICERS			
	Pilots & Navigators	27,321 $ (For line functions mainly)	3124 + (For all functions)	

7. EDUCATION LEVELS

Officers :		
(a) Below Graduates	0.1% *	19.7%
(b) Graduates	54.9%	62.9%
(c) Post Graduates	43.6%	17.2%
(d) Doctorates	1.45%	0.15%
Airmen:		
(a) Some colleges	44.35%	(Not readily available)
(b) Graduates	3.1%	
(c) Post Graduates	0.36%	

8. INVENTORY OF AIRCRAFT

24 +years	29%	8.3% $
21 – 24 years	12%	5.3%
18-21 Years	13%	6.6%
15- 18 Years	5%	10.6%
12-15 Years	5%	9.9%
9-12 Years	6%	14.3%
6-9 Years	9%	15.8%
3-6 Years	10%	18.5%
0-3 Years	11%	10.5%

Source:	**For USAF**	**For IAF**
	@ Military Balance, 1988	+ JD Stats
	* Air Force Magazine, USA May 1990	++ D Fin. P
	$ Air Force Magazine, USA	Y Budget from D Fin
		P GNP from Economic Information Year Book.
	$ Computed from data	Obtained from Maintenance Cells for each type of aircraft

Condition for IAF is extremely bad. IAF, operating the most modern and lethal aircraft and other weapon systems, could not recruit a single IIT graduate in the last about three decades, apparently due to low remuneration and career options offered. IAF had to make do with graduates from ordinary (capitation fee?) colleges and institutes. System is showing the strains! High accident rates in India are unofficially attributed to these deficiencies! The conditions in the other two armed forces are worse.

Manpower-distribution of Armed Forces of all developed countries has shifted to technology-savvy personnel, but we understand that accretion to personnel in armed forces in the India in last decade has mainly been in non-technical branches.

Traditional concept is 'army marches on its stomach', but Air Forces flies, albeit all armed forces operate, in highest technology environments! Armed forces, especially, Air Forces, invariably use the most modern marginal technologies, which come with high price tag. In mid eighties, USAF had a budget of around US $ 100 Billion, whereas total budget of the Armed Forces in India around the same time was just about US $ 6 Billion. Even now India spends the least amount per capita in the world for Armed Forces, much less than that of even a miniscule State like Singapore! Our economic policy stance did not permit adequate expenditure for national security and India is depending on diplomacy for protecting its national interests on the premise that brain is always stronger than brawn! Might be the lessons of Iraq II, or the evolving conflict in Iran, point to the other direction.

We are convinced that the leopard-like Government of India will not change its colours soon and go in for requisite mobilization of the nation in spite of the fact that mobilization is an immediate necessity from economic, power-projection, industrial, agricultural and cultural growth perspectives. There is a vast reservoir of talent in the pool of retired/ superannuated personnel of the Armed Forces. This manpower can be put to use in servicing the armed forces. US armed forces forks out to native civilian entities and heavily depend on aliens for BPO (Business Process Outsourcing), KPO (Knowledge Process Outsourcing), EPO (Enterprise Process Outsourcing) for all their routine/non-routine work. They even use the aliens for active combat work. They can use the aliens freely as dollar is a highly valued currency in all countries used by them. India does not have this particular advantage but simple alternative models are available. The techniques of BPO, KPO and EPO can be used by Indian Armed forces easily for utilizing the services of the ex-servicemen within the country. Armed forces, particularly Indian Air Force could take a lead by handing over all peripheral and non-strategic activities like: Inventory control, stocking and Stores Management, Tools Management and tools control and issue, Third and fourth line servicing, specialist laboratories, Transportation in all media, non-critical area Security, Pay accounting and disbursement, Air Traffic Control, medical services in static establishments, etc., etc. The air force (albeit all armed forces) will have full freedom to direct the civilian entities to meet all their requirements under all circumstances in 24*365 modes. The attached civilian entities will carry out legal orders of the authorized serving personnel without demur. The civilians will not resort to strike, go-slow and work to rule under any circumstances. For the first few years (till experience is gained), only ex-servicemen will work in armed forces bases and in armed forces establishments. Service decorum will be maintained but serving personnel will be entitled to issue orders to senior ex-service personnel also. Embedded civilian entities will carry out studies on various issues projected by services. Even after handing over custody of the stores to civilians, services will have full control for distribution, transfer and stocking of selected items. All the service bases will be interlinked and serving personnel will be able to determine status of any item anywhere in India and abroad (for expeditionary forces) from his desk top or laptop in his work place.

Relieved of routine mundane administrative and domestic chores, serving personnel will then be able to concentrate on their core jobs and will have enough time for inspection, supervision, monitoring, surveillance, war games, exercises, simulations, paper exercises, management games, evolving and exercising on innovative uses of available equipment and forces. After all, manpower is the greatest force multiplier. With support of dedicated ex-servicemen, serving personnel will be able to drastically reduce the turn round time of servicing and deploy much larger proportion of available resources for exercises and operations. There is indifferent use of Air Power in India, but manpower constraints could also be major factor. Defence forces cannot raise money from the market. Embedded private agencies have no such restraint. Such agencies will be able to raise funds from the market like any other business establishments. Stores handed over by services will continue to be service stock and these will be usable as required without payment; civilian agencies will only be entitled for inventory carrying costs and dispensing and distribution costs. They will be able to 'Bond' the stores and raise money from the Banks also. Thus these entities will not be requiring any budgetary support from the services or the government, except for rebates and tax holidays available to other businesses. This sort of arrangement would have been a win-win situation for all in India but our liberalized economists, administrators and ministers have other considerations!

One thing is very clear that highly developed states, irrespective of their ideological stance or nature of government, have high state of mobilization. This direct correlation between national mobilization and development needs to be impressed on the LDCs (Least Developed Countries). All the western and some of the Middle East countries are always complaining of low population but they still keep and maintain very large armed forces. There is a nexus between strength of armed forces and development. It is no use debating which comes first, development or armed forces, in the traditional configuration of the "Egg or chicken first" debate. Development process is tortuous and the outcome of any policy thrust is always beset with many vicissitudes and doubts. National Mobilization is a sure process, outcome of which is quite predictable. Although the social effect of National Mobilization is uniformly beneficial (if the example of the developed countries are to be believed), the political effect may be conjured in a different light by the entrenched elite. It somehow misses the calculation of these LDCs that developed countries are doing rather well with big armed forces. They seem to have grasped the significance of militarization albeit mobilization for the good of the country. Of .course, one argument is always heard. The developed countries have many international obligations and hence they must maintain big mobilization state. Their policy prescription for LDCs is to have minimum military or mobilized effort. It is never pointed out that the main source of power of the Developed countries (DC's) is the big mobilization. History is possibly testimony to this. I have not carried out, but if someone does carry out a study, it will be seen that the states of Alexander the Great, Taimur Lang, Mohamed of Gazni, Julius Caesar, Napoleon, etc., were highly mobilized states or at least more intensively mobilized than the countries they subdued. Modern history is, at least, replete with examples. Hitler's Germany, Mussolini's Italy and Tojo's Japan were highly mobilized before World War II.

There are various other compulsions for mobilization. It solves a great proportion of the unemployment. Apart from direct employment, something like 20 more persons are required to be employed for each soldier for manufacture of armament and in related industries, housing, food and Medicare of the troops and associated other requirements of the armed forces. The unemployment that we find in developed countries is of a nature quite different from that in the LDCs. In DCs that unemployment is engineered for keeping certain thrusts of the profit propelled economy intact. In order that the problem does not spill over, unemployment doles and social security are ensured in these countries for all. Further, mechanization and labour saving devices are manifestations of the labour shortage for supporting the mobilization.

Mobilization leads to industrial growth. Armed forces of all ages and countries thrived in high growth economies. It is a fact of life that all developed countries pursue high mobilization with concomitant investment in industry to keep the armed forces equipped. Also, all the armed forces of the developed countries are mostly equipped with indigenous equipment. Even in this case, the country which does not have full indigenous capacity has comparatively lesser mobilization states - contrast the position of UK with USA or for that matter UK with Germany and France. What a climb down by the greatest Imperial Power! It is a moot point to decide – which declined first: military strength or economic power of UK? But these developed countries are most vociferous in prescribing low mobilization states for the UDCs or LDC's. Even after the near collapse of the economies of Latin American and African states under debt burden under the tutelage of the World Bank and IMF, the policy being advised is the same: no mobilization, no independent industrial infrastructure for indigenous armament production. Result? No economic growth. How lop-sided western country arguments are, can be gauged by the analysis of the American economy without militarization published in a journal:

"— majority of Americans cling to the belief that a large cut in the military budget would plunge the country into recession or even depression".

The fear is not unfounded. When almost 8-9% of GDP goes in direct defence spending, switching to civilian production is just not easy. Look at the fiasco in Soviet Union and Russian Federation.

Country, wise study of mobilization status also reveals interesting facts. Highly mobilized states have more international power and can impose their will on contenders. Because of its low mobilization state, Indian power in international politics is disproportionately lower than its big size and population should have endowed it with.

To be reckoned as a big power in Asia, India should aim to have a mobilization status of 1 soldier in 100 population in next 3-5 years (within the span of current five year plan) and should aim to have active mobilization of one in 50 people in next decade. Indian economists and policy planners will just shrug and ignore because they have never been able to be receptive to Indian solutions to Indian problems.

But consider, if India had a 10-20 million armed force, however badly equipped, it would have given something to others to ponder. Three to five million of these would be looking towards west and south west, 2-5 million towards north, 2-5 million towards north east and 3-5 million towards south and south east with some of these stationed in far and near countries for international peace keeping strictly under complete Indian control (functional, administrative and provision of administrative services) but financed for equipping and maintenance by host countries or the UNO (troops wear only Indian uniform). Then, like Eden, PM of United Kingdom, the surviving super power could persuade itself to follow the 'doctrine of withdrawal from 'East of Aden' and leave the disparate countries of Asia, Australia and Africa, with inadequate leadership qualities to be managed by India. Composition of troops - whether Army, Navy, Air Force, marine, maritime, amphibian, special forces, intelligence, nuclear, anti- or counter-biological, chemical, psychotropic forces – will depend on the specific threat perception in area or theatres of operation in different countries in different time frames and seasons and culture of the host place or country (the last two factors being important for only peace time operations without any overt conflict of interests). Who would have thought of tangling with such a force? The perennial threat perception which India harbours now would have gone. Others would have developed some inferiority complex!

Thus India's perennial problem of unemployment would mostly have vanished. Two hundred to 400 million additional employed people would have been required to support 10 to 20 million soldiers in addition to other requirements for civil sector. The requirement of massive manpower in India would have stopped Brain/Brawn drains and reversed the flows! India would be then welcoming immigrants with work permits and grant citizenship after thorough screening. The industrial development and GDP growth rates would be in double or triple digit figures. Prosperity of the common men would be realized then. Economy will not be superheated, as is prognosticated for China off and on, if equity norms developed in this book are followed scrupulously.

This would have killed in one stroke the 'Smallness syndrome' successfully employed by Indian planners (or thinkers like C. Subramanian of 1950s) to give business to other developed countries. Because the burden of equipping 10-20 million troops would have to be borne by Indian industries only the question would have been so big that no planner could argue in favour of import.

Let us have a look at the dimensions of the industrial and agricultural growth we are envisaging for the desired mobilization of India. A soldier needs 2 kg of food per day. Hence, for 20 million men in uniform, the country would need to provide 40 million kg or 40 thousand tons per day or 14.6 million tons per year. The supply chain for the defence forces is pretty long with myriads of government, semi-government, public and private sectors involved. We have assumed that the long and tortuous supply chain with multiple stocking and storage points will lock up two to five times the food actually consumed. Thus, any thing from 30 to 70 million tons of food out of national stock will have to be kept earmarked for the armed forces per year, which works out to something like 10 to 30 percent of current production. An average Indian is also entitled to 2 Kg of food per day. Hence daily food requirement of Indian is 2 billion kg (in 2007) or 2 million tons per day or 730 million tons per year. Since supply chain is no shorter for a common

Indian (to cater to the profit and price manipulations of private traders and wrong and anti-national stocking and storage policies of government) the actual requirement is more than 800 to 1000 million tons per year against current production of hardly 300 million tons. Increasing Indian food production by three times is no big deal for a government committed to Indian interests and not committed for only protecting private profits. The shortfall in national strategic reserves of food can be procured easily from abroad with a proper FE exchange rate. Similarly, thousands of millions of metres of uniform and other clothing items will be required to provide proper clothing for the military and for fulfilling minimum requirements of other civilians.

Then accommodation for 20 million servicemen and their families will need minimum covered area 20 times more than what the military establishment has in its possession presently. The existing military cantonments, airfields, other service and domestic accommodations, firing ranges and other exercising and manoeuvering areas are already occupying a major portion of the land, water, air, economic, electronic and other national spaces of India. This is being strongly resented by liberated nationalists and big businesses. Already moves are afoot to delegalize national security endeavours and deny adequate space to the armed forces. Massive mobilization of India will be considered contrary to big business interests (although the reverse is true) and they will mobilize all their forces and rationales to prevent mobilization of India. Since Indian political system is just an extension of big business, we cannot expect a smooth progress towards a strong and effective India in the traditional manner.

Concurrently with commencement of mobilization, National Building Codes will have to be thoroughly recast. All low height buildings (excluding Heritage buildings certified by Indian national heritage and historical site preservation authorities) including new religious constructions or buildings will be prohibited. All buildings will have to be minimum 50 storied high (there being no upper limit) with minimum four underground levels (there being no depth limit.) Cantonments and military establishments should be in mostly deep underground structures and non-critical facilities in super-high rise buildings.

Intrepid economists and wise amongst the administrators will gleefully point out the paucity of sufficient land and air space for peacetime exercising/manoeuvering of 20 million troops. We also agree that exercising in the periods available after the crops have been harvested (as is the practice now) will not provide sufficient exercising time for 20 million troops. We have simple solutions in mind. Open seas and uninhabited islands, uninhabited lands and desert areas in Indian ocean, and of Indian ocean littoral states will be used for peaceful exercising with due approval of the states concerned, where required. All these states will be invited to send their (native) observers and in selected cases joint exercises will be conducted with these countries. Once India has more men in arms than that of America (i.e. more than five million for this purpose), then the neighborhood of India will give serious considerations to Indian desires – articulated or non-verbal. It will be then quite simple matter for exercising in sparsely populated and poor regions of Africa, Australia, Pakistan, Arab peninsula, Egypt, Iran and all countries in Sumatra region (countries with which we are supposed to have very close friendly relations now). After initial hostility and hesitation, when countries of Asia get convinced that we have only peaceful intentions of a mobilized soft super power (MSSP) and we do not have ulterior motive of exploiting these countries, then they will welcome India readily. India will first exercise in Africa and Asia, including Tibet, China and Asian Russia. After 20 million troops get in place, India will exercise in South America, European Union, Russia and Europe. By that time North America will be sensitized to Indian intentions and interests. All foreign countries will benefit as Indians will pay legitimate charges for all goods and services accepted from these countries. Since India will not be in exploitation mode, Indian foray can be a permanent feature of these countries – it will be immigration of a different kind (like religious tourism or ritual), where the immigrants pay for their stay! The upshot of this might be that India will be implored to gradually take charge of the geo-politics of the world.

Since there is a consensus amongst the economists in India that expenditure on Armed Forces does not add to the economic well-being of India, the conclusion from above statistics is what the (un-liberalized) economists know for a long time; large share of the defence budget is going away due to imports of equipment for the armed forces, especially, the Indian Air Force and the Indian Navy. Since there is a consensus of silence, nobody has questioned the justification for imports eternally. Or, no wise man has questioned the puerile recommendations of that C. Subramanian committee (must be filled with anti-nationals) of early sixties of last century that India does not need independent civil aviation aircraft manufacturing facility. No wonder aeronautical industry is so moribund in India and ministers/bureaucrats/private entities can make hay and merrily import billions of dollars of aircraft and other stores and make massive profits in the bargain. Also, economists and intelligentsia has never taken seriously the theory that indigenous low performance equipment in overwhelmingly large numbers can compete effectively with sophisticated imported equipment. Our planners have not applied their minds to the historical evidence that no country became powerful or victorious on imported equipment and technology. Canard was widely circulated in western countries that Bolshevik Russia/USSR was technologically inferior to the west. But this inferior-technology state had checkmated all western moves for control of the world economy till such time Gorbachev arrived on Russian scene. The law of Mass Action of chemistry is too easily forgotten by official and privatized planners and economists.

7

POLITICS FOR MOBILIZATION OF INDIA

National mobilization will solve economic and national security problems, but proper political and judicial environment need to be created for all-round development of the country. Politics in India has always been an open stage for enactment of charades of competitive global powers. Politics is conducted in India under shadow of economics and vice versa. Economics and politics in India cannot be studied separately in a realistic environment, as both are, individually and collectively, subject to external monitoring and control. When we discussed national security and economic issues, we have, in fact dealt with most of the Indian political trends and issues. We now wish to examine politics in broader global concerns, the activities of some principal actors in politics and the constitution mandated for poor Indians.

Democracy and Development

We, in India, have no doubts that Democracy is the ideal vehicle for expression of popular will. Where military rules, dictatorship of one form or other operates or where some form of monarchy or where degenerate progenies of monarchies thrive with consensus of elites from all parts of the political/cultural divides, there is an urgent need for establishment of genuine 'democracy of the people for the people and by the people'. But Anglo-Saxon model of democracy that is being practised in India is effectively scuttling real freedom of choice. In Indian scheme of constitutional democracy, all top constitutional authorities are either indirectly elected or nominated or selected by a coterie around the PM, who wields exclusive power on all matters - including economic preferences. Amartya Sen in his book has most comprehensively proved the linkage between Development and Freedom, but the book also points out the aberrations that can affect both development and freedom. Our worry increased manifold when we noticed that World Development Report 2000-2001 of World Bank started selling 'Democracy' as a panacea for the undeveloped countries. They totally forgot that genuine democracy cannot co-exist with 'uncontrolled Market'. The timing of publication of Prof Amartya Sen's book and World Bank's sudden renewed interest in democracy might be coincidental. People must consider whether democracy is being sold as 'brand equity' by the international operators. There is a need to focus the searchlight of intellect of great economists on the actual practice of democracy in poor and ever stagnating countries like India. It is worth considering whether 'controlled' or 'oligarchic' Democracy operating in poor countries, could be the means for enslavement of the people. Is Arundhati Roy really a crazy writer who called 'Democracy as the whore of the capitalists' in her speech in Harlem in New York, USA, on 13 May 2003? Logically, philosophically or operationally, simple solutions are available, but who needs to care?

This book (*Development as Freedom*) is quite unique in explaining various circumstances of incidence of starvation, destitution and famine and how divisive these can be. We consider that similar circumstances are already operating in initiating and perpetuating inequality and poverty in less developed countries. But Prof. Sen's unidimensonal 'development', we are afraid, can also be divisive like famine and we have many instances of this in India. Examples are, 'green revolution' in Punjab, 'white Revolution (in milk)' (mainly in Gujarat) initiated by well-meaning people, 'freight equalization' for development of production capacities far away from raw materials, 'deforestation' of Terai and Nainital and other Himalayan foot hills, 'deforestation' of Assam and Eastern India, 'Tehri' and 'Narmada' dams, establishment of SEZ (special economic zones, to permit free exploitation of labour and the poor), FTA (free trade area to pass on special benefits to foreigners, which are denied to the common Indians), especially, when free trade is not available within the country, etc., etc. - examples are galore. It is surprising that economists have not focused on these issues, except to applaud these developments, all for the wrong reasons, and hound out the opponents of these projects like Medha Patkar, Arundhati Roy or Sunder Lal Bahuguna from public space.

Will someone (and/or an esteemed member of the bench) please define what does this term 'Development' really mean? The anguished cry of the dispossessed runs something like this. When you take my perpetual asset, 'land', in exchange for a transient asset like, 'money', and you create an industry, how do I personally benefit by this development? Who gets the massive profit generated by development of my land? Why can't I get the major portion of the profit, since I contributed the only strategic resource? (Honourable Judges, can you understand what I am trying to convey?) Since I am an aged uneducated (in English medium school) agriculturist, I can expect (if I am extremely lucky and if the competition is not so intense) to get a lowest paid menial job of degrading nature, without any opportunity for independent decision making. This industry (in the garb of development) has ruined my economic security and independence and thrown me to the hounds like money lenders and mafias of the industry. I have been forced to leave my home and hearth and move into a dirty, filthy, stinking ghetto with my family with a liability of hefty monthly payments to the slum-lord (of an unauthorized colony) for an accommodation in which even pigs will be unhappy to stay. I invite judicial fraternity to kindly visit the 'Bhumihin (Bengali, translation being 'Landless') Camp, near Govind Puri, South Delhi (on the left side of the double-carriage road running between 'Kalkaji' temple near Nehru Place and the Mehrauli– Badarpur Road in South Delhi) and see for themselves how humanity has been treated by the modernized version of 'Development'. I have a sneaking conviction that if some members of the highest bench of the country could anonymously visit Bhumihin Camp, they will understand why we hate this irresponsible slogan of 'Development' for cheating the low income earners. Who will answer me as to why it is always that the low income earners are expected to make the sacrifice for 'Development', 'Protection of Tiger or other animals', big dams or big steel factory or power station or 'Environmental Protection'? I wonder why the lands, mansions and palaces or the farm-houses of the industry developers, affluent and elite or of civil society are never taken over in the name of 'Development'. I wonder why the constitutional protection of Article 300A 'Right to Property' is not available to the poor and how some laws or edicts predating the constitution can subvert the constitutional right (which earlier was a Fundamental Right)! Mind you, all this development and my impoverishment have been taking place in a so-called western model democratic country.

Gorbachev and Olympics

This heading may look incongruous but by and by you will see how the two are intimately related. Olympics 1988 was unique in many respects, but this was the only Olympics which showed how intimately the medal tally in Olympics is linked with the politics (Economic-Politics or Political economy) of a state. The media (as it is steeped in occidental culture) highlighted all its other aspects except the most important one. In Gold medals and in total medal tally Soviet Union and East Germany secured first and second places. Again Bulgaria was high on medal tally above Rumania and Czechoslovakia, Poland had done well but nowhere near the USSR, GDR, Bulgaria or Rumania. The two sporting giants Cuba and North Korea did not take part in this Olympics. If they had, the relative position from third place onwards would possibly have been different. These are the so-called Socialist countries. You might have noticed that countries, where the much maligned socialist fervour is stronger, has done better in sports. In these so-called iron-curtain countries money does not have all that power and access to resources is not hereditary nor can be commandeered by either wealth or prosperity. None of these countries has national wealth or GDP anywhere near the United States of America. But with its multi-billion (or trillion) dollar expenditure on sports from Government and private sources, USA had to be satisfied with the third place in medal tally. China, with its vast population and promise from past Olympics and sports meets ought to have performed better but did not. India, of course, did not get any medals and has remained out of reckoning as a sporting nation. Incidentally, India houses the second largest population in the world and follows capitalist economic model under a pseudo-name 'mixed economy' (unmixed curse for common Indians). Amongst the African countries, only those have done better which have some sort of socialist politics predominant.

This close correlation between socialist politics (or economics if you so desire) and performance in international competitive sports had intrigued me most as I watched the progress of the Olympics 1988 on T.V. A caveat is well in order here. The degree of excellence in sports cannot be judged solely by result of the Olympics alone. In Olympics (for that matter in any competitive meet) only quality does not win the medal. The carnival atmosphere, the foreign land, rules, regulations, habits, customs, culture of the host country and the competitor countries - all of these affect the performance. But all said and done, what succeeds better than success? Hence degree of success in Olympics can be taken as a rough and ready measure of the degree of excellence in sports.

International competitive sports demand the all-round best from the participants. Only the best sportsmen of a country can give the best. But do the best sportsmen get selected for representation of a country? It is not the superficial selection process of the pre-Olympics trials in the country. It is concerned with the process in which the sportsmen from the village level, low economic levels get thrown up to the national level. In spite of all the media hype and all the expenditure of GNP on sports, the access to opportunity is possibly grossly unequal in the market economy countries. Even in the non-socialist faith, those countries have done comparatively better where the grip of the market on the economy is lesser. This negative correlation between the force of so-called market and sporting performance should be examined by economists and political leaders. The under-privileged ones just fall on the wayside due to economic hurdles and social pressures which do not view devotion to sports as worthwhile economic pursuit. But the whole population can only be covered when the political mores are tailored to so-called socialist pattern and not on elitist syndrome with so-called individual initiative. A comparison of socialist and non-socialist countries will tell us in which system high performance sport can best thrive in a massive scale.

The conclusion that socialist system possibly gives best chance to performers may appear facile assumption when it is considered that USA, in spite of so-called market economy, has performed well, so much so that, it occupied the third place in the medal tally. Hence, possibly only the system-study will not do. Net worth of the country, per capita expenditure on sports and general level of well-being of a country has something to do with performance in sport. Also, it may not be lost sight of that in American contingent a good proportion was provided by the African-Americans who are the most under-privileged as a class in American society. The superior performance of African-Americans tends to belie that political or social system has something to do with excellence in sport when the whole country is considered. But the performance of the African-Americans has to be reviewed in the context of the per capita expenditure incurred in USA on their African-Americans sportsmen (also on white sportsmen including sports women) and their relative performance. The ethnic quality of the Negroes and the African's performance in arduous sports is now an accepted fact. American African-Americans possibly retain good part of this hereditary quality, which are being accentuated by superior technique, training and technology in America with massive expenditure of funds. But here again the doubt lingers whether the best African-Americans got selected from child hood in a systematic manner and the best survived. In the jungle of the Occidental civilization, the best need not be the fittest to adopt, adapt or adjust for survival.

But even all these African-Americans were not good enough to beat the Whites from other social systems. Thus, the example of America does not seem to invalidate the general hypothesis enunciated above.

Again, America is too rich and varied a country to be wholly under the influence of the market. Thus with all the high-pressure selling of market economy, USA has been able to keep a strong leash over the market. Public spending for the public scrutiny (nay Governmental and Agency control) of private enterprises is rather wide and invidious in America. But accountability for spending of public funds is not all that developed in America or has knowingly been kept vague and indirect for traditional control over overseas resources after the indigenous population was dispensed with and their resources assimilated by the colonizers. A touch of illegal vulgarity of masculinity of power had to be sustained and tolerated in American system for both historical and perceived civilization goals. An essential ingredient of this masculinity was the artificial creation and sustenance of disparities amongst (what the communists would call) 'classes'. Of course, these classes are neither Freudian nor Marxian. However, distinguishable distinctions had been nurtured in the name of Initiative of the Individual. But Olympic results are now staring in the face of the American systemic superiority.

But systemic deficiency ought to have meant much inferior result for America. But that it was not so can be explained by the rather high per capita GDP of America, the gross volume of the GDP and by the fact of presence of large immigrant population. Distribution of GDP in America is also badly skewed in favour of the top 10 percent as in undeveloped countries like India, Peru, Zambia, Zimbabwe, Bangladesh, Francophone countries, etc. *(This has changed for worse as per World Bank Report 2000-2001)*. Thus, in terms of distribution of purchasing power, America is non-socialist for bulk of its population as in some European and third world countries. This explains the reasonable performance of USA in spite of its dominant political stance.

After we have disposed of American case, we can consider the performance of China. A detailed study of Chinese scene is called for. The decline of Chinese independent distinctive stance in economic affairs which was heralded with the demise of Mao Zedong has affected its sporting performance as well. Chinese version of Perestroika (Restructuring) has been in operation for much longer than in Soviet Union, the economic growth rate, population control and distribution of wealth has become progressively adverse for Chinese population. What the Chinese had achieved in first quarter century of freedom (since 1950) got progressively reversed under Deng regime and China had not much to show of its sporting achievements in Olympics 1988. The Chinese case is a copy-book example of simultaneous decline of socialist fervor and decline in sports.

Here then comes Gorbachev for USSR. My hypothesis is that if Gorbachov succeeds in the way the western press is depicting, then Soviet sports performance will decline. Olympics of 1992 will see USSR removed from its dominant position if market forces really take a grip over Soviet economy. At present market forces do not determine which sportsman will go up - possibly merit has more to do with selection process in USSR and possibly all strata of society gets a chance at selection. As market economy takes root and money determines the hierarchy of preferences, the selection process will favour the progeny of the more elite and merit will take, at best, a second place.

Henry Kissinger had rightly concluded that the thrust of Gorbachev's Perestroika and Glasnost' was consolidation of personal power and Gorbachev was willing to break the backbone of his party to get his desired goal. But conditioned intellectual, Kissinger, had not delineated why Gorbachev had to take the course that he (Gorbachev) actually took. The great intellectual forgot that power in the communist state is not concentrated in a single individual. There are far too many presidiums, councils, commissions to circumscribe the power of the First Secretary. The First Secretary has to provide sinews of power but the actual exercise is through the President and the council of ministers. The Politburo can direct, criticize and advise but actual things get into the act through the Governmental machinery and not through the party bureaucracy. Gorbachev must have been chafing at his constraints seeing how the President of America and the Prime Minister of UK exercise total power both in the Government and party keeping a transparent veneer of debate and democracy. He must have been quite envious of the freedom of action available to the Presidents and Prime Ministers of so-called democratic countries. He must have envied how the President/Prime Ministers praises/appoints/transfers Judges, bureaucrats, Ambassadors, agency or commission heads, ministers and even the Head of State 'The President of the Republic'! He wanted to get absolute power but there was no way of getting it without destroying the existing order. And Gorbachev started by drawing conclusions from economic and political signals and articulating those in a way which will bring disrepute to the existing system. And he attacked the system where it was (like in any other countries) most vulnerable – military and consequently its economic structure, in that order. He either never understood Marxist/Leninist doctrines or intentionally mis-represented the same as he knew the party control could only be weakened by attacking the military and changing the economic structure. The attack had to be on the basic framework of the nation, that is, the distribution of the 'surplus produce of labour' and the allocation of resources. The talk of freedom of enterprise or value of the market was aimed at delegalizing the distributive justice, which distinguished the Soviet system from Western economic models. Gorbachev did not perceive but he touched off a change which could only push Soviet economy downwards (and records show it did), if not covetous of the wealth of the foreign countries, like his western counterparts. Thus, if Glasnost and Perestroika succeeds in the manner it is unfolding, the third world will be faced with another variety of Communist-capitalism, which in its virulence of attack or invidiousness, may not be less pernicious than the western capitalism. (Fortunately this has not been manifested till 2007). Internally Soviet Union will see rise of disparities and money deciding merit (which has actually happened). World should not be over concerned about what happens to the Soviet people but Olympic movement will be grievously affected, as best possible athletes or sportsmen and women will then not be representing Soviet Union. Hence, if Gorbachev succeeds in what he had set his heart upon, Olympics will be the greatest loser. (P.S. Olympic movement has been seriously affected, as results of subsequent Olympics showed. Russia and Cuba are no longer the principal sporting nations.)

Politics of India

Indian Republic, particularly after independence under the benign guidance of Mahatma Gandhi (fortunately, he was disposed off rather quickly before he could add further meat to his mischief), Jawaharlal Nehru duo have brought in abnormal political, economic, legal and constitutional systems which militate any action against poverty. Our monetary fiscal and taxation policies have been geared to ensure that certain level of poverty always remains. Elite would like to possibly call this as 'structural poverty' in line with the concept of 'structural unemployment' propagated in the capitalist societies.

The Mahatma ignored all lessons of history in conniving in partition of India and consigning India to economic and political stagnation and decadence. Nehru evolved a centric, bureaucratic controlled administration where every organ of the state got subverted to first the ICS (British indoctrinated Indian Civil Service) and then the IAS (the Indian Administrative Service, steeped in British doctrines of selective action/inaction) for control of the administration and the military. In retrospect, it can be said confidently that the present moribund state of Indian Republic is the outcome of the lack (or clouded) vision of the Gandhi-Nehru duo. No economic study can be complete without tracing the path laid out by these two stalwarts for Independent India.

This duo created such a culture of administration that minority communalism and subversion and the secession from India came to be recognized as mainstream activities with state finances going selectively to these States. Demographic studies[41] over the last 50 years show that the majority communities (the Hindu Religionists) are losing ground fast. The population of the minority communities (in the Semitic Religious groups) have seen unprecedented growth after independence, so much so that, although the Hindu Religionists are now contributing 80% of the population, but in next 50 years, this group will be in minority if the population growth remains at current rate. Muslims and Christians need not wait for their population percentage to reach 51% for proactive communal action. We apprehend that by the time the percentage of these minority religionists reach 25% to 30%, Indian political leadership will be controlled by these aggressive minorities and distress levels of Indians will increase manifold, as obscurantism, irrationality in statecraft and legal system will undergo unannounced shift to minority communal accommodation. This is already happening in vast tracts in Assam, North East, West Bengal, Kerala, Andhra Pradesh, Uttar Pradesh and J & K. The annoying sequel of this transformation will be that India will be pushed to more backwardness and decadence, as witnessed only in West Bengal now. 'Purdah' (whole body covering) will be the national dress for women and we will see exotic purdah designs in fashion parades – (life will be interesting)! There will be more starvation deaths, suicides by farmers and ever increasing number of other dispossessed due to proper legal action dispensed by those, who swear by the constitution. We want to explain to Dr. JK Bajaj[42] and other concerned Indians that this systematic shift in religious configuration of India is not a casual affair, as affirmed by the top secular and Hindutva-mouthing elder statesmen acclaimed in media, but a systematic effort planned by capitalists and their surrogate economic reformers, liberalizers and lovers of Anglo-Saxon variety of democracy! In economic field, a recent study[43] revealed that whereas, major States like West Bengal and Uttar Pradesh had negative job growth to the extent of (-) 4.6%, the terrorist infested and troubled States of Nagaland, Manipur, Arunanchal etc. had all more than 67% job growth in this decade as against national average job growth of only +4.6% over this decade. Central contribution in job growth, especially, in the most troubled state of Jammu & Kashmir, has been massive compared to the unfortunate States of West Bengal and Uttar Pradesh. All independent studies have shown that after succeeding in the north east and extreme coastal, southern and extreme north belt, the Semitic religious groups have targeted West Bengal, Bihar, Orissa and Uttar Pradesh for accelerated conversion to their religion and culture. Bureaucrat-controlled administration is helping this process as the job growth rate, Reservation policy twists and investment decisions of the central bureaucracy are demonstrating. Nehru-created/nurtured bureaucracy's control is now so pervasive that change of government in the Centre or States is not having any influence on the course charted by the bureaucracy. Of course, the political elements, in any case, are totally compromised.

If the population distribution of India changes ultimately, as indicated in the emerging data on population, job growth, growth-distribution and investment policy thrusts, India is sure to join the band-wagon of Semitic culture and suffering, in the third millennium, as experienced by Europe in first millennium, Africa and major part of Asia (excepting India, China, Korea, Japan) in the second millennium. This is the outline of the policy which Pope Paul II announced publicly in India about a few years back, when he visited India as an honoured "State Guest" of the Hindutva-mouthing Prime Minister! This Hindutva spouting PM did the worst possible crimes against national economy, Hindutva, national security, sovereignty and territorial integrity of India as we shall see later.

We need not rejoice that India will become developed like European States if the apprehensions expressed turn out to be true; we might find ourselves in bigger straits, than say Africa or the Middle East, or South-East Asian (earlier 'Tiger' and now 'Pussy Cat') economies.

The politicians do not ever dare to spell out clearly what exactly they intend to do while in power, because they know slogans of liberalization, economic reforms, labour reforms, restructuring for extensive privatization and such other fancy (puerile) ideas like that drive the voters away from the protagonists. They only hint at these, if at all, most obtusely in their verbose manifestos or action plans. When it comes to effecting so called reforms the power elite will not mind bending the Acts, rules or regulations or distort these to such an extent that no legal challenge is possible and in any case no question of legality is likely to be upheld by the legal fraternity as soon as they find that it has something to do with economic reforms or if it involves questioning administrative decisions. An example of such a mindless action of the economic reform programmes was highlighted in a (captured?) newspaper with a catchy headline

"Even one month-old FCCBs converted - Foreign Industries Make a Killing on Convertible Bonds".

World Bank and IMF reports have been ruing the low level of consumption and health. It is expected that the Indian produce will be first earmarked for consumption by Indians and then only the remaining could be exported. We have explained elsewhere that no such parity exists and Indians are net losers in exports and imports. The thrust for export after the liberalisation was let loose in India was mainly to facilitate exorbitant unnecessary imports at exorbitant and unconscionable prices. Of course, Indian administrators are not aware or would like to hide that they are always importing from grossly inefficient countries. This fact was also vividly reported in the newspaper (*E.T.*, Thurs, 20th Nov 03, New Delhi)

"NOW INDIA INC - escape cyclical swing in local market – exports growth faster than domestic sales since '00". For the last three years, exports have outpaced the growth of domestic sales for India Inc."

Indian Prime Ministers have traditionally been great politicians and they completely internalized the communist dictum "Poor are Always with Us". The corollary of this dictum is that a vast number of poor must exist to keep the voting support high. Hence perpetuation of poverty is high on the political agenda of all political parties. The way communists managed the affairs of West Bengal (which has reduced West Bengal in last half a century from a premier to a laggard State in all economic and social measures, with communist supremacy persisting) may prove that bad economics is good politics in India. Sound bytes for eliminating poverty have been high and corrective actions have been always in negative proportions. Latest (2006) communist victory for a record number of times tends to disprove Dr. Bhallas and our theory that economics decides the voting outcome in India. We, possibly, need to add a caveat that at least one side in an electoral competition must articulate economic issues relevant for the voters vigorously and will not resort to competitive politicking! We had noted earlier in the introduction to this book that the Supremo of Trinamool Congress was great in politicking but had hardly any clue about relevant economic issues affecting West Bengal. Aiming to win elections is not abnormal for a political party, but it is abnormal behaviour if the Party wishes to keep the loyalty of the voters after ignoring all their distress-calls. Municipal Corporation of Delhi Elections 2002 has confirmed the belief that: "Indians Vote with their Tummies". Voters like to take pride in the economy and national security but all the party combines at centre had disappointed them thoroughly. We believed in 2000-2001 and in 2007 as well that if the ruling elite chooses to continue with the current policy thrusts in the management of the economy and polity, we can confidently predict some unexpected outcome of next General Parliamentary Elections (in 2009) will be repeat of the 2004 elections, for the Hindutva combine. They will taste dust as ignominiously as the Hindutva parties did under Vajpayee and earlier Congress under Shri Narsimha Rao. We forecast that if the current UPA government gets another term, then the great reformer will show to the nation the back of Hindu India and capitalism, under reforms garb, will take over completely. But ruling combine may note that unless they can come up with alternative economic policies, ***"They will lose in Economic Rebound, what they gained in Political Swing"*** like the Trinamool Congress in West Bengal elections in 2001. All political outfits see immense possibilities of enrichment to themselves with the 'lawless rules of the game' of Economic Reforms and, hence, they do not want to significantly change the so-called Reform Policies or paradigms and try and solve the economic conundrum by political manipulations. But scope for manipulations by current ruling elite (across the party line) is, unfortunately, limited! We will be proved wrong if the contestants agree to keep basic economic and national security issues out of political discourses and engage in extraneous or ethno-communal issues. This was successfully (for themselves) demonstrated in India by all principal actors in Indian scene, particularly the following four.

Four Prime Ministers

PANDIT JAWAHARLAL NEHRU

Pandit (it does not mean scholasticism but is only a communal annotation in Kashmir) Jawaharlal Nehru straddled Indian political scene for more than six decades till his death due to natural causes in 1964. Out of this long period he was the PM uninterruptedly for 17 years (from 1947) till death separated him from power and pelf. He built up the fledgling Independent India as a poor, deprived and destitute country always looking forward to the erstwhile colonialists and their surrogates for administration, advice, assistance, food and succour.

He, with concurrence and connivance of the great Mahatma Mohandas Karamchand Gandhi, got India divided on religious grounds and conceived population exchange and took no steps to prevent or thwart (in fact, condoned) horrendous communal riots unprecedented in modern history. He and his supporting Congress Party had such deep grass-roots contacts that they had no inkling of the disgust, disbelief and discontents in the country side about the concept of 'Partition', its causative factors and the rationale. It was never articulated to the common man that British engineered the partition and the totally unviable and unscrupulous hare-brained idea of population exchange was British concept accepted with alacrity by two megalomaniacs (Nehru and Jinnah), unmindful of cost to the people of Indian subcontinent. This duo would have done anything to get control over Indian wealth and getting India fractured for this purpose was of no great concern to them. Megalomaniacs are demagogues also; these two leaders could easily consolidate their power in the portions acquired by them, only Jinnah could not enjoy that for too long and Chinese hastened Nehru's dementia and the end by their exploratory raid in 1962.

Nehru retained the British administrative apparatus intact and started behaving like a successor government forgetting that India is supposed to have attained independence after some struggle and suffering and the bureaucracy was the most visible oppressive instrument of the British. This venal instrument became symbol of independent Indian nationalism, just because during Indian so-called independence movement, the British (real visionaries that they were) always treated the common man with extreme harshness, brutality and evilly, but the top leaders were given five-star treatment with all considerations.

This great man was ever unprepared and was ready to be surprised always. He was surprised at the pre and post partition riots and did not think of using the massive British and British-Indian military stationed in Fort William in Calcutta and other cantonments to quell the riots. It will never be known whether Nehru was ever aware of the extent and clout of British/British Indian military. Although he tried to instruct his daughter about the history and legacy of India in his much-acclaimed book, "Discovery of India", he was incapable of learning anything from history. He did not have clue about the elements of power of the State and about essentials of exercise of state power. He was educated in British institutions of slave traders and drivers and ought to have known that military is the anvil without which the state hammer falls on feet of the uninstructed wielder. He just did not have enough liberal training to be aware that Rabindranath Tagore believed that "To be always prepared is the essence of civilization"![44] He was again surprised in 1962 when Chinese wanted to teach him a lesson for trying to show that he had grown too big for his pygmy shoes. I was posted in Leh then and I, possibly others, were totally ashamed at the tone, tenor and contents of his speech on (16th?) October, 1962, over All India Radio, once the Chinese ceased fire unilaterally after achieving their limited goals.

He became the epitome of 'Synthetic' (or Teflon) popular leader and became a role model for his dynasty and for all other PMs who succeeded him. Nehru ensured that his legacy continues even after he has left and groomed his daughter for the purpose and ensured that direct foreign rule can be slowly reintroduced in the country by the successors of his genre. For this purpose he retained English as the State Language and kept the citizenship provisions lax – whatever Indian could be thought of was subsequently obliterated by the British introduced judicial system by their unbridled right to interpret the constitution and create 'Case-Laws' and thereby amend the constitution as and when required.

Nehru got assembled in less than two years a Constitution for Indian Republic on the basis of British Indian Act of 1935 with such changes and additions which will completely delegalize any Indian effort for free development. This non-Indian at heart and activities appointed a British-trained colourful Dr Ambedkar to get a Constitution for India. Dr. Ambedkar is supposed to have given pride of place to secularism. But after getting the Constitution approved by the basically nominated constituent assembly, Nehru quarreled with the Constitution maker, who promptly went out and created enmity and fatal divisions amongst mother religion, Hinduism, Buddhism and other religions believing in fundamental doctrines of 'Religion of Man'. This divide is being freely exploited to the detriment of Indian ethos even today by all colonialists and countries professing some variants of Buddhism or Semitic religions. This development was god-sent opportunity for Nehru to practise his divide and rule policy learnt from the British masters to control the dispossessed majority of India.

The British judicial system, which only caters to the needs of the nobles and elite was retained by Nehru, and elitist judiciary with totally 'conditioned' mind-sets is still being recruited to man the apex courts. This Constitution validated every single exploitative British laws and rules. This Constitution introduced all the anti-people features of all the predatory or colonial countries. This British inspired constitution which does not accept any claim to equality and derecognizes equity for the majority of the population was retained by succeeding governments. He institutionalized religious, ethnic and communal divides in India through fundamental rights enshrined in the constitution giving special rights to the minorities (i.e. the erstwhile ruling class) and for pandering to the interests of this class so that India remained, and continues to be so till date, a fertile ground for secessionist forces. Nehru, during his rule, made secessionist forces so powerful that many areas of North East and Northern states of the republic became permanent base for anti-national and secessionist forces with liberal state assistance for ethnic cleansing and (constitution guaranteed) opportunity to Semitic religions for unchecked conversion of the majority community (i.e. Hindus the overwhelming majority) to Semitic faiths, as Hindus have an innate disgust of converting people of other faiths to Hindu faith. This situation could come about as neither Nehru nor the Hindu western educated intellectuals had/have any clue about the fundamental difference between Hindu faiths (which collectively are called Hindu religion) and Semitic and other non-Hindu religions.

His proverbial vision extended to his pockets and to his immediate family and friends. This proclaimed socialist was the greatest supporter of big avaricious businesses. The hiatus between his words and deeds was unimaginably wide. His success in his chosen line emboldened his successors, mostly his progenies and progenies' progenies and admirers, who rode roughshod over Indian aspirations and got away lightly also. Only his daughter and his one grandson were felled in the march of history by their foolishness buttressed by Nehru's own version of 'discovery of India'.

As usual, he did not believe in any lessons of Indian history, even to the extent he wrote to his daughter, poor Mrs. Indira Gandhi, in his well-publicized book "Discovery of India". If he had slightest knowledge or comprehension of any history, he would have known that poor countries are always dependent or that source of national power and well-being flows from national mobilization, as the famous saying of the great (rather, the greatest nationalist in human history, Mao Zedong) succinctly brought out: "Power flows from the Barrel of the Gun". Nehru was so enamoured of western jazzy culture of selective affluence and he had such pathogenic hatred of anything of the East that he could not comprehend what Mao, his contemporary, was trying to convey. He, in line with western opportunists, misunderstood and decried Mao's 'Great Cultural Revolution', 'The Great Leap Forward', or "Let Thousand Flowers Bloom" (for unprecedented diversified ecology-sensitive mass industrialization of the countryside), 'Four Modernizations', and other such initiatives. He could not comprehend that Mao was trying to break the stranglehold of the traditionally entrenched bureaucracy and power elite so that real freedom could flow to the people. It is another matter that internal capitalist-inspired forces represented by Deng Hsiao Ping could rob the popular contents of Mao's revolutions and modernizations, but military component continued to benefit even after demise of Mao, as Mao's military was and continues to be a potent force in China and in the world. Even in the life time of our great J L Nehru, the beneficial effects of Mao's policies, thought processes and activities started throwing up startling positive results for China, but Nehru and his troupe of clowns turned their faces away and did only what their foreign masters dictated. The Pandit, his cohorts and secularists interpreted secularism as delegitimization of claims of Hindus to their religion, culture and national resources. Nehru's thought processes have been fully imbibed by the communists amongst others. The most intriguing is the peculiar and self-defeating behaviour of the Hindu majority Communists since the time of Nehru. Parties believing in some sort of communist ideology are handicapped by their economic and national security concepts. These parties are not able to create any ripple in the mind-space of the minorities also. Common men of all religions are quite aware of the antics of Gorbachev and Yeltsin and Indian replica of the sinister GYS syndrome virulently manifest in the persona of communist chief minister of West Bengal (in 2007 also), Buddhadeb Bhattacharya. People should ignore Noble laureate Prof. Amartya Sen's mindless praise of communist rule in West Bengal, as this rule has been an unmitigated disaster for Bengal, which has descended from a premier state of India to one of the most laggard one.

Nehru's mixed economy concepts and Fabian variety of socialism sanctioned inequity to such an extent that India has joined the ranks of 'Terminally Sick States' (as we have noted earlier) so far as equity is concerned. Equityless mixed economy has been and continues to be a curse on India by perpetuating poverty and demobilization of India. In the morrow of the independence, he retained the British-devised administrative systems, placed the Indian military under the straitjacket of the civilian administration and the military withered away to be fit for marching on ceremonial occasions only. He and his successors brought ignominy after ignominy on Indian military in every action against inimical forces and laid the foundation for further division of truncated India on religious, ethnic and language divides.

Indians are ever thrashing around to get out of the cesspool in which Nehru's legacy had consigned them without their premonition. It is like being raped by the betrothed and sold in the market.

DR. MANMOHAN SINGH

About four decades after Nehru, a soft-spoken Sardarji burst forth in Indian political firmament with economic pretensions. Dr. Manmohan Singh held every single economic/political apex posts in India, like, Governor of Reserve Bank of India, Vice Chairman of Planning Commission and Finance Minister of central government and ultimately the Prime Minister. People sat up and noticed to their mortification when he launched economic reforms and structural adjustments to open up India for free exploitation by Indian private enterprises and by foreigners like in colonial days, on the plea (without clearly verbalizing that, though enough hints and innuendoes were circulated) that previous Congress and some other assorted governments have mismanaged the economy to the detriment of 'Aam Admi' (common man). Common men quickly found out that they were least of his concern but they were rendered helpless because such a 'cacophony of lies and deceit'[45] was created that all rationality and logic got buried in mounds of garbage of reforms. Before someone joins issue on these or similar issues, they will be well-advised to scan the relevant headlines of national dailies, as the information furnished in these dailies show how much anti-national and counter-national debilities are being heaped on Indians by Indian government of Manmohan Singh and governments led by people of his ilk.

Dr. Manmohan Singh understood that Nehru had successfully divided India along all nascent fault-lines of caste, community, religion, region, language and cultures and only what was left to give a final push to restoration of colonial control was economy, and he set out to do that, first as a Finance Minister and then as the Prime Minister under a foreign leader. The Military, which would have necessarily played the spoil-sport, having been successfully debilitated by Nehru and by all governments after Nehru, Dr. Manmohan Singh could have his way. His restructuring and reform measures to pander to the interests of the affluent and foreign exploiters (in the garb of businessmen and traders), disinvestments of public assets, other privatization measures to cripple the public sector, constant devaluation of rupee against foreign currencies, building up of unsustainable massive 'international reserves' ($400 billion in 2008) in foreign banks by starving the indigenous sectors, constant emphasis on exports at the cost of Indian consumption, fillip to high cost imports, ignoring the requirement of having proper pricing of exports and imports, paying no heed to the demand for equity and equality, nuclear co-operation treaty with the super-power as a long suffering faithful, are all intended to do India in as a powerful independent nation. Indian power elite are working overtime to make a success of Dr. Manmohan Singh's counter-national activities.

Chapters 2 and 3 of this book depict the debilities heaped on Indians by Congress Party variety of politics and the economics of Dr. Manmohan Singh. He, like Gorbachov/ Yeltsin, was shrewd enough to project the economic debilities created by managers of the economy as an excuse to launch his variety of economics, with the same type of managers at the helm. His economic ideas were liberally borrowed from the half-cooked economic theories of his western masters. We tried to explain in introduction and first few chapters of this book and our readers are aware how irrelevant and unnecessary western variety of exploitative economics were for India and other undeveloped countries. Common men might understand the significance, but our 'aam admi' loving elite have placed their full faith on western economic concepts and the denouement for the aam admi to be, per force, adverse!

To my experience wise men are easily fooled, but common men have also got a nasty habit of giving a long rope to every devil, forgetting that all devils might not 'hoist with his own petard'[46]. Further, a devil supported by a super power devil cannot be easily banished. Hindu religion explains that all evils have long tenures and AXN TV channel some time back presented in a movie that a new evil creature gets created from a small body part of the vanquished evil. Manmohanics and mobilization/welfare of the people are anti-thesis of each other. My anguish is that as and when we banish Manmohanics, Indian political system will create another greater evil substitute for this brand of economics, if we fail to compel the power elite to appreciate the inescapable need for adequate mobilization of India and consequent changes elaborated in this book.

I tried to understand how the mind of this so-called great reformer works by reading his published speeches and by reading his books and books on him. I was at a loss to make out what to communicate with respect to Dr. Manmohan Singh. Then *'The Economic Times*, 25th October, 2007, New Delhi', came out with a leader page article titled:

"Equity no alibi for inefficiency

In order to operate in open and competitive markets, with all the contingent uncertainties and risks, firms need long-term strategic thinking and organizational flexibility to adjust to change, says Manmohan Singh".

At the end of his article it was clarified that, "This is an edited version of the speech delivered by the PM at the McKinsey directors' meet in New Delhi".

Only an amputated brain (as defined by Hodu)[47] or only a sterilized economist[48], could consider that western colonizers are his constituency, could make such a speech and that also to the directors of a reasonably suspect service organization (which all foreign consulting/advisory services are). Manmohan Singh is in his eloquent best when talking to big business or their 'managers' (this word of mine has also double meaning). I noticed that he has a set of currently popular words which he uses in his speeches appropriately depending on the audience but his ideas mean nothing to the common bureaucrats nor to the common men but these give sufficient directions to the big businesses to devise newer exploitative techniques. He wants inclusive growth, which apparently means 'talk populist and work against the people'. He considers equity as destructive of efficiency – his criteria of efficiency, apparently, is generation of unbridled profit. He is the un-proclaimed authority, having a doctorate in that Voodoo science/art, called economics. His heart bleeds only for private profiteers and other exploiters! Many portions of his published article depicts what ought to have been done but has not been accomplished and he takes credit for non-achievements. He believes external liberalization (i.e. induction of more and more foreign exploiters in India) has lessened the chance of development of native oligopolistic or monopolistic tendencies. He is supposed to be an authority on international dimensions of economics and essence of globalization but he is non-cognizant of the fact that all external and internal exploiters have a competitive collaborative relationship. He, of course, assumes that no literate Indian reads the statistics doled out by government, private and other agencies and the graphics copied and depicted in a chapter earlier in this book does not exist. It is really a wonder that such mind-set of the FM and PM is acclaimed by intelligentsia of India! It is a waste of time trying to criticize such neutered scholars! Dr. Manmohan Singh has broken down completely all legislative, administrative, legal and constitutional barriers to development of monopolistic and oligopolistic aberrations in economy, as the growth of assets of the top business families of India reported in media[49] depicts. Incidentally, the year of 2007 was bad year so far as suicide of farmers and other indigent people of India are concerned. Who needs to care, as 'Bharat Mahan Hai' or 'India is shining'! Of course, we consider this shine is due to the reflected glory of the marauding businessmen and totally liberated PM or under the arc lights of the image builders! Our liberated intellectuals never tire of repeating how honest and scrupulous Dr. Manmohan Singh is. Strenuous efforts of his admirers to convey this impression left me unimpressed and I could not forget the story of the drum beater and his anguish when the enemy General awarded him the death penalty while the fighting soldiers, who actually carried out the bayonet-charge, were given lesser punishments. He was pleading that he only played on the drum as required of him and he had not physically harmed any one. But the General explained that the drummer was instrumental in deadening the conscience of the soldiers and induced them to carry out the dastardly bayonet charge and he deserved the most severe punishment. Dr Manmohan Singh has been able to, by deft management, to deaden the conscience of the judges as well, as they do not find anything amiss in such trends in the country in spite of our attempts to put forward the contrary views. We can only keep lamenting that even with these backgrounds no legal challenge to economic reforms or arraignment of main perpetrators/ culprits thereof, is likely to be upheld in courts.

I was wondering whether his ethnicity, nativity, his cultural moorings and his up-bringing had any influence on the evolution of his mind-set. He was born in Punjab, literally the land at the cross-road of civilizations and in the access route to the riches of Indian plains. Hilly Afghanistan and undivided Punjab had to withstand the fury of every marauder, who took a fancy to loot Indian wealth and violate the women and girls at ease, as India, from the time of the successors to The Chanda-Asoka (reformed as the Asoka, the Great, after Kalinga war) forgot or under-estimated the value of large strong military. Repeated visitations of the violators had left their genes in the areas they operated — more in the frontier areas than in the hinterlands. Cruelty, masochism, sadism, oppressiveness, servility, uncaring attitude and all other disruptive behaviour are all hereditary traits with wide variability. When gene-patterns for all Indians or, at least, of statistically valid representative sections or, at least, of the power elite are completed, it will be seen that frontier people have genes, consequently behaviour response, patterns reasonably distinct with high anti-national attributes. I have a feeling that Manmohan Singh, because of his gene-patterns, cannot behave any differently even when he has opportunity to act otherwise. Only way to convince him is to present him with vulgar show of masculinity by defeating his missions demonstratively.

I am convinced that there are many individuals and youngsters (not corrupted by call-centre/software practising cultures) are chafing at the constraints of modern liberal economic and liberal administrative practices. They might be planning some radical alternatives but they will have to take care that their activism should not get converted to adjuvant dated Naxalism and they ought not to resort to senseless assassinations. My aversion to political assassination is due to the established fact that assassination and physical liquidation of an evil gives longer life to a greater evil. Indian experience of political assassination is uniformly bad. Assassination of Gandhi gave absolute power to Nehru, and assassination of Indira Nehru Gandhi and Rajiv Gandhi gave us Dr. Manmohan Singh! Pakistan tried disposing off their tyrants but they could not get out of the political quick-sands and each successor, like in India, turned out to be worse than the previous one.

Heed thee, awakened Indians, there are many alternatives available! Arise and move your limbs purposefully!

ATAL BEHARI VAJPAYEE

The only important PM outside the Nehru dynasty or Congress party, who let India down as comprehensively as his moral guru, Pandit Jawaharlal Nehru, was Atal Behari Vajpayee. He or his image creators and companions have on more than one occasion let it be known that Vajpayee was a great admirer of Nehru. It is natural also, as he also aspired to get absolute power like his model, unmindful of what it entails for the country and its welfare. In the best traditions of Indian PMs, he comprehensively sacrificed Indian interests in all spheres where his influence could be spread in the short time available to him. Atal ('the steady one', in Bengali), possibly, holds the world record in remaining in highest elected office heading a coalition for the least amount of time (13 days). He also might be holding the world record in leading maximum number (three) of successive coalition governments to general elections. His tenures in office of PM reads like fairy tales – Ist term: 13 days, 2nd term: 13 months and 3rd term: four years or so. We have already analyzed elsewhere in this book about his compulsions for calling for last early general elections in 2004 and the resultant fiasco for his party. In fact, most of his initiatives resulted in fiascos for his party and for the mother organization (Rashtriya Swayam Sevak Sangh, acronym, RSS), to which he used to pay convenient ritualistic obeisance, without observing or caring for their value systems or tenets. He was a sartorial artist – he could put on the garb of nationalist, modernistic liberal of the Congress and communist variety, a Swayam Sevak, a devout RSS apparatchik or a universal man depending on the demands of the situation.

There was maximum massacre of Hindus in J&K during his tenure; maximum number of incursions into India across the LOC, a line lying wholly within Indian territory (made into a disputed territory by followes of his moral guru, Nehru), and across the border, maximum Indian casualties in international border, LOC and J&K. He had a colourful Home Minister (a deputy PM later), who allowed his personal image-makers to create a halo of a 'tough Iron man' and would promise, with clenched fists and other appropriate facial contortions of a toughie, to banish terrorism etc. and forget about it till the next massacre and repeat the pantomime. After Hindus of J&K had tolerated this drama for a few occasions, they heckled him to force him to retreat to normal politicking in the Capital. Within about a month and a half of assuming office of PM, Atal forced the scientists/engineers in nuclear establishment to carry out some 'big bang', without carrying out any study of the necessity or cost-benefits of such bravado or taking into confidence his cabinet colleagues, Armed Forces Commanders or other top functionaries of the State. The nuclear scientists/engineers, a neglected lot till then, took the opportunity to have some exposure, promptly carried out six partially successful nuclear tests and had no more ready devices to counter the counter-measures of the inimical forces. The outcome of Vajpayee's nuclear tests were that Pakistan, which was itching to demonstrate their acquired nuclear prowess, promptly carried out seven nuclear tests of their ready-made devices and America and other western powers imposed crippling economic sanctions on India. Vajpayee's bluff about Indian strategic capabilities were tested by Pakistan by occupying large tracts of Indian territory in Kargil and other bordering areas and, on top of that, threaten India with nuclear weapons (as confirmed by Pakistani President Musharraf in 2007). During Kargil operations Vajpayee succumbed to Pakistan's belligerence and American arm-twisting. His complete lack of any respect for the country's interests was repeatedly manifest in his readiness to sign the CTBT and sending troops to Iraq to help out the Americans to subdue recalcitrant Iraq. Change of American government saved India from the ignominy of being declared a surrogate of America by signing on CTBT, which no powerful country wanted. Domestic political pressures saved the country from being dragged in to a conflict in Iraq and getting Indian soldiers killed in shame, as intended by Vajpayee. Although as a Swayam Sevak he was expected to know of the necessity of adequate national mobilization/militarization, he did his best to delegalize the armed forces. He allowed implementation of the grossly unjust (to the armed forces) Fifth central pay commission awards and had the distinction of being the first government to countenance open demonstration by serving Air Force personnel. He took the bureaucratic approach of just getting these dissenting cries crushed. He was the first PM to sack a serving Chief of Naval Staff and the serving Chief of Joint Staff, that also improperly, if not illegally, and without any trial. As already mentioned elsewhere, he kept the Army standing on the border for a full year and then forced it back to barracks, causing immeasurable damage to Indian Army's morale and fighting abilities and causing irreparable damage to civilian control over armed forces. Armed forces now know that civilian managers only want bravado and no real action and, consequently, the morale of armed forces are on fast decline.

Vajpayee's antics with foreign policy and national security issues could embolden the succeeding PM to let India down in every fora and, comprehensibly, at that. The nation expected Vajpayee not to be clone of the Nehru dynasty or of the Congress party, but he exactly acted contrarily to national wish. He could never comprehend that if people wanted him to be a successor to the Congress PM, they would not have reposed faith (though, partial at that) in his party. People possibly had suspicion that he will not live up to their expectations and he did his best to prove the people right by betraying their trust. He left India in worse condition than he inherited in all fields, viz. economy, national security, strategic options, status of the landless agriculturists, and other poor, dispossessed, destitute. He has the distinction of continuing the aberrations of the economy started by Congress governments and gave fillip to inequity, as evidenced by mounting GINI index. This Index had become so high, thanks to the mindless shenanigans of Vajpayee and his successor, that India is now adorning the ranks of the Terminally Sick States. He and his ministers ignored all the calls of the RSS to ponder and avoid walking the paths charted by Congress stalwarts, particularly, that of Dr. Manmohan Singh, but all were in vain and he dragged himself and his party and conglomerates (NDA) to utter ignominy in 2004 General Elections. People are so disenchanted with Vajpayee variety of politics that it would have been a miracle if BJP/NDA forms the government after next General elections in 2009. Thus Congress/UPA conglomerate got another chance. The leading lights and all the poster boys and girls of BJP and NDA, basically bereft of any nationalist feelings, have infinite faith in efficacy of Manmohanics to lift India out of the current morass! We prognosticate that India is in for bad times for quite a few years now.

MRS. INDIRA NEHRU GANDHI

The only issue of JL and Kamla Nehru was the second effective PM of India after Nehru, the interregnum between Nehru's death and ascension to office by his daughter, Indira Nehru Gandhi (not a niece of Mahatma MK Gandhi, as believed by common Europeans; she got her Gandhi surname from her husband, Feroze Gandhi), was filled by the diminutive Lal Bahadur Shastri, a devout camp follower of Nehru, who took India to war with Pakistan in 1965 and signed the Tashkent Accord with the Pakistani PM, under the watchful eyes of the USA and USSR. Lal Bahadur Shastri, as is the usual practice of Indian PM so far, bought peace with Pakistan by gifting away some more Indian territory (especially the militarily strategically important Pir Panjal Range) and imposed a new international boundary on India through the inviolable LOC (Line Of Control). From the time of Mrs. Gandhi, USA is ensuring the inviolable nature of LOC for India, although Pakistan freely violates this line and sends raiders and infiltrators across LOC. Indian PMs, since Mrs. Gandhi's time, are accumulating evidence against Pakistan but are not able to get American concurrence for retaliatory raids across the LOC against Pakistan. If you ask Indian PMs as to why they need American concurrence for discharging their constitutional duties, they will first ignore the question and then mutter something about reality of international diplomacy, the last resort of the nincompoops!

Mrs. Indira Nehru Gandhi lived up to the reputations of anti- or counter-national mindsets and activities of her two role models whose names she adopted in her surnames. Although she incessantly visited the Hindu temples and religious places, she displayed totally illiberal mindsets and activities of a diehard Semitic bigot. She declared emergency (1975) when she was unseated by Allahabad High court for electoral malpractices and let loose a reign of terror by arresting or incinerating the opposition leaders and other opponents and continued in power. She lost power in 1977 General Elections held after lifting of Emergency. But the ragtag opposition parties filled with capitalism loving gentry and clones of capitalists (i.e. Socialists of different hues and nomenclatures) was no substitute for the strong-willed and wily capitalist, with a thick teflon coating of impeccable socialism, that Madame Indira Gandhi was. She came back to power about three years later and continued her reign till felled by the bullets of a misguided Indian patriot in 1984. How mis-informed and misguided this assassin patriot was that Indians were repelled by this wanton display of vulgarity of killing of a woman, however evil that woman might be in the eyes of the assassin. Moreover, this assassination ensured foisting on India a PM, through landslide victory in next general elections, of her surviving only son with a foreigner (from mafia-land) wife, a psychologically and intellectually ill-equipped pilot of a civil airline. This liberated PM delivered India as a supplicant to America, which Mrs. Indira Nehru Gandhi had been opposing all her life, at least, verbally.

She meant well for India but she could not control her power-hunger or her imperial propensities of achieving her ends unconcerned with the means needed to be adopted. For a good part of the reign of her father, JL Nehru, she was the main background controller and manipulator of the party and government machinery. She learnt all the tricks of keeping the flock under absolute control. She had very good idea of the strengths and weaknesses of all the top and real power–elite of all departments of the government, bureaucracy, security and other agencies and apex organizations of the state and private entities. This intimate knowledge and her innate qualities made her indispensable to her party, which fact the elder leaders (nick-named the Syndicate) of Indian National Congress had to learn after a bitter internecine fight joined with gusto by both the sections, which Mrs. Gandhi won convincingly. She also convinced the masses of her fine Socialist qualifications by coining appropriate slogans like, Garibi Hatao; Bank, Coal, Mining Nationalizations and such other socialist pretensions, which her successors, particularly, Dr. Manmohan Singh, comprehensively reversed.

PROACTIVE MOVES

An impartial analysis of Indian economic scene reveals that Indian economy is not being managed for the Indians, but subserves only the interests of foreigners, their collaborators in the country, and Importers/exporters! Super Power and their surrogates will resist any change.

A line of pro-active action could be in India allowing the Armed Forces, especially, the Indian Air force, to cross the LOC at will to impose massive collateral damage in POK for even a small terrorist transgression in any part of India. India should officially treat the POK as 'Demilitarized' and 'No Fly' Zone for Pakistan. Unofficially India would expect Pakistan (for good neighbourly relations) to observe 'No Fly" Zone in 20 Km territory in Pakistan all along the Indo-Pak Border as a quid pro quo for interacting with Musharraf or such regimes. This will not be done till India has a significant military strength. Then India will be confident that it cannot be short changed as it has been happening under all successive governments since JL Nehru. Viable and demonstrative move for militarization will send necessary signals of serious intent. India should unfold a set of "Sanctions" against select "Nuclear Weapon States (as defined in Article 1 of the totally illogical Nuclear Non Proliferation Treaty)" as a proposed counter-measure against any adverse reaction from the surviving super-power(s). India should hold out credible threat of taking the defaulter to the WTO DSB for imposing Sanctions/Control/Denial regimes against India. It is also axiomatic that DSB will not rule against super/Big powers on sanctions/ control regimes etc. and India can gleefully go ahead and erect some sanctions/control regimes against the defaulters. For example, India can deny the convention country status for Patents for some P-5 countries and deny them any patents protection or derecognize their claims on the basis of TRIMS or TRIPS. We are also realist enough to know that current ruling elite (in 2008), being totally compromised, will not dare to take any proactive action, as begging from the super/big powers is so much more convenient for all concerned with ruling the country.

Economy Managers, especially Ministers, ought to be aware, after analyzing the World Development Reports, that India has very strong potentialities, which are not being exploited. It is not God's wish that India should remain poor; India is being intentionally or due to sheer ignorance and incapacity of the power elite, being kept poor. Under the cover of the anti-terrorist tirade, India should go ahead and give a 'Shock Therapy' to the Indian economy.

OUTLINES OF THE SHOCK THERAPY

INTRODUCE PURCHASING POWER PARITY (PPP) EXCHANGE RATE FOR ALL INTERNATIONAL TRANSACTIONS: In the first instance, the PPP exchange rate will be the Rate established by "Bretton Woods" Agreement or if more reality is desired then by the formula: STATUTORY MINIMUM HOURLY WAGES FOR INDIAN LABOUR IN INDIA IN INDIAN RUPEE = STATUTORY MINIMUM HOURLY WAGES FOR FOREIGN LABOUR IN RESPECTIVE COUNTRY IN THAT COUNTRY'S LOCAL CURRENCY.

INCREASE PURCHASING POWER OF THE GENERAL POPULACE: The best way to turn around the economy is to ensure sufficient purchasing power with the general populace. Income Tax should be payable only on Yearly Incomes of Rs. Five Lakhs and above. All high-income earners must be brought under tax net. All producers, whose estimated Excise duty liability in a year are less than Rs.1 Lakh or so, should be exempt from Excise Duty. Expenditure on tax collection will also come down considerably, thereby increasing the disposable tax revenue. Customs duty for any imported item cannot, under any circumstances, be lower than that for Excise or service tax for same or similar item.

STOP DIVESTMENT AND VRS: Conventional economic wisdom would specify that when the economy is in downswing and employment growth rate is falling, the Government should increase Investment for increasing employment. Stop the uneconomic measures of Divestment and VRS. Rechristen Ministry of Divestment as "MINISTRY OF INVESTMENT".

INCREASE CUSTOMS DUTY COLLECTION TO INTERNATIONAL STANDARDS: India collects very little Per Capita Customs duty. Go back to Customs Duty rates prevailing prior to 1995. Tell supporters of WTO to sing 'Ave Maria'!

CAPITAL CONSUMPTION TAX: India is supposed to be facing shortage of capital. Hence this Tax on Withdrawals of Rs. Ten Lakhs or above per year by individuals or businesses.

CAPITAL EFFICIENCY TAX: Efficiency in usage of capital can be measured by the following economic measures, viz.: a) Income Velocity of Money, b) Capital-Output Ratio, c) Capital-Labour Ratio, d) Labour-Output Ratio. There shall be a progressive tax on all industry/business/trade/other commercial entities, varying from 2% to 10%, depending on how far Indian overall and individual ratios are less than international/ Indian Standards. These cannot be add-on to the price of the product or service. Price of all products or services to be net of all taxes, cess or other contrivances conjured up by the government and business.

DEGENERATE ELITE

How degenerate Indian political and constitutional authorities have become can be glimpsed from the episodes narrated hereunder.

EARTHQUAKE IN GUJARAT

Respected Rashtrapatiji, (c.f. After devastating earthquake in Gujarat in 2001),

Media reports show that the Government, after agonizing whether to go through with the "Beating the Retreat" ceremony as culmination of the Republic Day celebrations, has ultimately cancelled this. It would have been grotesque and nauseating, if the Government had been celebrating in Delhi and other unaffected State Capitals, whereas Gujarat was desperately fighting with Death, Injuries and Devastation!

May we humbly request you to kindly ascertain and make your findings public, as to:

a) Whether the Prime Minister and Home Minister (whose constituency is in Gujarat) had arranged for the Central Crisis Management Team to effectively organize relief and rescue operations before the commencement of the Republic Day Parade on Raj Path? We believe that enough time was available, if only the high-ups in the Government had any comprehension of the magnitude of the crisis situation.

b) Why relief and rescue arrangements by the Central Government started only after the Parade was over? Why Relief, Rescue, Medical teams and heavy earthmoving equipment started moving to the affected areas many hours after the devastation?

c) Why Satellite Imageries were not used for instant assessment of the damage? Why Indian Air Force strategic (MIG- 25) and tactical Photo Reconnaissance aircraft were not launched immediately on receiving report of the damage and obtain detailed pictures and precise assessment of the damage in different areas of Gujarat? It ought to have been possible for Air Force to come out with an assessment of the damage long before the "Parade" was over. If anyone dares to contradict this, we are willing to prove them wrong.

Rashtrapatiji, we are concerned that the Government machinery remained paralyzed for several hours in Delhi because of the Republic Day ceremonies and vital hours, when many more rescues could have been effected, were unnecessarily wasted. We implore you to particularly consider the national security implications of the inability of the civil and military components to react effectively and decisively in time of crisis. We do hope you appreciate that such matters can turn out to be of grave national significance, as India has declared itself as a Nuclear Power and, apparently, has no worthwhile capability to assess instantly the damage caused by a pre-emptive attack!

With regards and best wishes

Note: The President of the Republic of India was unmoved and he or his secretariat, as is the time-tested practice, maintained total silence in spite of several telephonic reminders. Why should they stir themselves when there is no fire in their premises?

GODHRA CARNAGE IS A DIRECT ATTACK ON INDIAN NATIONALITY

AN OPEN LETTER TO NHRC

Activism of the NHRC (National Human Rights Commission) should normally be welcome. But flexible norms in handling different complaints raise doubt. For example, the NHRC earlier (1997-1999) had declined to properly examine the complaints of gross discriminations against and gross violation of human rights of serving armed force personnel in the aftermath of the discriminatory awards of the 5th Central Pay Commission. It appeared that the significance of the Godhra carnage was underplayed and the subsequent riots overplayed, thereby, bringing into disrepute the legally constituted Government of Gujarat and also the retired members of the apex court, the chairman of NHRC being invariably an erstwhile member of the apex court! We would beg the Commission (in 2007) to kindly consider that Godhra carnage has national significance of unacceptable consequences.

We have examined the recommendations of the National Human Rights Commission after their visit to Gujarat (in 2007). We beg to submit that these recommendations, even if implemented at all (and hardly anyone will guarantee that these will be fully implemented!), will not remove the scourge of communal riots in India. We consider these as bureaucratic half-measures to ensure status quo ante.

Godhra incident is doubly cursed. If it is accepted that the abominable act was the handiwork of the Indian Muslims, then that represents a diabolical mentality unrelated to the general Indian consciousness and a communal bias of horrendous proportions and evil possibilities! Then it calls for not rationalization of the event in Godhra, but initiation of drastic action to erase the cancer of communalism latent in Muslim community. There is no question of any accommodation from Hindus in that effort. It must originate and end in the Muslim community. The minority communities must internalize that they are Indians first and Muslim, or of other faiths, thereafter. Minorities must shed their extra-territorial loyalties and must consider seriously the suggestions of the RSS ideologues for evolving suitable Indian philosophies and idioms for their religious practices and not blindly follow all the obscurantist philosophies and practices of the Middle East or of the Vatican. With respect to Christian faiths, the Church of England declared independence from Papacy in 16th Century, as also tellingly depicted in a movie by Shekhar Kapoor.

We would like to believe that the Muslim community could not be perverted enough to perpetrate such a massacre and some misguided elements were used by international agents for this heinous crime. Of course, such a conclusion will involve holding Pakistan culpable and punitive action against it becomes imperative then. Compulsions of the fight against so-called (by Americans) "International Terrorism" forbade any action against Pakistan, and the innocents of other places in Gujarat had to pay with their lives for the convenience of the power elite!

Massacre near Godhra Railway Station in 2002 of Ram Sevaks of majority community returning from their pilgrimage in Ayodhya, is a defining event in the history of Independent India.

a) A communal massacre of such a proportion has not happened in India after Independence, outside that lawless/hapless Muslim-majority State of Jammu and Kashmir!

b) It has taken place in a Hindu-majority State, where the Muslim population (and immigrants at that) had a local majority in that small region around Godhra near border with Pakistan (- a portion of India forcibly got detached by the British for perpetuating division of India into two fighting organs of the same entity.)

c) The minority community was either convinced that the majority community will not have the gumption to react violently or they anticipated that national and international pressures would prevent any significant reaction. The minority community again erred in this respect - as they erred while initiating the Bombay riots after demolition of Babri structure in 1992.

d) Apparently, the minority community again wanted to terrorize the majority community and the state apparatus into accepting their terms for social and religious interactions.

e) The minority community allowed itself to be co-opted by the forces inimical to Indian interests.

f) Reaction of the power elite, intelligentsia and media managers in India and abroad was on the lines expected by the minority community, in that, the sinister significance of Godhra carnage got submerged in condemnation of the majority community, by all and sundry, for the mutual battle between the political parties for political space in Gujarat.

g) Grisly burning of Ram Sevaks in an Indian state neighbouring Pakistan has shown up the strategic weaknesses of Indian state for dealing with the inimical neighbour and their foreign handlers, especially, since the armed forces were supposed to be in full alert on the borders.

h) The power elite in India and abroad seem to have internalized the concept that Muslims can be expected to react communally and irrationally violently on the slightest pretext in any given situation. Muslim nationhood is not limited by any state boundaries but is determined by their religious affinities only![150]

i) Knowing (or they ought to have known) that such a dastardly act could not have been carried out without cross-border support, inspiration and motivation, the

> power elite and the top functionaries forgot to see any terrorist connections and promptly converted this incident into a communal strife, thereby, inviting Hindu communal riposte.

It never appears incongruent, and it is conveniently forgotten by all the so-called thinkers, erudite persons and leaders, that all countries with majority of population affirming faith in some Semitic religion, has invariably a Theocratic state-structure. That international terrorism is always associated with the practitioners of Semitic religions is axicmatic. The newfound great admiration for Pakistan displayed since Iraq II, as a bulwark against international terrorism, is a manifestation of the convenient tactical compromises of America; of course, mostly at the cost of India! So-called 'International Coalition against Terrorism' is not expected to be available for ending terrorist depredations faced by India! India has been left high and dry in facing up to the regional component of the terrorism without full freedom of action, as is normally available to a sovereign country, not to speak of countries like Israel!

However much we may condemn the communal strife in Gujarat, it is also acknowledged by all rational Indians that some sort of reaction to Godhra incident was called for, as otherwise, the perpetrators of Godhra carnage would have been emboldened enough to pull asunder the Indian integrity. Since official apparatus could not take action against the 'Exporter' of international terrorism, the people had to take the law in their hands! Already, Think-tanks in America are busy making war/management-games to create situations for Balkanizing India in the manner they succeeded in Soviet Union, Rump Russia, Yugoslavia, Albania, Balkan States etc. We must not forget that "Market Economy" and "Divestment of PSUs and Public Utilities" were some of the preferred tools used to break up these States. Same tools, which have already been introduced in India, along with escalating civil strife, would give a handle to the international operators to try and break up India. If India chooses to convert an international problem like Godhra incident to an internal civil commotion problem, India is begging to be a candidate for Balkanization and loss of its strategic space. Truly, Godhra carnage is a direct attack on Indian Nationality! My friends who claim that Gujarat saved India, might be correct!

All neighbouring countries of India are Theocratic States and most of them have systematically carried out ethnic cleansing of Hindus. Even the Indian State of J&K, has carried out ethnic cleansing by driving out the Hindus, i.e. the original inhabitants. In all border areas of India, adjacent to the neighbouring countries, vast tracts have been occupied (in about 20 km or more depth in Indian territory) by the immigrants, from where the original inhabitants, the Hindus, have been driven out and in these places (with Muslim majority now) "EXCLUSION ZONES" have been created which are "OUT OF BOUNDS' for Hindus. Even in urban conglomerates or in metropolitan cities, Muslims have been able to create "Exclusion Zones" where Hindus are prohibited from or are unwelcome. In the context of Godhra incident, this matter assumes great significance and Government can afford to ignore this at their and country's peril!

Immediate steps need be taken to desegregate the Muslims from such exclusive areas and ghettos and bring them into composite living areas and into the national mainstream. But the calls for economic development on the basis of the antiquated and pernicious doctrines propagated by the lobbyists of WB/IMF and WTO signal disaster for India. Till India chooses a different Reform Programme, there is no escape from internal strife as seen in Gujarat. Only the most perceptive and erudite persons will accept that Gujarat conflagration was due to a combination of factors and most important of that was the peoples' frustration with the current economic and national security policies which can only increase the distress levels further in years to come! Seen from the elite perspective, Gujarat fiasco had also a positive fall-out so far as economy-managers are concerned. The patently bad Budget 2002 got passed without much ado, as everyone's attention was glued to Gujarat and related events.

In the post-Godhra riots in Gujarat, both the dominant communities fought with abandon and the major targets were industry, business premises and other economic facilities even of the communities not involved in the conflict of interest. This sort of targeting of economic sinews of the communities has a historical compulsion. Godhra incident brings into focus the historical fact as to how economic disparities give rise to social tensions and strife and how that strife takes the shape of inter-caste or inter-community conflict. We should not forget another historical fact that revolts or violent dissents against the economic dispensation arise mostly in the favoured States and Regions. It is useful to recall that the Bengal region gained maximum from the initial period of British Raj, and colonial Capital, business and industry was first concentrated in the Calcutta and Bengal regions. The initial lead for rebellion and armed conflict with the British was provided by Bengal and Bengalis mainly, the prime beneficiaries of the British Raj then! In the later period of British Raj and in Independent India, Bengal suffered baneful or benign neglect and lead for rebellion also got passed off to the regions favoured by the official dispensations. Leaving aside the post-partition riots, it is therefore no wonder that serious communal carnage took place in Delhi in 1984, Bombay in 1992 and now in 2002 in Gujarat - all the States and regions favoured in the last few decades. We wish to disagree with all media-savvy elite and we can prognosticate that unless effective economic programme for balanced development of different States, regions, communities, are initiated immediately (time is not on your side and this moment is the most opportune) - Action-Plan, totally different from the time-eaten and moth-eaten pseudo-economic measures mandated by the denizens of WB/IMF/WTO or Foreign Advisors - India is headed for more communal conflict, as that provides a catharsis for the society. And these conflicts will mostly arise in the favoured regions. You can have your pick but our prognostication is that the most favoured one will be the scene of next drama and the cycle period might be shortened.

We would beg the Commission to kindly review the Godhra carnage from the perspectives highlighted by us and provide proper guidance to the Central and State Government's in the overall national interests and not for satisfying the bruised ego of some minority interest groups! If the intention is to punish the rioters of all the communities involved in the carnage and consequent riots, the Commission could deviate from the beaten path and recommend that these crimes be tried by 'Military Courts (Court Martial)' only for speedy trial and exemplary punishment. The Armed Forces Acts can be extended, as it is, or through Presidential Ordinance or Act of Parliament to cover the perpetrators of the communal carnage and riots in all states, including J&K. We consider such a recommendation will add welcome 'teeth' to the Commission's recommendations. We also know that we should not expect any nationally relevant recommendation from NHRC or other such commissions till they have public trust.

CONSTITUTIONAL IMPEDIMENTS TO SECURE PROSPEROUS INDIA

Indian Constitution is elaborate in peripheral matters but it is reticent or deficient or silent on essential matters concerning the national interests and national security. After observing the way so-called democratic constitutions were assembled for Afghanistan and Iraq (after Iraq War II) we know what was the compulsion of the leaders then to foist such a constitution on India. In these latter countries the respective founding fathers acclaimed all the shenanigans of the intelligence/counter-intelligence operatives of the conquering power and installed patriots (who operated from the conquering country all along) into power with contrived, obviously constitutional, election under conquering country military supervisions and killing forays into un-reconciled Afghanis and Iraqis. Indian constitution had in the morrow of independence, distorted Indian ethos so significantly that it is of utmost importance that we try and decipher how Indian constitution can be made to serve basic Indian interests.

India was divided on communal lines. The great visionary and (synthetic) charismatic leaders even agreed for a population exchange. The communal carnage as a result of these ill-conceived ideas was of horrendous proportion unmatched in Indian or world history. Although, India was divided on communal lines, the leaders and founding fathers totally forgot this instantly. Their distrust of the majority Hindu population and of Indian history was total.

The constitution is couched in so arcane and artificial language that all major provisions could be interpreted in such a manner that actual "Prime Ministerial, Chief Ministerial /Bureaucratic Dictatorship" has evolved in India. The Prime Minister (Chief Ministers, in case of States) is now having absolute powers over all areas/ organs and segments of the state without any accountability what so ever. Since only low calibre, self-seeking individuals without any demonstrated administrative, military, combat/operations experience or acumen/capability were thrown up by the partially democratic polity, the dictatorial powers got gradually transferred to the British-trained and indoctrinated, in-bred, self-sustaining bureaucracy with accountability to no institution or organ of the state. The observed decadence of Independent India is rooted in this "Bureaucratic Dictatorship" made possible by the interpretations of the essential constitutional provisions. Bureaucracy evolved from the elements with average (55%) educational attainments, low IQ, and very low OLQ (Officer Like Quality), and they became amenable to all sorts of external manipulations in detriment to national interests and security, territorial integrity and sovereignty of India. Important elements like the strategic capability and powers of the state, including the armed forces, got completely side-lined, demoralized and decimated. The constitution is silent on the role, functions, funding and control of the "Heart, Soul and Iron Fist of the

Nation – the Armed Forces". The Indian constitution has even called the 'Armed Forces' as 'Defence Forces', thereby precluding or prohibiting any external role or strategic relevance, significance or capability for the armed forces. The supreme court interpreted the constitution and the laws in such a way that defence force personnel are left with no constitutional, legal or natural rights (for further elucidation please refer to the judgment on Wing Commander Hazara Singh vs. Union of India case). Bulk of the defence force personnel being from the poorer strata of society, neglect of defence force became an economic means for perpetuating poverty in undeveloped country, like India.

Compromises with national interests in all fields have been made possible because the constitution is conveniently silent on ratification by Parliament of all International Agreements, Treaties, Covenants, Conventions, MOU's or Protocols, etc. Things have come to such a pass that even long term effect on Indian welfare, national sovereignty and national security interests have been given away for free in pushing the 'bilateral (under covert superpower insistence and continued compliance) Simla Treaty between India and Pakistan', W.T.O. agreements, NPT, CTBT, Paris Convention and Sanctions/Control/Denial Regimes directed against India, massive devaluation of the Indian Rupee with respect to foreign currencies (for benefiting the foreigners and a small segment of the Indian entrepreneurs, by exclusion of the general populace of India) etc. – the list is pretty long! The most depressing fact is that Indian power-elite or intellectuals are not overly concerned about these deficiencies or dangers!

A so-called Hindutva party in India which lost office in the elections of 2004, in the flush of their first ascendancy to power, had constituted a Constitution Review Commission with top available legal brains and a renegade of the main opposition party. The expectation in the rank and file of the ruling combine was that the commission will suitably amend the constitution to debar foreign nationals from making a bid for prime ministership. As is the practice with top legal functionaries, they played politics and refrained from commenting on this important issue.

Judiciary: It has been estimated and mentioned in the media that it will take about 324 years to clear the existing backlog of cases in the courts, if no more new cases are admitted. Judicial delays are now a common event in India and even central cabinet ministers use this alibi to push their pet legislative or other measures! Even though there are only small number of Judges in the apex and high courts, the courts observe long holidays, other than weekly and gazetted holidays and other lay-offs due to political and social upheavals. The courts, often, are not overly concerned at judicial procrastination and often deny justice by delays! The courts have been less than fair to the defence force personnel. They have developed such procedures that common men or armed force personnel cannot get any succour from the apex court even. Hereunder is a first hand report.

JUSTICE AS METED OUT TO UNKNOWN SOLDIERS

There has always been a strong undercurrent of discontent in the armed forces personnel in India regarding pay, promotion, privileges, perquisites, tenure in the services, condition of service, post-retirement benefits, Medicare, food/clothing, domestic accommodation - gross discriminations have been brought in by the bureaucracy under the patronage of their nominal civilian elected leaders in all spheres of existence. After the Vth Central Pay Commission (headed by a very geriatric retired Supreme Court judge, with one member being a highly conforming economist, and all the decisions being taken by the member/ secretary, a civilian bureaucrat) award came out, the Chiefs of the defence forces dutifully welcomed the award. But rank and file of the defence forces exploded in disgust at the more heightened discriminations. To fob off the mounting clamour, the government (the home minister, under whose domain was the Pay Commission, was then a communist stalwart) constituted several committees under civilian bureaucrats to study the different instances of gross discriminations, but soon it became clear that these committees had no charter or intention of doing anything positive and these quickly resorted to time-tested bureaucratic procrastinations. Towards the end of October 1997, when I was away from Delhi on a visit, I read in the newspapers about public agitation by men and officers in different major air force bases and there were unconfirmed reports of open expression of discontent by serving personnel in other two services. After I returned to Delhi a few days later I found that the print and electronic media had been giving quite wide coverage to these unique and sensational occurrences. I got involved as my close friend, and my compatriot in all our socio-political activities, had lined up a TV debate in one of the channels with my erstwhile boss scheduled to air the contrary views supporting the government. I was having misgivings but all my service friends, erstwhile colleagues and subordinates, who were close to me then, insisted that I should not run-away or give any quarter! They apparently were a better judge of my character! I waded in. We won that round (the only one we won). Since I became known a little, some other channels also broadcast some sound bytes and projected my visages. That's the end! The media lost interest as quickly as it took up the issue and steadfastly refused to portray our views any further, when news of torture and incineration of the agitators started in earnest. We then started writing/projecting the gross and wanton discriminations against service personnel to all constitutional authorities - the President of India and supreme commander of the armed forces, prime minister, defence minister, home minister, attorney general of India, chairman of national human rights commission, service chiefs, members (all chief ministers of Indian states) of the committee formed to examine the welfare (or some such thing) of service personnel, etc. We had opportunity to meet the defence minister and chairman of the human rights commission (twice and his secretary once). Some chief ministers even wrote personal letters!

In the meantime aggrieved serving service personnel approached the courts in droves. We made a cardinal mistake of approaching the apex court (CWP 329/99?) We spent Rs. 30,000/- (a very handsome payment in India, though a pittance to the elite) to hire a senior advocate. We made (what we thought) a bullet-proof case about gross, persistent and burgeoning discriminations against service personnel. The division bench (of three judges, headed at that time by a judge, who a little later became the chief justice of India) ruled that service matters cannot come to the court, apex court was not the proper forum for agitating such issues (implying that administrative channels must be explored, notwithstanding the fact that all efforts made in that direction had been elaborately recorded in our case file). We were livid with anger and we were pillorying the advocate in his chamber, when one of his young juniors, who carried the files and papers to the court, said, "Sir, we have been told that the supreme court is the last resort of the oppressed and the suffering, but after today's verdict people might think that this court is the house of comfort of the thugs, crooks and scoundrels only". I was taken aback at this impunity and the senior loudly and sharply rebuked him. I forgot my anger and was concerned that the young man will not go much far in his profession if he did not overhaul his mind set and language! When the 'legal aid society' secretary/office assistant told us that there was no bar in pleading our case ourselves, but courts do not like non-advocates lead arguments and the apex court would have made the legal aid society to provide legal aid, we thought of appealing to the chief justice to get the case reviewed by another bench. Although the registrar of Supreme Court was very encouraging initially, he completely cooled off, possibly, seeing the import of our appeal. Nothing happened for many months and all our telephoning could not elicit any significant response. After waiting for many more months we visited the office of the registrar and to the registry. Several attempts to elicit the actual position got thwarted.

Ultimately, one office assistant took pity on us and directed a clerk, who promptly pulled out two massive files. Many officials had commented and made learned observations about our appeal. The registry could not give us access to the files, but told us 'off the record' that our appeal was barred by Rule 6.1 of 'rules of procedure of the supreme court'! That was the denouement of our efforts to get justice for the servicemen!

CRIMINAL JUSTICE

This is how justice is denied in civil suits with very convenient contrivances. A magazine[51] carried an article titled "Murder of Justice", in which KTS Tulsi, Ex-Solicitor General, Prakash Bhushant, Advocate, Supreme Court, and others have brought out that criminal justice system ensures that the victim is denied all rights in the trial time and justice system has been so systematically subverted and criminalized, with active participation or connivance of judiciary and all parties (other than the victim), that the powerful are literally getting away with murder. This has been publicly demonstrated in the case of murder of Jessica Lal, a Model turned bar tender in a super modern bar owned/operated by well connected husband/wife/daughter (the trio possessing foreign passports), because the murderer was legally (must be with ill-gotten wealth) rich and his father was well connected. The beautiful part of this is that the judge, after acquitting the murderer and his accomplices, immediately got promoted to the high court, the very court, which was seized with the Jessica Lal case once again (in 2006) and some criminals ultimately got punished! Even the court broke tradition to reopen the case after huge popular outcry. The outcry for justice for Jessica was raised by the affluent internet-savvy youths with a sprinkling of cinema personalities, media-savvy elite and leaders joining force and by flooding the media with SMS and e-mails, chat-shows, etc. The same Delhi high court or Supreme court cannot be expected to revisit the Narmada dam controversary, as the victims in this case are deprived, dispossessed and persecuted tribals and other poor, and their champion is a frail woman (Medha Patkar) fasting for weeks in summer heat of Delhi (in 2006) and her only known famous supporter is a frail woman (Arundhati Roy), a fearless writer of repute. This duo had fallen foul of the apex and other courts earlier for their cardinal crime of seeking justice for the poor displaced in contravention of even the Indian constitution! Some years back the SC or HC (?) punished Arundhati Roy to jail term and in her post-release press conference, she roundly and soundly criticized the courts and the judicial procedures (which to my reckoning was more scandalous than what she had been punished for), but the courts took it with equanimity, as any action consequent to her press conference would have excited media and elite outcry. After all, discretion is better part of justice! This piece in magazine (Endnotes 34) has once again demonstrated how inadequate Indian constitution is and how venal the judicial system is.

The Poor, the Constitution and the Legal system

Broad consensus but no willingness for taking any action

14.8.2003

S.C. BANNING 'STRIKE' IN GOVT SECTOR

Newspapers reported gleefully with banner headlines a few years back that a two judge bench of the SC had banned 'Strike" in Government Sector. The business/industry class and power elite acclaimed the (most pernicious ever of) SC verdicts. The political leaders were nonchalant (though with some suppressed happiness). The labour leaders and the legal community are still confused and sharply divided about how to react or act. The communist leaning group (with existential compulsions of supporting a most reactionary/ totally anti-labour party in power) felt that the so-called verdict was just an 'obiter' (wishful thinking or a cursory remark) and has no operative or legal or constitutional significance and potential mischief can be contained by some public debate.

The first Group felt that petitioning the President or the SC or ILO will be counter-productive, knowing the 'Class' inclinations of the present ruling class and international organizations! All are convinced that portents are pernicious.

The net losers will be the labour and lower level Government employees, who are in any case the target of the power elite and legal system alike, so that, for example, "Hire and Fire" policy can be sanctified for killing of more local jobs, without providing for any unemployment/indigent compensation or any social security. A review of the verdicts and edicts of the SC, gives us the notion as if we are still a conquered country and the 'justice' that we are getting is a gift of the powers that be. There seems to be no consciousness of Indian ethos or interests in the judgments handed down from time to time!

Trade Union leaders and common Indians are either ignorant enough to know or understand or are naïve to hope that political leaders and other elite in all fields are convinced that the second phase of "enslavement of Indians" started by the VP Singh-Manmohan Singh duo are totally bad for India. It is understood by very few people in India or in the world that the current activism of the legal system is an extension of the subversion of basic Indian interests. It is worth noting:

1. The judgment is Unconstitutional, Illegal and wishes away the whole concept of collective bargaining enshrined in labour laws and ILO conventions and other international conventions. It needs to be remembered that the SC judges cannot, in isolation without any consideration of the relevant prevailing circumstances, quote/misquote any article of the constitution or any of the statutes in support of their judgment or loud thinking, which itself lowers the dignity of the apex court.
2. The judges forgot that they are not entitled to pass moral or ethical judgments.

3. Dichotomy and apparent discrimination of banning strike in Government Sector while allowing same in private sector will be pointed out sooner or later and ultimately an effort will be made to take away an important tool of collective bargaining.
4. Is it possible that the coterie-selected low IQ/OLQ/ Social Consciousness judges with God-like immunity and job-security have become completely inured of the travails of the working class in the liberalized economic scenario?

The economic reformers, globalizers and liberalizers have raised such a concerted cacophony (in the words of Arundhati Roy: "a multi-tiered edifice of falsehood and deceit, coordinated by the Government and faithfully amplified by the corporate media") that the judges, being ordinary mortals, have been rendered insensitive to the needs of the common man and the working class. Judges do not know or care that Indian Labour is the lowest paid and most productive in the world! This truth has been ignored with vicious venality by the Sixth Central Pay Commission in spite of our protestations.

It is necessary to consider a series of apex court judgments to get a picture of the evolving situation, viz.

a) Wing Commander Hazara Singh vs. UOI (for denying all fundamental, statutory, natural rights to the defence force personnel).
b) CNG for mass transport vehicles (for disrupting the transportation of the masses, livelihood of the poor, facilitating massive imports and consequent job losses and reordering the economic booty).
c) Displacement of the poor and the downtrodden from the central and privileged areas of the metropolises.
d) Mass Displacement of labour to inhuman, unhealthy, undeveloped areas (in the name of ecology/ environment protection and cleaning up the city centres).

e) Tehri and Narmada Dams (to facilitate destruction of ecological balance, facilitate massive imports, displace and decimate the tribal and scheduled tribes and create constant flood threats in the downstream areas and create interstate and international disputes, with the prospect of manning arbitration panels and commissions providing for life-time employment to superannuated judges and bureaucrats. Colourable exercise of ,judgment is transparent here.

f) Interconnection of river valleys (for facilitating subsequent PRIVATISATION AND INTERNATIONALISATION OF WATER), facilitate massive imports, destroy the ecology unalterably in the catchments and down stream areas and along the canal routes, which will all be over ground (our liberalized fantastic governments cannot consider having sub-terranian tunnels for long distance carriage of water); displace the tribal and scheduled tribes, impoverish India in general and the riverine people of the east and north-east of India in particular, create perennial water shortages all round and create transfer of earthquake possibilities to hitherto unaffected areas. We wonder whether the judiciary is alive to the fact that God showers enough rainfall per year (some estimates put it at 400 million acre-feet) sufficient for all the water requirements of India (estimated at about 20 million acre-feet per year) for more than a decade or so. Also, the Judiciary seems reasonably unconcerned that most of the natural water bodies, man–made lakes, aqueduct and aquifers have either been filled up or badly degraded for private profit and all water channels, river systems, natural and man-made drains systems and run-offs have been allowed to be unacceptably degraded and polluted. Of course, no one has ever been held responsible for such cognizable crimes. If only the judiciary had given some thought to restoration of the water channels, rivers, drains, traditional and extensive rain and flood water harvesting systems and upgrading these before launching the super costly, super polluting river interconnection systems, they would have left some worthwhile legacy for posterity. With all the solemnity that we can command, we wish to declare that we are sanguine that the apex court will bequeath only misery and bondage to posterity if they do not retrace their path and recall their edict for interconnection of rivers. We beg the Apex court to consider these comments as a PIL application.

g) Privatization of BALCO, (without first determining whether privatization and consequent fillip to profit-taking, i.e. extraction of labour and production surplus for private gain, is constitutional), the near certain possibility of approving the privatization of profit making oil companies (to impoverish India in general, increase India's vulnerability to external manipulations, massive outflow of Indian wealth, and debilitating further the already grievously debilitated Indian security systems). Incidentally, BALCO was involved in some national security related projects, which have been effectively sabotaged.

h) The recent judgment of the SC clearing the way for the educational institutions to charge whatever they like from the hapless Indians is another step to push India further into educational black hole! We are amazed that the learned judges could not think of some parity of the charges in India as compared to developed countries, especially, the grossly inefficient and costly USA! Is it illegal to demand that charges in India in Rupee should bear the same ratio of the Minimum Statutory Hourly Wages for Unskilled Labour in India as the educational charges in US Dollars bear with respect to minimum wages in US Dollars in USA? We assure the SC that the enthusiasm for private institutions will then vanish like camphor in air! We have also doubt whether majority apex court judges can even comprehend the significance of the simple equation mentioned above.

We apprehend that the political parties controlling the trade unions would not allow the trade unions to mount any joint moves, at this juncture. (This is exactly what happened till the summer of 2006, when anti-Quota agitation reached its peak and led to massive shut downs in capital and other cities. The courts were mum at the peak protest time, because discretion is better part of judicial immunity!). SC moved in at the opportune time and gave a life-line to the beleaguered government of reformists! But without any joint move the SC will not be inclined to listen to the trade unions. The proactive moves, we recommended:

a) The trade unions publicly demand from the Chief Justice and from the judges who made the 'Obiter' about banning of strikes, which had been wildly publicized in media, that they immediately clarify that no ban order has been issued or none is envisaged or considered necessary in the Indian context.

b) If the judges fail to clarify this in their open courts, the trade unions should first boycott the two involved judges and after a month, all the SC benches, till an authoritative pronouncement is made by them on the desired line.

c) Since the present members of SC benches are all selected by a coterie without any accountability, the judges should volunteer to be cleared by Two-thirds majority of both houses of Parliament and all the legislatures of the country, with members voting compulsorily without any whip. The judges must voluntarily resign if not cleared by Parliament or legislatures. The President of India should arrange for such clearance immediately.

d) In order to clear the lingering doubt about the IQ/OLQ/Social consciousness of the SC judges, the judges themselves should volunteer to be tested by three independent national agencies. Also the judges must volunteer to resign if their ratings are not equal or above the average of the top 10% Indian or top 10% of ITT graduates or armed forces officers (especially, for OLQ), for whom ready data ought to be available.

e) Since the SC has run up a massive backlog of cases (some media estimates put it as 324 years of work if no new cases are added), the SC should work in three shifts 365 days in a year, like all other essential services, which it is. Till all backlogs are cleared there shall be no whole-sale closure of SC as at present in the name of holidays.

We are aware that these are simple nationalist steps but very difficult for the political parties, the judges and the elite. Who cares for India or Indians, when foreign attraction is there!

POOR SHOULD DO WITHOUT EDUCATION – does the judiciary really imply that?

World Bank Report 2000-2001 (subtitled "Attacking Poverty") gave some revealing statistics, which indicate that management of Education and social security systems in India could do with some thorough-going reforms; of course, not the type now being seriously attempted. WB and other UN organizations have chided India repeatedly for low expenditures and most inadequate support systems for education of the masses. Ishihara Shintaro (a thinker of the class of Rajni Patel) (currently, 2006, Governor of Tokyo) in his article titled "A Nation Without Morality"[52] made a significant point that phenomenal growth of Japan in post-WWII period was mainly due to the high and universal education standards of Japanese people. (It is another matter that same Ishihara Shintaro, on becoming Governor of Tokyo, turning all logic on its head, privatized the most famous Tokyo University, against all advice of academics. After all, private profits always succeed against society in every capitalist country)! Privatization ultimately makes higher education so costly that it gets restricted to only the rich upper strata of society, as we are seeing in India. After cutting back on access to higher education, there will be pressure and economic rationale to depict expenditures on education as an avoidable waste. No one need be complacent. There are examples galore on this in undeveloped and so-called developing countries in addition to India.

After studying the situations in India and other undeveloped countries it was concluded that only economies in terminal phase of decline attack blatantly weakest and defenseless people – viz. the old (i.e. the pensioners) and children. These classes of people need most benevolent considerations from society. But the IIM fees issue will demonstrate that Indian leaders in all fields and Indian judiciary are trying to improve on "Mother Nature"!

We made a 'brief' but could not motivate (with small amount of fees) a single senior advocate to accept our brief for a PIL in Supreme Court. It is given hereunder in the hope that it will catch the attention of some public spirited judge or legal luminary.

IIM FEES

Seeking impleadment (or review, in case matter already disposed off) in the case in Supreme Court – CJI bench

We consider that the IIM Fees case is being fought in Court in an unreal condition and that also in an unreal world scenario! This case has no relevance to the Indian context for the following reasons:

a) Fees to be charged in an educational/training institute are essentially economic and administrative issues falling within the domain of the executive and courts have been reluctant to intervene in such issues in the past.

b) Quality of any education cannot be neutral or unrelated to general milieu of existence in a country or it cannot be neutral to the culture, ethos or national purpose of the country. The question which begs an answer is: whether the so-called slogan of quality-education is a mere camouflage to produce talented persons for manning the enterprises in foreign lands at, almost, slave rates of wages/compensations, even though, some of these enterprises and countries might be inimical to national interests, sovereignty and territorial integrity of India.

c) Fees charged by an institution cannot be (and should not be) a measure of the quality of education in that Institute. If this were correct, then the IITs and even Central Universities could not be providing quality or relevant education to the students currently. In fact, Faculty of Management Studies (FMS) of Delhi University, with token fees, as per IIM standards, have uniformly produced very talented and well placed managers.

d) Fees to be charged by an institute for providing education cannot be divorced from the economic standards of the country or relative cost of living or earning capacity of the average man.

e) Mal-distribution of resources is already being done by the authorities in India and the IIMs are creating an enabling environment to perpetuate the discriminations on economic grounds.

f) Poverty is already being perpetuated in India by the authorities through their discriminatory financial, taxation, monetary, FE Exchange Rate, FE management, food management (whereby foreigners, businessmen, middlemen, rodents/insects have first charge on the Food Reserves of India), Banking regulation policies and now the IIMs, by creating the bogey of quality education selectively at great expense to the nation, are literally adding to the burning hunger of the underprivileged millions.

g) Some wise men are hinting that funds for paying the exorbitant fees are no problem as banks are willing to give loans at very useful terms. It needs to be examined which policy framework or legal provisions permit such discriminatory distribution of national wealth.

h) Some wise men have also hinted that IIM graduates always earn more than even engineering or medical graduates. The elite could not, as yet, think of demanding and the Government has, so far, refrained from having any national remuneration/compensation policy for the entire employed, in private and public, or Government sectors. Do we want to convert India into a service centre for foreigners or should it be a self supporting, manufacturing country? IIMs cannot be permitted to assist in converting India into a dependent country.

i) The IIMs should confirm what their basic objectives are (of course, if they have any specific objective at all) and whether their training and quality objective is really fulfilling the national purpose for which these institutes were formed.

j) We are convinced that the instant case in Apex Court is only to sanctify the perpetuation of inefficiencies, discriminations, denial of access to opportunities to the majority of the population practised by the IIMs with (tacit?) approval of the administration. The timing of this case, when general elections were announced or contemplated (in 2004), has significant political connotation.

k) One major issue which should be settled is: whether the IIMs are entitled to claim per capita expenditures more than in other educational or training institutes in the country.

l) Claiming of high fees for teaching a non-technical subject is not considered rational.

m) IIMs' per capita expenditures on different expenditure head needs to be compared with that of IITs and other major universities.

n) Per capita income of Indians is about US $ 500 per year. In Rupee terms, this works out to about Rs. 23000 (500×46) per year. Thus a student will have to pay more than six times his income per year for his training in an IIM! The moot question is: whose income will the student consume for advancement of his career! He can do this by putting his other close relations in enhanced penury. This cannot be a desirable national objective.

o) Even the fee limit of Rs 30,000 per year specified by the Government is roughly 1.5 times the average yearly income of Indians, and is an administrative fiat which needs to be declared contrary to the principle of equity. As the fees are not indexed to differential income levels, Government and the IIMs are guilty of encroaching upon the 'Right to Equality' enshrined in the Constitution. (Of course, we are acutely aware that our foreigner-inspired great constitution is silent about social or economic equality! We are depending on the 'Preamble' and 'Directive Principles of State Policy' of the constitution for our claim for equity and equality).

p) World Development Report 2000-2001 of the World Bank (Titled 'Attacking Poverty') reports that lowest 10% of the population in India get only 3.5 % (i.e. just $ 15 Billion or $ 150 [Rs. 6900.00] per capita per year) of the national GDP (of the order of $ 500 Billion), whereas the highest 10% of the population corners 33% of the national GDP (i.e. $ 165 Billion or $ 1650 [Rs. 7,59,000.00] per year). A Pareto analysis will show that Lowest 1% of the population earn hardly $ 6 (Rs. 276.00) per capita per year. IIMs have ensured by their high cost operation that lowest 1%, or the lowest 10% or 20% or even 50% of the population can never hope to access the services of these elite institutes. Equity demands that fees are suitably differentiated/indexed with respect to per capita and per family income.

(Note: Indian Budgets, Economic Surveys or even the World Bank Reports do not give dependable national Income or its distribution. Hence, we have taken the GDP figures as roughly representing the national Income).

q) The WB Report also records that GINI Index (a rough and ready guide to measure inequity in a country, the higher the Index worse it is) for India is extremely high compared to all large and populous countries which are conscious of their social responsibilities.

r) The Apex Court may also consider that India has the most skewed distribution of national income as is evident from the GINI Index as determined by the World Bank in their Development Report cited above.

s) Incidentally, fees for an MBA course in an IIM in India costs the Indian student 2.5 times more than that in Chicago Graduate School of Business, USA, which institute harbours many Nobel Laureates.

t) Might be these students are fronting for other vested interests, as we wonder how could they succeed in obtaining the services of famous advocates to plead their case.

u) The court may wish to throw out of court any suggestion that they, RBI/ MOF, are not able to put in additional money in circulation to incur sufficient expenditures for social sector due to inadequate Reserves, when in fact, Indian Reserves of FE is being parked abroad for comfort of foreigners and foreign countries and are being encouraged by government to squander Indian hard-earned FE in foreign countries. We honestly suspect colourable exercise of judgment by the power elite (we shall explain who all constitute the power elite in India, if the court so desires).

PRAYER

We pray that:

a) The case be deferred till the Government spells out its policy for establishment of any National Institutes, whether for education, training or pursuit of national objectives. The Government should evolve a national wages/remuneration/compensation policy to cover all employed people in all sectors to end the discriminatory remuneration as we have highlighted above. Till then, this case should be kept in abeyance.

b) In the interim, IIMs could be permitted to charge fees in line with the fees currently being charged by the IITs or Central Universities.

Matter is in limbo, to the best of my knowledge.

AMENDMENT TO THE CONSTITUTION

We felt very strongly about the aberrations and deficiencies in the Constitution of India and we submitted a memorandum to the commission. We reminded the secretariat of the commission several times and every time we were assured that the commission will consider our memorandum in due course, which moment, it seems, never arrived! The commission went over the well-beaten track of such commissions and made some innocuous recommendations, which the party in power shelved for posterity. Some aspects of the memorandum is given hereunder to demonstrate the urgent need for thorough going constitutional reforms for ensuring enduring welfare of Indian populace.

EXTRACT OF MEMORANDUM TO THE NATIONAL COMMISSION TO STUDY THE WORKING OF THE CONSTITUTION. (All references in this section are to the constitution of India and all suggested amendments are for the Indian constitution.) These should give a general idea of the debility which Indian people are suffering. We are convinced common man in other developed and undeveloped countries suffer similar or more serious infirmity).

PERSONS ENTITLED TO HOLD HIGH OFFICE

Amendment No. 1 **Add clause 11 (a) after Article 11, as follows:**

Article 11(a): Only natural born Indians or where both biological parents are natural born Indians, can be elected to the Houses of the Parliament or state assemblies or hold any high statutory or constitutional appointment.

Amendment No. 2. **Equality before law: Add Sub-clause 14 (A) as follows:**

14 (A) : Every natural born Indian will have inalienable right to proportionate share of all classes of land, all natural, other resources and biosphere in India or in alien territories under control of Indians in full or part.

Amendment No. 3. **Amend Article 15 by adding three words.**

Amended Article 15. Prohibition of discrimination on grounds of religion, race, caste, sex, place of birth, social and economic status.

Amendment No. 4. **Add three new Articles after Article 16 and renumber the Articles suitably.**

Amendment No. 5. **Article 17. Right to Equity - a) The income distribution of the population should be such that the GINI Index is less than 10%.**

(b) Ratio of income of highest 10% of the population to the income of the lowest 10% of the population cannot be more than 2.

© Highest all world individual income cannot be more than 15 times the lowest all world individual income of any one, native and aliens included.

Amendment No. 6. **Article 18. Right to rational distribution of wealth and income - Nation-wide distribution of wealth and income will follow the norms given hereunder:**

(a) Primary Sector comprising of actual farmers, fishermen, village artisans, direct primary workers, sweepers, midwives, armed forces personnel, central and state cabinet ministers, judges of supreme, high and lower courts, creative artists of repute, engineers, medical professionals, teachers and professors, Ph.D. and doctorates in any discipline and such like direct workers. Minimum pay (all world income) will be five times mw (where mw is the minimum statutory wages for unskilled labour) and maximum pay (all world income) will be 15mw.

(b) Secondary Sector comprising of personnel engaged in manufacturing, construction and fabrication, secretaries and other staff of the government of India and state governments, municipal and local government employees, judicial support system personnel, public/private sector undertakings, utilities in public sector. Minimum pay will be 4mw and maximum 13mw.

(c) Tertiary Sector comprising of service sector, utilities in private sector, non-manufacturing entities, chartered accountants and their support staff and all those who do not belong to the primary or secondary sectors. Minimum pay will be 3mw and maximum 10mw.

(d) Distribution along the scale in each sector will be on the basis of IQ, OLQ, experience, academic/scholastic/ professional achievements and not only on the basis of appointment, office or nature of job.

Amendment No. 7. New Article No. 19. Social Security - Every man/woman/ child whose income level is low and male child upto age of 18, female child upto age of 20 and unemployed adult will automatically get (without any paper work) every month from central treasury or central bank (i.e. RBI) an amount equal to the 'Monthly Statutory Wages for Unskilled Labour', as social security payment.

Amendment No. 8. Right to Freedom of Religion: Add an explanation after Article 25(1)

Explanation: To 'propagate religion' does not imply Right to 'Conversion' of people of other faiths or religions to another faith or religion. Religious conversion is prohibited.

Amendment No. 9. Taking cognizance of the fact that 'Profit-taking or Profiteering' is the most worrisome form of exploitation, as other exploitations arise from the 'desire to extract Labour and Production surplus for private gains', add a new Article 25 in the Section "Right against Exploitation" and renumber the Articles.

New Article 25. Prohibition of Profit – Extraction of labour or production surplus for private gains, i.e. Profit-taking or Profiteering is prohibited. All labour and production surplus will devolve on the State.

Amendment No. 10. Article 26. Freedom to manage religious affairs: Add after Article 26 (c): ***, provided land and wealth is not acquired disproportionate to the number of people of that faith or belief;

Amendment No 11. Insert a new Article 21(A) as under.

New Article 21(A) – Right to medical and health care. State shall provide full and free medical and health care to all citizens of India. Medical and health care will be a priority charge on the resources of the state. State shall ensure that there is no profiteering in provision of medical and health care.

Amendment No. 12. Insert new Article 28 and renumber existing Article 28 as 28(A).

New Article 28 – Right to education. State shall provide free education at all levels. Education upto Class VIII standard will be compulsory for all Indian citizens. State will ensure there is no profiteering in provision of education. Education will have first charge on the resources of the state, even ahead of the requirements of the armed forces.

***Amendment No. 13.* (A) Protection of interests of minorities: Amend Article 29 (2) by deleting the following words, as Indian State is merrily privatizing State institutions and hence the following limitations are putting excessive burden on the majority and minority alike:**

Words to be deleted from Article 29 (2): "maintained by the State of receiving aid out of State funds"

***Amendment No. 14.* Article 31A. Saving of laws providing for acquisition of estates etc. Add after "shall be deemed to be void on the ground that it is inconsistent with, or takes away or abridges any of the rights conferred by [article 14 or article 19],"**

Add: "provided it is not in conflict with article 14A."

***Amendment No. 15.* Article 300A: Amend this Article as follows:**

Amended Article 300A will be: Persons not to be deprived of property save by law – (1) No person shall be deprived of his property acquired legally and with due diligence after 15 August 1947 save by authority of law.

(2) Property can only be acquired from persons holding in excess of limits specified in Article 14A.

ELECTION OF PRESIDENT

We should not forget that the written words of the constitution envisaged that all executive powers of the State will be exercised by the President of India, but the Courts, by some weird logic, made the President as the titular or name-sake Head of State (in the model of the British Emperor), which, of course, is without any constitutional basis. Even now the President is more popularly elected than the Prime Minister – both being indirectly elected. *Indirect election of the President is an aberration,* which needs to be corrected by the Commission.

Hence, amend Article 54 (Election of President) as follows, keeping the requirements of Article 52 uppermost in mind:

Amendment No. 16. "Article 54. Election of President - The President shall be elected by the people of India by direct voting. The winning candidate must secure 51% of the votes of the total electorate of the country, with three or more serious candidates, with compulsory voting. If necessary, a second ballot will be taken with all serious contestants), if in the first ballot no one secures 51% or more votes of the electorate. If the candidate securing the majority votes in the second ballot still does not secure the required majority votes of the electorate, the votes will be counted state-wise. The candidate securing majority of 'popular votes' in a state will be considered to have secured all the 'popular votes' polled in that state. Accordingly, the candidate securing the majority of 'popular votes' on All-India basis will be declared as the President.

Explanation: a) Voting will be compulsory for all eligible voters. Non-participation in voting, except in cases of medical or health debility or other specified emergencies, will be cognizable offence, entailing graded (not Indian judicial equality but real progressive, we mean) financial penalty depending on social and economic status and graded jail terms, depending on social and financial status, for repeat default.

b) A candidate will be considered as serious, if he secures 10% or more votes of the electorate.

c) In a single serious candidate constituency, the winning percentage will be 61%; for a two serious candidate constituency, the winning percentage will be 55%; and where the number of serious candidates are three or more, the winning candidate must secure 51% votes of the electorate.

d) For purposes of this Article, votes polled by the winning candidate in first or second ballot, as the case may be, will be divided by 1,00,000 and approximated to the nearest whole number to calculate the 'popular votes'.

Ministers to be Accountable to the Parliament/Assemblies

At present the Ministers of the Union or of the constituent States are responsible to the Prime/Chief Ministers only and not to the legislatures, as nominally mentioned in the constitution. They are appointed and removed or their offices are changed at the pleasure of the Prime/Chief Ministers. The legislative bodies, to which they are supposed to be accountable, have no say in the matter. This has created unacceptable levels of sycophancy and the ministers cannot and do not freely discharge their constitutional duties. They can and often do ignore the Parliament/Assemblies. Prime Ministers have been raised to the levels of absolute Emperors and the Chief Ministers to the status of absolute Kings. For the sake of democracy, such a state of affairs cannot be allowed to continue.

Amendment No.17. **Amend Article 75 (1) as follows: -**

"Article 75. Other provisions as to Ministers

1) The Prime Minister shall be appointed by the President after the nominee has been approved by both Houses of Parliament. Other Ministers shall be appointed by the President on the advice of the Prime Minister after both Houses of the Parliament have approved them individually for a designate office. If a nominee has been rejected by the Parliament, he will not be re-nominated for duration of one year from the date of rejection of nomination.

2) The Council of Ministers collectively and Ministers individually shall be responsible to the Parliament.

3) Prime Minister and other Ministers shall only be removed from office with prior concurrence of Parliament. The President will remove a minister from office, if majority in both Houses vote to remove the Minister on a motion by a Member of Parliament.

Explanation: **1) If there is divergence of opinion between the Houses of the Parliament, the issue will be settled in a joint sitting of the Parliament where decision will be on**

the basis of total votes polled counting the value of each member's 'popular vote'.

2) Value of each member's popular vote is the total votes polled by him in the first or second ballot, as the case may be, divided by 100000 and approximated to the nearest whole Member for Lok Sabha and for Rajya Sabha Members.

Naturalized Citizens not to be Member of Parliament/ State Assemblies

Citizenship provisions of the Indian constitution are rather lax and it is the whim and fancy of the foreigner to obtain or not to obtain citizenship; interests of the Indian Republic do not seem to play any part in according or refusing citizenship rights. The great constitution review commission under a superannuated Chief Justice of Indian supreme court, along with a few more retired judges of apex court, with the sitting Attorney General and other luminaries of India, played politics and left this matter in limbo.

Amendment No. 18. **Amend Article 84(a) as follows:-**

"Article 84(a): ...is a natural born citizen of India or one whose biological parents are both citizens of India. Naturalized citizens cannot be Member of Parliament or state assemblies.

Members of Council of States to be directly elected

The present system of indirect election of the members of the Council of States is scandalous, as any person of ill-repute can get elected to the important Council of States, if the prime minister/ leader of the party or any one who can influence the power that be, can get convinced of the utility of the person concerned. The selection of candidates is without any criteria or basis, but strictly on the basis of likes and dislikes of the power-elite in the party. Further, the council of states has virtually no power of decision on the activity of the council of Ministers, or for protection of national interests, national security, sovereignty or territorial integrity of India. This council of state has been modeled on the pattern of 'House of Lords' of Great Britain and has the same popular relevance in a democratic set-up and acceptance and esteem as the House of Lords. This state of affairs cannot be allowed to continue.

Amendment No. 19. **Amend Article 80 (4) as follows:-**

"Article 80(4): The representative of each state in the council of states shall be directly elected by the people of the state.

Explanation : The assembly constituencies of the States to be equally, as far as possible, divided amongst the designated number of Council of State members for election to the Council of States. Hence, the constituencies of the Council of States (Rajya Sabha) will be roughly two times bigger than the constituencies of the House of the People (Lok Sabha).

Article 80(5): Procedure for Election to the Council of States: The procedure for election will be the same as that for the President i.e. there shall be a second ballot with the serious contestants, if no contestant secures the desired majority of votes of his (or her) constituency in first ballot and if second ballot is also indecisive, (all ballots will be with compulsory voting), the candidate securing the maximum number of 'Popular Votes" in the assembly segments of the constituency will deem to have won that constituency. The value of 'popular vote' in a constituency will be calculated by dividing the votes polled in first or second ballot, as the case may be, by 100,000 and approximated to the nearest whole member.

Election to the House of the People (Lok Sabha)

Enough studies have been made and enough has been written about the absurd results thrown up by the "First Past the Post" type of ballot with low voter turn out, in the absence of compulsory voting, held in India.

Amendment No. 20 **Amend Article 81(a) to incorporate an explanation as follows:-**

Explanation after Article 81(a): The procedure for election of members to the House of the People will be same as that for the members of council of states except that they will be voted by the constituents of the Lok Sabha constituency.

(b) The selection of candidates for both Lok Sabha and Rajya Sabha to be notified before the date of publication of election schedule by election commission. Parliament may specify that candidates are selected by secret ballot of the eligible voters of the constituency, there being no requirement for compulsory voting by electors.

House of the People will exist in perpetuity

Five-yearly general elections to the House of the People (Lok Sabha) do not adequately represent the wishes of the people as the MPs can conveniently forget their promises once elected. Since there is no method of recall, the Parliament has been generally insensitive to the demands of the people, as the MPs remain sanguine that they can do whatever they please for four years or more and then start agitation on some issues just before the five-yearly so-called general elections. In the present dispensation, the capricious Prime Minister/Chief Minister can, and do, dangle the threat of dissolution of the Parliament/Assembly to keep their flock under their tutelage. Further, the administration of the country goes into a limbo for many months before and after the general elections and long term strategic interests of the country suffer. Hence, it is essential that the House of the People must exist in perpetuity.

Amendment No. 21 **Amend Article 83 to delete sub-clause (2) and substitute, as follows:-**

Article 83. Duration of Houses of Parliament:

2) the House of the People (Lok Sabha) shall not be subject to dissolution, but as nearly as possible, one-fifth of the

elected members of this House and one-sixth members of the Council of States (Rajya Sabha) shall retire as soon as may be on the expiry of every year in accordance with the provisions made in that behalf by Parliament by law.

Explanation : For the first time as a starter, the seats to be vacated and re-elected after first to fifth or sixth year, as the case may be for Lok Sabha and Rajya Sabha respectively, will be decided by lottery, provided, the seats, as far as practicable, to be divided equally/proportionately amongst all States and Union Territories for every such election.

If the public is annoyed with the performance of the MP(s) of any particular persuasion or party, they can demonstrate their anger/frustration by punishing that party/individual in yearly elections. Since, roughly half the electorate will give their verdict every year, the party(s) in power or opposition cannot take things for granted, as the Indians have the nasty habit of proving the poll-pundits wrong. We are convinced that elite minds are so crooked that even these comprehensive constitutional provisions will be attempted to be subverted. Hence a provision for recall of parliamentarians and legislators needs to be incorporated.

Amendment No. 22. **Add a new provision as Article 83(A)**

Article 83(A). Recall of elected representatives.

Demand for recall of elected representatives will be made by a written petition to the President of India by 20% eligible voters of the concerned constituency citing the reasons for recall. The election commission will examine the petition and hold a referendum in the constituency, where voting will not be compulsory (provided that election commission certifies that there is no possibility of false or deviant voting practices). A simple majority vote will determine that a recall motion should be initiated. The President will order recall proceedings and voting will be held within six months. 70% votes in favour of recall (with compulsory voting of the eligible electorates

of the constituency) will carry the recall motion. The President will dismiss the concerned parliamentarian and order the vacancy to be filled up within six months. The recalled member will be debarred from seeking election for the next six years.

Parliament must have time and opportunity to consider all national issues, bills, reports, and submissions etc.

At present, Parliament and assembly sessions are just perfunctory and no systematic discussions or decisions take place. The Sessions are always overloaded with a surfeit of bills, reports and ad hoc and scheduled discussions and announced and unannounced interruptions. Elected representatives and the government behave, as if, all concerned are doing free and part-time service to the nation by condescending to attend Parliament or Assembly. The elected representatives need to comprehend and internalize that legislative work is a full-time job and they are subject to some discipline and time-constraints. The informal arrangement for conduct of business in Parliament and State assemblies must give way to some definite constitution-mandated arrangement for attendance and conduct inside the house.

Amendment No. 23. **Amend Article 85. Add after sub-clause (1) as under**

Article 85. Sessions of Parliament, prorogation and dissolution (1) —— the Parliament must sit for minimum 1440 hours in a year, i.e. minimum 180 days in a year and minimum eight hours per day, excluding any period lost in holidays, interruptions, disruptions, prorogation, adjournment etc. Each member must attend, at least, 75% of the time of sitting. Members attending less than 50% sittings in preceding two years will lose voting right for the current year. Members attending less than 40% sitting over a five years period will not be entitled to seek reelection for 6 years thereafter. Members falling short of attendance below 75% will lose double the hourly attendance fees for the period of non-attendance below 75%.

Amendment No. 24. **Delete sub-clause 2 (b) of Article 85, as the House of the People will continue in perpetuity, if amendment to Article 81 is accepted.**

All International Treaties, Agreements, Protocols, Covenants, Conventions, MOUs etc., to be ratified by Parliament.

At present, the executive enters into international Treaties etc. behind the back of the Parliament and the country is presented with a *fait-accompli*. Even Indian Territory has been virtually ceded to the enemy or inimical countries, in violation of the constitution, without taking the so-called representatives of the people into confidence. **The Government or Executive should not make any binding commitments without prior approval of the people.**

Amendment No. 25. **Insert Article 108 as under and renumber the rest of the Articles:**

New Article 108: All International Treaties, Agreements, Protocols, Covenants, Conventions, MOUs etc. are to take effect only after approval by Parliament. These are to be submitted to each House of Parliament and state legislatures for approval, with or without any amendments, additions/alterations, as required. Important treaties etc. to be passed with amendment, additions/alterations, as necessary, with 2/3rd majority in each House as in the case of amendments to the constitution.

Explanation: Whether a Treaty etc. is important or not will be decided by each House on the basis of majority vote. In case of difference of views between the Houses, the matter will be resolved in a joint sitting of both the Houses where the majority with value of each member's 'popular vote' will be taken. Such procedure will be followed in all cases of difference in views of the Houses.

Amendment No . 26. **Delete Article 109, as Council of States will also be directly elected.**

Have appropriate consequent changes in Articles 113, 114.

Amendment No. 27. **Amend Article 124 as follows;**

Article 124. Establishment and Constitution of Supreme Court (1) There shall be a Supreme Court of India, consisting of a Chief Justice of India and other Judges in the proportion of one Supreme Court Judge per ten million of population or part thereof, with the proviso that Parliament by Law may prescribe a larger number of Judges.

Qualification of Judges of Supreme Court

At present, anyone may join the Apex Court if only the powers that be become convinced of the utility of the person concerned. Judges of the Supreme Court need not be acceptable to the people at large, so long as they are acceptable to the power-elite. Whereas they need not, or should not, be involved in day to day political humdrum, but they ought to have political and cultural/social consciousness. The apex Court judgments have finality for common man, but the powerful ones can always get a review done. There is no system of review or social evaluation of the apex Court judgments. At present, the Judges are appointed by the executive and the legislatures and peoples' representatives have no say in selection or confirmation.

Amendment No. 28. **Amend Article 124(3) (c) as follows.**

Is, in the opinion of the President, a distinguished jurist with IQ and OLQ ('Officer Like Quality', as measured for Armed Forces Officers) and cultural consciousness of not less than the average of the topmost 10% of Indians, with a PhD (Doctorate) degree in humanities, or sciences, or medicines or engineering or law.

Amendment No. 29. **Amend Article 131 by adding the following at the end of Article 131:**

131. Original jurisdiction of the Supreme Court.

Provided that every judgment of a bench of the Supreme Court shall be subject to peer evaluation by same or more number of judges of the Supreme Court before issue of judgment and provided that the Supreme Court will make full use of computers and other such technologies for eliminating subjective element of judgments, as far as possible. The Supreme Court will operate 24 hrs a day, 365 days in the year, like all other essential services. The Supreme Court will evolve effective means for elimination of backlogs and expeditious dispensation of justice equally to all. The Supreme Court shall have interconnected (with IT) benches in major population centres and outlying areas, as decided by Parliament by law.

Judges of Supreme Court and High Courts are to be responsible to the people.

At present, the Judges of the S.C. and H.C are appointed by the executive and they, often, display unconcern about peoples' aspirations and interests.

Amendment No. 30. **Amend Article 124 by adding sub-paras (d) and (e) as follows.**

Article 124(d): The appointment of the judges of the Supreme Court is to be approved by both the Houses of the Parliament and the legislatures of the States with two–thirds majority of the total number of members of the Houses. In case of divergence of views of the Houses in Parliament or in States, the matter will be resolved in a joint sitting of the respective Houses, wherein two–thirds majority will be decided by the 'popular votes' of the members. If a nominee is rejected once, he will not be re-nominated for the same office. For removal of the judges, similar procedure to be followed, except that removal procedures can be initiated more than once.

Article 124(e): The appointment of the judges of High Courts are to be approved by both the Houses of the Parliament and the legislatures of the respective States with two–thirds majority of the total number of members of the Houses. In case of divergence of views of the Houses,

the matter will be resolved in a joint sitting of the Houses, wherein two–thirds majority will be decided by the 'popular votes' of the members. If a nominee is rejected once, he will not be re-nominated for the same office. For removal of the judges, similar procedure is to be followed, except that removal procedures can be initiated more than once.

ARMED FORCES OF THE UNION

Amendment No. 31. **Amend Article 53(2a) to delete the words 'Defence Forces' and substitute by 'Armed Forces'.**

The Constitution is silent about the creation, roles, control, funding, and methodology of usage of the Armed Forces, its duties, responsibilities, privileges and protections. This is a black spot on the Constitution.

Amendment No. 32. **Insert three new Articles, 76, 77 and 78 and renumber the rest of the Articles suitably.**

Amendment No. 33. **New Article 76: There shall be a Military Commission for raising/command/control/maintenance/ victualling of the Armed Forces, Intelligence/Counter–Intelligence agencies, Para–military and Auxiliary Forces and other forces, as decided by the Government from time to time, and shall consist of the following:**

a) The President

b) The Prime Minister

c) Defence Minister

d) The Supreme Commanders of Army, Navy and Air Force.

Explanation: Till such time Supreme Commanders are appointed the Chiefs of Staff of the Army/Navy/Air Force will discharge the functions of the respective supreme commanders.

Amendment No. 34. **Armed Forces of the Union – (1) there shall be three Armed Forces of the Union - Army, Navy and Air Force, each commanded by a Supreme Commander of the respective force and responsible to the President** and Supreme Commander of the Armed Forces, through the Military Commission. The Parliament by law may create other armed forces, if required.

(2) Other Formations of the armed forces will be:

a) No. ... Army/Navy/Air Force Group (each with roughly three million officers and PBOR), as appropriate. There shall be several such groups for respective services, depending on the state of mobilization of the nation

b) No. ... Army, Navy and Air Force (each with roughly one million officers and PBOR), as appropriate. There shall be several such army/navy/air forces, depending on the state of mobilization of the nation.

c) Other lower formations will continue as at the time of this amendment to the constitution.

(3) The armed forces, while so commanded by the military commission, shall be responsible for safeguarding of territorial integrity and sovereignty of India and whenever required by Council of Ministers/Parliament, for internal security.

(4) The Supreme and Group Commanders of the armed forces will have the status of cabinet ministers and will take oath as set out in third schedule for ministers of the union. Army/Navy/Air Force Commanders and GOC-in-C of Commands (and the equivalents of the Navy and Air Force) will have the status of Minister of State of the Union and will take oath as set out in third schedule for ministers of the union.

(5) The Supreme and Group Commanders of Army, Navy and Air Force shall be ex-officio members of the House of the People (Lok Sabha) and shall attend the sittings of the House as many times as possible, without compromising other duties and commitments. Every Commander shall have the right to speak in or otherwise to take part in the proceedings of either House, of the centre or state, as applicable, any joint sittings of the

respective Houses, and any committee of Parliament of which he may be named a member, but shall not by virtue of this article be entitled to vote.

a. The Speaker of Lok Sabha and Chairman of the Rajya Sabha, may require the Supreme/Group Commander(s) of the services concerned to be present in the House on specified occasions and respond to queries of the members on national security issues, with proviso that he shall not be required to divulge state secrets or compromise the armed forces or do or say anything prejudicial to national interest/territorial integrity/ sovereignty.

b. Army/Navy/Air Force Commanders and GOC-in-C (and the equivalents of the Navy and Air Force) shall be ex-officio members of the Assembly of the State of the Union where the HQs of the formation is located and shall attend the sittings of the assembly as many times as possible, without compromising other duties and commitments. Every Commander, GOC-in-C and equivalents shall have the right to speak in or otherwise to take part in the proceedings of either House of the state, as applicable, any joint sittings of the of the respective Houses, and any committee of Assembly of which he may be named a member, but shall not by virtue of this article be entitled to vote.

Armed Forces personnel are citizens of India and they are not potential participants or initiators of 'coup'

In order to obviate the possibility of 'coup' or 'Military take–over of administration', it is necessary to bring the armed forces in national mainstream of administration and legislation. It is an established fact that there has never been a 'coup' in a big country with large (one million or more strong military) and especially where the armed forces are integrated with the executive and legislative wings of the state. After Independence, the British trained and indoctrinated bureaucrats, with the help of compliant and complementing political elements, have isolated and placed the armed forces in administrative ghettos and denied or deprived them of protection of the constitution and from normal pay/promotions/perquisites and privileges which ought to have been entitled to them. Although implied, but not clearly spelt out in the constitution, the armed forces are required to be under Parliamentary control, but the interpretation of the constitution by courts and administrative procedures evolved by the civilian bureaucracy, has ensured that the Parliament has no access to service matters. At present, the legislative wing has no control, what-so-ever, on the armed forces.

Presence of armed forces personnel in Parliament will enable Parliament to have realistic assessment of the national security scenario and it will no longer be possible for the bureaucrats and ministers to keep Parliament in the dark and mislead it or pass on lies/half–truths/untruths to the representatives of the people.

It is high time that the power-elite may wish to accept that the armed forces are the **"Heart and Soul of the Nation and its Iron Fist"**. The bureaucrats and elite need to internalize that armed forces personnel are **Not** potential mutineers or initiators or participants of 'Coup' and that armed forces personnel do not cease to be citizens of India as soon as they volunteer to join any of the armed forces.

Amendment No. 35. **Add new Article 77 as under.**

New Article 77: Representatives of the armed forces to participate in Parliament – (1) President shall nominate one Principal Staff Officer from Supreme Headquarters of each of the three Armed Forces - Army, Navy, Air Force - from the branch/arm/cadre with maximum number of men and officers in the respective service, as ex-officio member of the Council of States (Rajya Sabha).

(2) The President shall nominate one Principal Staff Officer from each Supreme Headquarters of the three Armed Forces – Army, Navy, Air Force - from the branch/arm/cadre with

second largest number of men and officers in the respective service, as ex-officio member of the House of the People (Lok Sabha).

(3) Two serving Armed Force personnel (one officer and one other ranks) from each of the three armed forces will be elected to the House of the People (Lok Sabha) by election from a joint special constituency of the serving and retired personnel of the three armed forces, Para–military forces, central intelligence and counter-intelligence agencies and serving members of the auxiliary forces and such other forces as the government, with approval of Parliament, may decide from time to time. Voters in this joint special constituency will not vote in any other constituency, but retired members of the armed forces, Para–military, intelligence, counter–intelligence and auxiliary forces may contest elections from any other constituency as a civilian.

(4) Election commission will conduct the elections and all other procedures will be same as for elections to the House of the People (Lok Sabha).

(5) The speaker of Lok Sabha and Chairman of Rajya Sabha, may require the nominated member PSOs (Principal Staff officers) of either House to be present in the House on specified occasions, and respond to queries of the members on national security issues, with proviso that they shall not be required to divulge state secrets or compromise the armed forces or do or say anything prejudicial to national interests/territorial integrity/ sovereignty.

(6) The nominated–PSO members shall attend the sittings of the House as many times as possible, without impairment of their other official duties and commitments. They will have right to speak in or otherwise take part in any joint sitting of the Houses and any committee of Parliament of which he may be named a member, but shall not by virtue of this article be entitled to vote.

Amendment No. 36. Add new article 78 and suitably change the other Article Numbers:

New Article 78. Armed forces to have special responsibilities and protections: (1) The members of the armed forces shall have to work and live in hard, adverse conditions and environments and shall be ready to make all manner of sacrifices, including the supreme sacrifice and may demand supreme sacrifice from those placed under them and inflict all manner of punishments, including death and injury to the enemy (as decided by Parliament) and damage or destroy property, as deemed necessary or punish violators of the territorial integrity and sovereignty of India or for preservation of internal security, as required by Parliament.

(2) The members of the Armed Forces may be denied protections of some of the fundamental rights and privileges on occasions of national emergency or on other occasions, as decided by Parliament. There shall be no omnibus denial of rights to the armed forces personnel.

(3) The armed forces will have first charge on the revenues and resources of the nation. The Parliament will ensure that the armed forces have adequate manpower, resources and funds for fulfilling their responsibilities.

(4) Members of the armed forces shall get better terms of service, pay, allowances, perquisites, facilities and privileges than comparable civilian employees in public or private employment for same year of service.

Explanation : Commissioned Offices of the armed forces will get better terms of service etc. than the Class I, Group A Civilian Gazetted Officers or their equivalents in the civil (including private sector) for the same year of service. Similarly, warrant ranks and non-commissioned personnel of the armed forces will get better terms and facilities than corresponding Class-II Gazetted or non-Gazetted personnel of the civil for the same year of service or those in private business. Non-gazetted personnel of services will get better terms than corresponding civilian non-gazetted personnel.

(5) All courts, organs and entities of the state shall ensure that no discriminations against armed forces personnel shall be continued or created in any manner. All existing discriminatory provisions shall stand annulled or be expeditiously removed, keeping in view the exceptional conditions of service of the armed forces personnel.

(6) The Warrant of Precedence (W.O.P) for armed forces personnel shall be same or better than that at the time of Independence in 1947. The WOP to be reworked expeditiously.

Explanation: No civilian employee (serving or reemployed or re-engaged after retirement) shall have warrant of Precedence higher than corresponding armed forces personnel or higher than that at the time of Independence.

(7) Armed forces and their supporting Para–military, intelligence/counter-intelligence, auxiliary forces, or civilians in support of the armed forces, shall have freedom of unhindered movement, operation and communication in all media and environment – land, sea, sub-marine, air, space - throughout the territory of India and abroad, whenever required. All states, public, private agencies/ organs/entities shall ensure full service, without demur, to the armed forces, whenever required.

Amendment No. 37. Official language

The unkindest cut and insult inflicted by the Indian constitution on India was the designation of English as the official language of the union of India. This single act consigned Indian languages to dung heap of neglect and delegalized the languages of expression of the common Indians. India is the single largest country in the world which has a barbaric foreign language imposed on it by the exploiters in concert with the topmost leader of the country for convenience of the elite, power-usurper and foreigners. This part of the constitution is a standing shame on India.

Amend Part XVII.

Article 343. Delete existing text and substitute as follows: Official language of the Union – The Official languages of the Union shall be all Indian languages listed in Eighth Schedule of the constitution.

Delete subsections (2), (3) of Article 343.

Delete Articles 344, 345, as these provisions are unnecessary after amendment to Article 343. In any case these Articles were cruel jokes on the common Indians.

Delete Article 346 and amend as follows:

New Article 344 (after deletion of existing articles 344 and 345): official language or languages of a state – The legislature of the State may adopt one or more languages of Eighth Schedule or other language in common use in the State as language or languages to be used for all or any of the official purpose of that State.

Delete Article 346 and amend and renumber as New Article 345 (after deletion of existing articles 344 and 345): The language(s) of the State shall be the official language for the State in communication with the Union and other States, with the proviso that while communicating with another State, authorized translated scripts in the language(s) of the receiving State to be also sent along with the original letter in the language(s) of the dispatching State.

Delete the words "shall be in the English language" in Article 348 subsection (1) and substitute with the words: "shall be in the languages listed in Eighth Schedule".

Delete Articles 348(2) and 348(3).

Delete Article 349, as this is irrelevant after amendments to Article 348, as above.

Delete Article 350A and reword as follows: Medium of Instruction in schools, colleges, universities and other

institutions will be in languages listed in Eighth Schedule and/or language(s) recognized in any of the State of the Union or Centrally administered territories throughout India. Students and parents/guardians will have the option to choose any language(s) of Eighth Schedule or any of the language recognized in any of the State of the Union or centrally administered territories as medium of instruction.

CASE LAWS AND INTERPRETATION OF THE CONSTITITON

Indian constitution being loosely and vaguely worded, the courts have created many case laws and have handed down many newer and novel interpretations to the constitutional provisions. These, in fact, have substantially amended the constitution without popular support (viz. legislative concurrence). Add a new Article as follows and renumber the Articles of the Constitution.

Amendment No. 38. **New Article ***: 1) Courts will refrain from creating new Case Laws and give new interpretations to the constitutional provisions, as far as possible. Case Laws/ interpretations will remain valid, provided Parliament/Legislatures approve these as constitutional amendments within one year from the date of issue of verdict.**

2) Registrar of Supreme Court in consultation with the Law Commission and Law Ministry will draft suitable constitutional amendments after Collegiums of Supreme Court judges have examined and determined which all old case laws and interpretations still needed. All such case laws etc. will become invalidated provided Parliament/ Legislatures do not approve these as constitutional amendments within one year.

Explanation: Such review of old cases to be completed within one year and legislative (popular) sanctions to be obtained within one more year.

OTHER IMPORTANT AMENDMENTS

Amendment No. 39. We had sought the indulgence of the review commission to consider following important amendments and entreated the commission to suitably incorporate these in natural, commonplace English, as has been tried by us in our suggestions given above (Note: The great commission, of course, in its exalted wisdom, ignored all of these also) :

a) Legislative Assemblies of States to continue in perpetuity with one-fifth members retiring each year.

b) Legislative Councils to continue in perpetuity with one-sixth members retiring every year. Members will be directly elected from constituencies bigger than that of the Legislative Assemblies.

c) Other consequent changes in the Constitution due to above two changes, particularly in respect of Money Bills etc.

d) Election Commission to be made responsible for prevention of bogus voting and ensuring distribution of Smart (Electronic-compatible) Identity cards to all eligible voters expeditiously.

e) Smart Identity Cards of Voters to have all information, like, full name, age, date, time (where available) and place of birth, height, colour of eyes, identification marks, other significant identity, such as distance between the IRIS of eyes, distance between the ears etc., name of both parents, present and permanent address, Income level, digital finger and palm prints, ration card (where applicable, of the guardian), driving licence, credit card, PAN/GIR, passport, identity card issued by employer, details, if any.

f) All non-elected constitutional authorities, all members of the Commissions, Regulators, Joint Secretary and above in central bureaucracy and their equivalents in State governments and CEOs/Chairmen in public and in private enterprises operating with public money from Banks, FIs,

FIIs of all descriptions, will have to have IQ, OLQ and Social qualities equivalent to that of judges of superior courts and will have to be cleared by both Houses like the judges and removed in the same manner.

g) There will be no Three-line whip by parties or groups or conglomerates of Parliamentarians or legislators. Whip can only be issued for attendance and voting but no direction or indication can be given for voting for or against any motion or bills etc.

Note: a) Once the Election Commission is made to move out of its bureaucratic protective shell, it will find that it can prevent bogus voting by having facilities in conjunction with Electronic Voting Machines to read the vital particulars of the voter through the smart I-card with bar-coding also. Don't tell us we still need foreign funds, technology and equipment for this or that we should wait for a decade to see whole of India covered! Actually the job can be done in a few months' time, but we are willing to give you so much time (2 years) knowing the bureaucratic and economic mind-blocks.

b) The Constitution Review Commission and the courts ought to have noted that acts of omissions and commissions of the Election Commission are, to a great extent, at the root of crisis of confidence in the Indian polity. The extent of false voting, rigging and booth-capturing is a direct measure of the conceptual, systematic and continuous failure of Election Commissions to discharge their Constitution-mandated duties and responsibilities. Here again, lax constitutional provisions, in the absence of public accountability (like the judges of superior courts, the Election Commission members are chosen and foisted on the republic by a coterie around the Prime Minister and the President of the Republic signing on the dotted line), permitted the Election Commission to get away with virtual murder of democracy! An ill-conceived and executed constitution, with the additional burden of conniving Election Commission, made a mockery of democracy; the most pathetic part is that the joke has been on majority Indian!

Amendment No 40.

(h) Delete Part XIV of the Constitution, or, at least Chapter 1 of this Part, as this is incongruous when contrasted with the fact that the Constitution is blissfully silent about the armed forces, excepting for imposing restrictions and constraints on their service, life and liberty! Purpose of Part XIV could have been easily fulfilled by Laws enacted by Parliament or by Government Rules and Regulations.

The Constitution Review Commission ought to have discovered that Part XIV of the Constitution is an imposition on the constitution by the entrenched British-trained and indoctrinated bureaucracy, which pressure, the great founding fathers could not resist.

Note: - We strongly feel that the judiciary is individually, collectively, morally, legally and constitutionally responsible to restrain or caution the other two major organs of the State to remain within limits and also prevent the misuse of Armed forces for acts of omissions and commissions against national/security interests, territorial integrity and sovereignty. We have highlighted many instances of deviations from the straight path by the principal constitutional authorities, which ought to have been apparent to an alert judiciary also. We consider that judiciary in India has been less than fair to the Indian interests and they have sizable responsibility for the moribund state of the country. We had earnestly requested the Commission to forget conventional wisdom on economic matters (as, in any case, these so-called economists and elite do not have the interests of India at heart!) and kindly accept our contention that **repeated voting and elections is a GDP–enhancing activity, as election expenses give high Income-Velocity of Money**. We had also advised the commission that if anyone cared to contradict they could confront us first before wasting time of the commission. Of course, we ought not to have expected the commission to let down the vested interests or the elite!

8

SHANTI PARBA

SECURITY IMPLICATIONS/SIGNIFICANCE OF DECLINE OF RELIGION OF MAN

The religion of man enjoins that every human being (nay, every creature in the world) has the inherent right to develop in all fields upto its fullest potentialities. Recognizing that humans can develop infinite capacity for doing good and mischief alike and often do that, the religion of man from earliest times specified that humans must work for common good without expecting or accepting particular care of its own interests. It was, hence, ordained in the original Hindu religion that humans have 'only right to work and not to specified or expected result'. Hindu religion also distinguished amongst 'Karma (work or fulfillment), aKarma (useless work) and biKarma (negative work). A work done for self aggrandizement or for achieving a desired result is classified as useless work as per Hindu belief. All exploitations for private gains are biKarma and fit for condemnation.

In this context it is relevant to recall the contributions of Buddha in the development of religion of man. Buddha is the greatest leader of supreme eminence, who gave new dimensions and meanings to religious, spiritual and cultural issues critical for mankind. All miseries and deprivations of humans are result of human failures. But he, in line with other Avatars of Vishnu, did not specify a set of edicts or doctrines for conduct of humans in specific circumstances, because he knew that all doctrines and edicts lose their relevance over time and with cultural flux. Man's competition is really with his inner being. It is noteworthy that more than a half millennium earlier to the rise of the sotereological Semitic religions, Buddha had anticipated the denouement of such thing occurring for furthering human sufferings. It is all too clear to see the outcome of deviation from Buddha's path.

Buddha being a teacher could not stay away from the people. Alas, Buddha, in spite of being a Mukta Purusha, made fundamental mistakes by trying to reach out to the common men by ignoring Brahminical concept of Param Brahma, and de-recognize concept of God as relevant or necessary. He allowed his close disciples to spread his messages. Hence, the well-meaning disciples like Anand, Javala etc. had to start the Sotereological methods. All westerners while getting out of their tribal and barbaric roots of origins got trapped in Semitic religious, social and cultural beliefs and mores. As a result, all Middle Eastern and Western and westernized educated people developed great admiration for (what Hindus call) as aKarma and biKarma (useless and negative work) and disdain and enmity for those who believe otherwise. God had given infinite powers and freedom to creatures, but he did not thereby forsake any of his own powers of creation or destruction. Liberated minds (Mukta Purushas) understood that human capacities and powers, however infinite those, are not even infinitely small fractions of the power of the Param Brahman. Unlike in our physical, known or perceivable world, His action-reaction system is quite indirect. All Hindu Munis, Rishis, Sages, teachers and preceptors spent their life in understanding His schemes of things in various situations. The more they understood, the more awe-struck were they in comprehending the complexity of Lord's ways and means. Semitic religions got over this problem by having a partisan as their God and Director, who is ever ready to solve human problems as and when they arise. It seems that the work of Kalki, the tenth Avatar of Vishnu, who is ordained to destroy the Human race from the earth, cannot be much delayed or avoided. Note carefully, only the human race is earmarked for extinction like the dinosaurs or the Dodo. The tenth avatar will not be of human form at all but some concept, idea or theory, as God, possibly, wants to try out all options.

Increasing use of Semitic religious and cultural beliefs to divide people into antagonistic and exclusive groups and creating administrative and economic structures with edicts of supreme human authority being inviolable, gives the impression that even with the experiences of last millennium, when two wars of world significance were fought inconclusively, with total misery level in the world increasing considerably, no correct and relevant lessons have been learnt. When the pay-back times comes that might be also remorseless.

Muslims cannot be ignored or excluded from what we call Indian being in any circumstances, as contribution of Muslims in Indian (nay, Hindu) culture has always been overwhelming; Indian five fine arts: Literature, Music (including drama, cinema), Sculpture, Architecture and Painting have been always and are ever dominated by that group which professes or believes in Muslim faith. Indian cinema particularly has always been dominated by Muslims. Currently in 2007/2008 four Khans are the heart-throbs of India – Shah Rukh, Aamir, Salman and Saif Ali. Meena Kumari is yet to be excelled in Indian (possibly, world) cinema by any lady star in sensitive portrayal of pathos and emotions. That lovable crazy painter, Maqbul Fida Hussain, has a fixation for Hindu gods and goddesses and paints them in all sorts of poses (some compromising) and he is a permanent hate-target of Hindu-zealots (the self-appointed saviours of Hindus), though I personally think that Hindu gods and goddesses must be quite amused at the antics of Madhuri (the most beautiful Hindu actress ever) - Fida Hussain! In BR Chopra's traffic-stopping serial on

Mahabharata, the role of the most important character (that of ARJUN – the third Pandava) was played with unequalled brilliance by a Muslim. But all eminently successful Muslims have to operate in Hindu idioms and Hindu format. Muslims are unable to break out of this constraint and some rebel. That creates Hindu-Muslim enmity and tensions in the society. Muslims forget the cardinal facts that Hindus take them to their hearts because of basic Hindu liberalism and tolerance of diversity. But Hindu political leaders (because of their Semitic inclinations) benefit at the cost of the Muslims and perpetuate the division. These leaders must be stopped, as otherwise, they will stop India!

CENTRAL TRUTHS

Study of growth and decline of civilizations, economic thought processes attending on civilizational progress and prognostications on the future led unknown soldiers, like me, to some conclusions regarding the central truths of human interactions, which I am presenting hereunder:

a) Poverty is an essential component of growth of western civilizations, especially, in the CE.

b) All states, especially in Asia and Africa , with Muslim or Christian majority, are invariably small, theocratic and generally poor or disadvantaged. USA is the only exception, because of its abundant natural resources, with native population completely eliminated as competitor, with opportunity for unbridled exploitation of near and far countries with brute force sanctified by capitalism and Semitism.

c) Equity has been the greatest sacrifice at the altars of civilization.

d) Western model of development and equity are antithesis of each other.

e) All instrumentalities of modern states, without exception, ensure perpetuation of poverty. The executioners are the political systems and bureaucracy.

f) Western model of development has always been at the cost of ecology and had put excessive and untenable demands on the biosphere.

g) Low overall productive efficiency of white races vis-à-vis Indians, black and yellow races, have been the motivation for plundering and colonization of India and other unfortunate countries of Asia, Africa, Latin America, elimination of native Red Indians and natives of Australia.

h) Conquering and occupation of peace-loving and non-militant nations were easy as such nations (like India) never understood the real significance of adequate and overwhelming national militarization or mobilization. Only militarily weak nations keep whistling in the dark, denying, like self-righteous Bengal-origin historians, the fact: "Bengal was over-run by 17 Horsemen of Mohammed Ghori"! The imperative need for massive mobilization of India is apparent to all except the liberalized Semitized power elite of India.

i) Indian belief systems enshrined in the Hindu Religion is actually a product of Indian ecology, environment and bounties of Nature.

j) Hindu belief system was the bulwark which prevented conversion of India to Semitic belief systems. Indians were not much bothered about their abundant material assets (because of their belief systems). Marauders concentrated on material aspects, were amply rewarded and were mostly overwhelmed by sophistication of Indian ideas, social engineering and belief systems. They made many attempts but found their efforts not very productive and left Indian cultures alone.

k) Europe, Middle East, Africa, Australia, Japan, Korea or even a vast and materially rich country like China did not have very strong liberal, all inclusive, tolerant belief systems and lost their traditional cultures.

l) White and Yellow races gained in material benefits at the cost of their traditional cultures, which in any case was exploitative. Black Africa did have optimum population, had no worthwhile sustainable indigenous value systems or technology and was exploited ruthlessly by all invaders and colonizers.

m) Semitic belief system has to get subsumed in Hindu belief systems if humanity is to continue into 4th millennium CE.

n) Semitization of Indian belief systems started about half a millennium before CE, even in the life time of Gautama Buddha. Buddha ensured the arrival of crucified Christianity and other more aggressive forms of Semitic religions that had only belief in coercion to achieve their ends.

o) What the marauders and colonizers could not do in more than two millennia of occupation of India, has been almost accomplished in about six decades since independence by Indian leaders converted to Semitic belief systems, like, Mahatma M K Gandhi, Pandit Jawaharlal Nehru, Dr. Manmohan Singh, Atal Behari Vajpayee and Mrs. Indira Nehru Gandhi (arranged in descending order of their venality in harming the Hindu belief systems) and other minions as prime ministers.

p) Indian traditional religion or cultures will not survive beyond 2050 CE, if Indian leaders continue in the same path.

q) This loss of Indian or Hindu identity will be hastened and will be completed, as soon as Muslim population in India reaches or crosses 30% of total population. India will be declared an Islamic State with Shariat rule coming about sooner than expected. Poverty will be more virulent with all fundamental rights (as we know of these now) abrogated.

r) Indian variety of secularism will be a dead letter or a despicable concept with Islamic rule

s) WWIII may be inevitable then, as billion plus converted Semitic people may not be happy to be contained within 2% of world geographical area and may claim lebensraum with renewed ferocity. This is not the clash that Huntington envisaged but western nations may find the temptations to join battle with Muslims an enchanting prospect. Since Muslims suffered in earlier engagements with Christians due to lack of numbers and ideas, they will be well equipped in this round. The prognosis is gloomy for the western nations.

t) Hence western nations may want WWIII to take place earlier than 2050 CE, provided Congress or Vajpayee variety of secularism and liberalism survive till then. But demands of capitalism in the current permissive economic environment may come up against impregnable wall of popular disenchantments well before end of next decade. But if conflict does take place due to intransigence of power elite of India that may turn out also differently than that envisaged by Huntington, as any conflict involving Hindu India may turn out to be really clash of two totally opposed civilizations, viz. Hindu vs. Semitic (Christian portion). Aroused Hindus may term this conflict as one for Hindu rationality and liberalism against Christian irrationality and obscurantism! The war may turn out to be one against exploitation and inequity in world order.

u) Possibly, there will be two types of conflicts of civilizations. One, as envisaged by Huntington: an internecine one between two Semitic civilizations well before 2050 CE. Outcome of this conflict is more or less predictable and Christian civilization will again prevail but with lesser clout and elbow room for manoeuvres.

v) World War III will give a renewed push for completion of Islamization of India and WWIV (assuming that WWIII had already taken place due to vaulting greed of private enterprises) will be unavoidable with Islamization of India.

w) But these scenarios are neither necessary nor inevitable nor the march of Semitic cultures inexorable.

x) Profit propelled capitalist system and Semitism is complementary, interdependent and can only co-exist.

y) Since profit has tenuous rational and legal basis, profit can be shown to be dispensable without affecting production processes or progress of civilizations. Such models of growth are already available but greed of the power elite of India is preventing implementation. Once greed and profit is removed from production function, capitalism will collapse under its own weight of absurdities and take Semitism down with it.

z) Demise of capitalism will herald the elimination of poverty.

We have examined these issues at great length in the book and suggested simple solutions

BASIC PROBLEM OF INDIA

External factors

Indians carrying the "White Man's Burden"

Productivity of the economies of the developed and super–developed countries are only a fraction of that of India, but these countries take away the Indian wealth by selling products and services at highly inflated prices and buying Indian goods and services at highly deflated prices. Gross inefficiencies of the economies of the developed/super-developed countries in the use of resources and capital ensures that poor Indians have to toil so that the rich foreigners can enjoy good life!

Super developed countries and international agencies have imposed cripplingly punishing F.E. exchange rate and fiscal, monetary and taxation policies on India and Indian power elite have happily compromised. External agencies have crippled the manufacturing sector, especially, defence production sector, by constantly haranguing the power elite, who, in any case, was not in a position to oppose.

Internal Factors

Indigenous vested interests and their influence on Indian economy and society

Indian ethnic democratic, egalitarian, equitable, productive social, religious, cultural, technological rationale drives/productive efficiencies were completely thrown away during successive colonial rules. From about 8th century AD, Indian society got distributed in rigid economic strata with an entrepreneurial class consisting of landlords, Zamindars, pawn-brokers, money-lenders, businessmen, agents and their henchmen in administration and con-men taking dominant control. This entrepreneurial class gradually gained economic clout, so much so that, during alien rule, basic administrative and economic decisions had to be synthesized with the interests of this group. After Independence, this class became so bold and blatant that all administrative, constitutional, judicial, political and economic decisions have been primarily serving their interests at the cost of the general populace of India. This is the fundamental difference between India and the other developing/undeveloped countries of the world. This auto-immune deficiency (AIDS-like) phenomenon explains the peculiar spectacle of India languishing in poverty in spite of vast natural, technological and human resources. The vested interests have subverted and distorted every single organ of the State and its instrumentalities, resulting in acute disparity in income and resource allocation. These aberrations and distortions have reduced India into supplicant of the developed and super-developed countries or their surrogate countries, like, China, Malaysia, Singapore, Taiwan, Israel, South Korea etc. Indian top leadership of all classes is constantly manipulated by the foreign inimical authorities and agencies.

Constitutional Impediments

Anglo-Saxon model of democracy has perpetuated oligarchy, coterie or crony control without any accountability or responsibility to the peoples' representatives, not to speak of the people. In Indian constitutional scheme of things and as interpreted by the apex court, all principal constitutional functionaries are either indirectly elected or are selected or nominated by the coterie.

Major changes are required in the Constitution. Constitution Review Commission missed a great opportunity, as they, apparently, had no clear idea on what is needed in a self–respecting independent country. Major changes are required in selection of and criteria/qualifications of top bureaucrats, Judges of Supreme and High courts, the Election Commission and other high functionaries and Constitutional authorities.

Indian Constitution is such an odd document that Parliament and Legislatures have no authority or locus-standi to vet or approve or disapprove international treaties etc. executed by coterie bureaucracy in connivance with the ministers, who are constantly at the mercy of the coterie around the Prime Minister.

International Trade and Interaction with foreigners

Indian share of international trade, which was more than 50% of the world trade even during mid Muslim rule and which at the time of independence was above 2% of world trade, has now sunk to abysmal depth of around 0.6% to 0.2% of world trade. F.E. exchange rate with Dollar which even during British rule was about Rs. 2-3/- per dollar has now came to near about Rs. 50/- per dollar and RBI will be happy if it goes above Rs. 60/- per Dollar. It is another matter that Indian manufacturing, per capita food availability, job growth rate and all other economic parameters have all nose-dived during the last 50 years, more precipitously in the last 5 years.

India has been made import-dependent and its export earnings (after deduction of export and import subsidies and reduction in duties/cess etc.) have gone down to intolerable uneconomic levels. Indian importers and exporters have been ensuring that Indian interests are always sacrificed for increasing their own profits. India's national, especially, security interests have been always sacrificed for the sake of private profit.

In the name of IT export, the well known figures of IT business have been selling Indian labour at slave rate of payment. Even Malaysian IT specialists earn 2/3 times more per hour than Indian IT specialists. These IT exporters have been selling the 'Source Codes' of their exported programmes and have been directly responsible for very low growth of computer industry in India. India is importing almost double the value of IT products from abroad (mostly surrogate production from the Asia Pacific and East Asian regions) and paying unreasonably uneconomic high prices. They are profiting at India's cost. Indian Government is silent on creation of a "Source Code Holding Authority of India" for all IT exports/imports. IT exporters have been grievously hurting India's economic and security interests by inviting overt and covert surveillance by foreign authorities on our economy and security.

An unique feature of Anglo-American exploitation of India in last about 50 years is that they adopted straightforward methods, which any average human being should be able to understand and counter. This simplicity of exploitation procedures of the foreign inimical powers thus can be easily countered within the existing framework by a new Group/Party provided its basic motto: "Indian Interests First in India and in the world". This new Group/Party should internalize that "India can afford to ignore the world, the world cannot afford to ignore India". This Group/Party also should comprehend that "Growth Flows through the Barrel of the Gun, provided the gun is in the Hands of the Real Nationalist Indian and not pseudo-Swayam Sevaks!"

Indian interests have been sacrificed in all sectors since independence (we need not shed tears for period before independence) and more since "Globalization/Privatization" credo took root from the time of that Mondal-Messiah V.P. Singh and more aggressively during the last 10 years! It will be interesting to note some of the sectors where we have yielded without resistance, viz. Economy, Education, Hindutva, Secularism, National Security, Territorial Integrity and Sovereignty, Ecology, National Interests in Trade, Intellectual Property Rights, Economic Freedom and Sovereignty, Nuclear and Missile development, Bio and Chemical Weapons, Health and Medicare, Labour Welfare, Agriculture, Manufacturing, Urban Development. You name it, and the Government and the Party(s) in power in the last 50 years have blatantly compromised and sacrificed national interests.

Even the much trumpeted 'Nuclear Tests' were a 'Command Performance'. It was done at the behest of the foreign power(s) in order to legitimize Pakistan's clandestine acquisition of nuclear weapons from big powers. No self respecting country would have stopped at six Tests with indifferent results. The way India declared unconditional Moratorium on further nuclear Tests and rolled back the Nuclear/Missile plans, and the way India responded to the Sanctions, Control/Denial regimes and assorted embargoes demonstrate that the 'nuclear Tests' were done to make India totally defenceless in the very hostile and inimical environment and also get the economy debilitated as a bonus.

UTISTHATA JAGRATA, PRAPYA BARAN NIBODHATA

(ARISE, AWAKE! EXERT TO GET DESERVED BOONS AND BLESSINGS)

KLAIBANG MASMA GAMA, PARTHA! Judges, power elite, administrators, economists, shake off your unmanly habits of unconcern for common cause and pursuit of narrow private profit! Arise! Follow the path of Dharma!

We have examined in detail the ailments of Indian Republic; any more details will only add gore to the sordid tale of betrayal of India by its leading lights. There is no time to be lost in initiating corrective action, if we are not bargaining for massive social upheaval against 'Advanced Gujralitis Syndrome' and 'Advanced Gorbachev-Yeltsin Syndrome' or enactment of WWIII or WWIV. We have these apprehensions on valid grounds. Though our scheme is non-intrusive, non-invasive, India-centric only but any reordering of economic order inside India, will intimately affect the slave drivers, slave procurers and slave-traders in India and the beneficiaries abroad. The foreign powers will bring to bear all their means and guiles to thwart any re-ordering in India. They will use their hit men (the media, intellectuals, elite, the slave traders, etc.) for sabotaging from inside, while they bring their military might in the contention. Since India is not Iraq or Iran and Hindu majority, and Hindu ethos is still overwhelming, path of intervention is expected to be extremely uneven and the reluctant western powers might be sucked into the vortex of WWIII. Common Indians can rest assured that they have nothing much to lose other than their poverty and destitution!

Perceptive people know that the imbroglio in land acquisition for a private profiteer (under the garb of industrialization) in Singur in West Bengal could continue for so long, as SC considers that the people of Independent India are bound by laws enacted by Lord Clive, Lord Cornwallis or some such colonial rulers and courts and executive can operate in 'eminent domain'. Colonial laws and rules are supposed to overrule all the protection on land rights supposed to have been provided by written Constitution of India enforced in 1950. They will escape retribution if they remember that what affects Indian common man, Indian national interests, national security, sovereignty and territorial integrity, affects the apex court mortally ultimately. We apprehend that courts are fast approaching irrelevance in public psyche.

It is necessary to immediately review the fundamental rights and determine which all are superfluous in a harmonious construction of the constitutional scheme of things, always keeping in mind that the constitution could have been assembled for perpetuating poverty and for keeping India subservient to foreign interests.

President of India should immediately issue edicts that the courts henceforth will not sustain the legacy bequeathed by Eliza Impey (that infamous judge of Calcutta Presidency court, who sent an Indian money lender, Nanda Lal, to the gallows, on trumped up charges by applying a defunct inappropriate law imported from England, for demanding refund of money from a Britisher), or by the Anglo-Saxon masters. The guiding principle for determining culpability (for same or similar crimes/deviations) shall be on the following lines, corresponding to Hindu concept of Chatur-Varna (four Varnas or Classes, as determined by Yudhisthir in the epic Mahabharata):

a) Those (individuals and their dependents) getting highest 10% share of GNP or GDP of India, ministers and top bureaucrats, high court and supreme court judges – Highest culpability and highest permissible punishment (4P, i.e. four times the punishment for lowest category).

b) Those (individuals and their dependents) getting less than highest 10% but more than 50% share of GNP or GDP of India, high level bureaucrats – Second highest culpability and quantum of punishment shall be three times that for lowest category, i.e. 3P.

c) Those (individuals and their dependents) getting less than 50% and greater than lowest 40% share of GNP or GDP of India - Third highest culpability and third highest quantum of punishment (two times the punishment for lowest category, i.e. 2P)

d) Those (individuals and their dependents) getting lowest 40% share of GNP or GDP of India – Lowest culpability and lowest quantum of punishment (say,

P). Lowest punishment mentioned in relevant Articles of the Cr. P.C. will be the maximum punishment for the guilty of the lowest 40% of income earners.

This single amendment will drastically reduce the backlog of cases in courts and the jails will not be filled with the poor and dispossessed (the misery immortalized by Victor Hugo in his book "*Les Miserables* – The Miserables"), as it is happening now.

Amendments to the Constitution and elections

Incorporate all the amendments to the constitution as elaborated in this book (without any change or correction or explanation, which is not approved by this author[53]) with the existing Parliament and assemblies with the current procedures. This shall be completed within one year. Both Houses of Parliament, assemblies and the legislative wings of the centrally administered and other such territories shall be immediately dissolved after passage of the constitution amendment bill and completion of delimitation and fresh elections held as per the provisions of the amended constitution. Delimitation of constituencies, especially for the Council of States and for legislative councils and such other representative Chambers and consequent additions and alterations to the voters list of all the constituencies shall be completed within one year. All necessary financial, administrative and human resources shall be made available to the election commission. It shall be the personal responsibility of the Chief Election Commissioner, Prime Minister, Chief Ministers, Chief justices of Supreme and High courts, Chief Secretaries to the Centre and States and the Chiefs of Staff of Army, Navy and Air Force to ensure that all necessary action needed to complete amendment to the constitution and election of the peoples' representatives are completed within the time periods mentioned above. It shall be the personal responsibility of the President of India to ensure that all the high functionaries discharge their functions diligently and expeditiously without demur. The President shall continuously monitor the progress and the laggard shall be summarily dismissed and replacement sworn in immediately to ensure timely completion. Borders of India will remain sealed as long as required and all inimical forces to be warned of withdrawal of 'most favoured nation treatment', withdrawal of protections under TRIMPS AND TRIPS and all violators of Indian territorial integrity and national sovereignty shall face massive retaliation with all means in all media at the time chosen by India.

TIMELESS INDIA – INDIA WHICH CAN BE RESURGENT

Indian Religion, culture and society dates from pre-historic periods. India is the only big country in the world, which has an unbroken line of religious, cultural, ethical and social value systems operating for more than one hundred millennia. This timeless quality is India's basic strength and has been cause of repeated invasion on its land and value systems. Now Indian economy stands seriously debilitated. Indian polity, society and culture are also showing unacceptable signs of strain and have yielded or are yielding in many places.

Political parties of all hues are totally unconcerned about these debilitating factors. Most of them have been compromised and they are willingly collaborating or justifying foreign control over our economy, religion, culture and society. These collaborating politicians, bureaucracy, judiciary have created a situation in India whereby the common Indian has been rendered voiceless and their protests are being ignored with impunity. Our intelligentsia and leaders are constantly ignoring the fact that economic domination is the main motivation for the control of the culture and polity of the target country by the controlling the country. This has to end!

NANNYA PANTHA BIDDATE!

(THERE ARE NO ALTERNATIVE PATHS, BUT TO ANNIHILATION!)

India for Indians

This effort to understand why military remains debilitated and poverty gets perpetuated in India and how this is bound to change should excite all well-meaning Indians. Very simple remedies for the self-inflicted maladies of India are: a) massive mobilization of India with Indian means and b) thorough-going amendments to the Constitution to make India really independent in the polity of nations.

Indian politicians need to recognize that India and its resources are for Indians first, and no one, other than natural born Indian,. can claim lien on India or its resources. No domestic or international treaty, convention and covenants, understanding can deny the Indians the first charge on Indian heritage and resources.

All these considerations will form the bedrock of our agenda for purposeful action and should illuminate all our future action plans.

This labour of love is dedicated to the people of India and of the world.

END NOTES

1 Prof. Amartya Sen has explained this in his writings especially in "On economic inequality" and "Development as Freedom" and his, possibly, is the lone recognized feeble voice in IMF, World Bank and in other UN fora. But even he could not assert the real remedy!

2 Some geriatric marginalized gentry mimic the military and exercise in open spaces in the mornings and afternoons and seriously and solemnly discuss issues sent down the elaborate hierarchy. This is one organization filled with below par majority with highly accomplished real leaders of men with exceptionally high spirituality, ecclesiastism and rational intellect (as distinct from animal or functional intellect). The RSS is the only secular nationalist organization in India today. All other political parties, organizations, socio-cultural and religious bodies are totally converted to the Semitic belief systems and are totally anti-national or counter-national. They always project themselves as secularists and do majority-community-bashing in and out of season. These latter groups showcase their liberal and secular credentials by decrying anything traditional Hindu and Indian and try and cozy up to the westerners!

3 "American dream of unlimited consumer choice has become universal dream" Dr. Murli Manohar Joshi *ibid*.

4 Shri Aurobindo, "The Foundations of Indian culture".

5 Letters of Swami Vivekananda.

[6] Page 86 (Table 4-4) "The Clash of Civilization and remaking of world order", S. Samuel P. Huntington, Simon Schuster, Paperback edition, 2003.

[7] "The Wealth and Poverty of Nations etc.", by Davis S. Landes.

[8] 'Saving Capitalism from the Capitalists: Unleashing the power of financial markets to create wealth and spread opportunity'; Raghuram G Rajan and Luigie Zingales, Crown Business, New York, 2003, 1st Edition).

[9] A full scheme for creating a "Source Code Holding Authority" for holding and creating newer programmes from the programmes already made by different agencies in India or Indian controlled agencies or entities in India or abroad and to ensure that repetitive low value softwares are not created. Also this authority was to hold all source codes of all imported softwares and other software or hardware programmes, so that repetitive imports could be prevented. This scheme was forwarded to two successive IT ministers of NDA government but they could not be woken up.

[10] A paper on this line was prepared on the advice of a top religio-cultural leader in 1988, who claimed to be socially-engaged, but after reading the paper he developed cold-feet.

[11] This disease was first manifested in Shri Inder Kumar Gujral, when he was the Prime Minister. For anything important he had two excuses for inaction: i) I was not aware; of course no one need be held responsible for it, ii) I am helpless, where I am aware. This is the famous "Advanced Gujralitis Syndrome".

[12] This article was written in 1987 when the author was still in active service, but could not be sent for publication as necessary permission of the controlling ministry could not be obtained. In retrospect, we do not blame the bureaucrats, as they really have no independent minds and were merely following the lead given by their controllers. In any case, if any one had dared to publish, it could not have much stirred the English-created Indian political/economic cesspool.

[13] *'Timeless India, Resurgent India'*, Dr. J K Bajaj and others.

[14] Dr. J K Bajaj *ibid*

[15] Wing Commander H R Seetharam in Bangalore (a most rational, unassuming, liberated mind one might have encountered).

[16] ILO Report.

[17] Kaushik Basu, 1998, in *Analytical Development Economics: The Less Developed Economy Revisited.*

[18] Kaushik Basu *ibid.*

[19] This idea has been taken from an English picture, 'The Nights of Iguana (?)', which I saw in mid-fifties of 20th century, when I was under training in Air Force Technical College, Jalahalli, Bangalore. What I remember now is like this: Rex Harrison (?), one of the finest male actors of foreign films, was the free-loving, free-drinking very popular pastor in a village. He once took the elderly ladies of the Parish on an excursion to a hill-resort with magnificent view of the sea below. There the Pastor meets his old flame, Deborah Kerr (?), (a very fine female actress of that time), who also had come to the resort nursing her very old grandfather. The old man was always on a wheel chair reciting John Dunne's poems appropriately for the occasion (like "The wood is dark and deep and I have many miles to walk before I sleep". (Readers may recall that this particular piece was a favourite one for Jawaharlal Nehru also. Of course, both Nehru and the wheel-chair-borne old man left the world with unfulfilled ambitions). Rex tried to renew his contacts and Kerr was mellowing. But one morning Kerr noticed that Rex was boisterously and heartily drinking the local brew and cavorting with the local sultry sirens on the sea beach below. When Harrison returned in the evening tanned and inebriated, they had a discreet, soft but strong argument about Harrison's conduct during better part of the day. During this altercation Rex Harrison uttered the fundamental truth of life: "Human beings operate in two planes – Realistic Plane and Fantastic Plane. But the beauty is that when humans operate in the fantastic plane, the realistic plane appears as fantastic!"

[20] Kaushik Basu *ibid.*

[21] Amartya Sen in his book *"On Economic Inequality"*.

[22] 'India 2030: A farewell to poverty? World Bank MD sees India as No.3 in the world', *HT*, New Delhi, (Page 23), 28 October, 2006, Business & World.

[23] See GINI Index analysis in page 73 of the text of the book and also endnote 31 below.

[24] This story was narrated to me by Group Captain Vimal Kumar Jain of Asiad Village. A washer man had a beautiful daughter

and a donkey to carry the clothes and other heavy stuff. The donkey used to work very hard and happily tolerate all punishment and slights by the washer man, as he was convinced that his future was bright. This vision for his future was buttressed by the fact that whenever the washer man was angry with his daughter, he used to proclaim solemnly that he will definitely give her away in marriage with the donkey.

25 "Saving Capitalism from Capitalists" etc., Raghuram G. Rajan & Luigie Zingales.

26 *The Hindustan Times*, New Delhi,

HOW EQUAL ARE WE?

You thought India fared badly compared to developed economies? Think again. The income ratio of our richest 10% to poorest 10% is 7.3 Compare that to US' glaring 15.9

RANK	COUNTRIES	PER CAPITA*	GROWTH RATE(%)	INCOME RATIO**	GINI INDEX
1	US	39319	3.4	15.9	41
2	China	5453	10.5	18.4	45
3	Japan	[illegible]	2.8	4.5	25
4	India	3113	8.5	7.3	33
5	Germany	28215	2.2	6.9	28
6	UK	30315	2.7	13.8	36
7	France	28758	2.6	9.1	33
8	Italy	27905	1.6	11.6	36
9	Brazil	7968	2.8	57.8	53
10	Russia	9822	6.6	12.7	40

Source: Human Development Report 2006 & World Bank

Countries with highest income ratios of richest 10% to poorest 10%

BOLIVIA	168
NAMIBIA	129
LESOTHO	105
SIERRA LEONE	87
BOTSWANA	78

Countries with lowest income ratios of richest 10% to poorest 10%

AZERBAIJAN	3.3
JAPAN	4.5
CZECH REPUBLIC	5.2
BOSNIA & HERZEGOVINA	5.4
HUNGARY	5.5

27 Kaushik Basu *ibid*

28 Kaushik Basu *ibid*

29 Kaushik Basu *ibid*

30 Borrowing a term from the vocabulary of our Shri Jaswant Singh, the venerable Foreign Minister in NDA regime.

31 *The Economic Times*, New Delhi, 2 Aug, 2006.

32 *Hindustan Times*, New Delhi, August 03, 2006.

33 *Hindustan Times*, New Delhi, 30 Dec. 2006)

34 *India Today*, New Delhi, 26 June, 2006, weekly magazine

35 *HT2 Business & World, Hindustan Times* New Delhi, 25 Oct 2006

36 Written for a top leader alluded to in prologue and submitted to Tehelka Commission

[37] Dr. Srimati Chakraborty, *CHINA*.

[38] According to us, any single-point authority without accountability is unmitigated evil and condemnable – it does not matter whether the dictatorship is proletarian or democratic as in USA and Britain.

[39] Taxi-drivers in any country are the intrepid sychoanalyst who can determine the predilections of their passengers with some deft innocuous questioning, observation and deductions and tailor their main theorems for benefit of their passengers. Taxi-drivers are the most voluble interpreters of national and international events, affairs, and predictors of emerging trends; they often turn out to be uncannily correct. Taxi drivers in Moscow in 1991 and 1992 freely declared that Gorbachev got 15 million US dollars and Yetsin 5 million US dollars for debilitating their countries and for bringing in western model of democracy.

[40] So far as India is concerned, it renders only financial help through Indian business tycoons, so that China in turn can service the super and western big powers.

[41] *"Religious Demography of India"*, Dr J K Bajaj and others.

[42] *"Timeless India: Resurgent India"*, Dr J K Bajaj and others

[43] *Economic Times* of Delhi for the 1990-1999 decade

[44] As mentioned in Rabindranath Tagore's lyrical Novel "Sesher Kavita ('The Last Poem')"*: an inadequate translation of the name by me.*

[45] Phrase borrowed from author Arundhati Roy.

[46] Borrowed from *'As you Like It'* of William Shakespeare.

[47] Hodu (nick name, which was only known to close relations and some in Hamburg, Germany; his actual name being Amiya Chakraborty) used to make this observation when he used to find any thing amiss or irrational in activities of German central or local governments or local bodies; for example: when he was driving us to witness the 'dancing fountain (Fontain Beau?)', he found something wrong with the orientation of a traffic island and traffic flow, he muttered "These German's have amputed brains". We were sprawled on the grassy bank of a biggish lake and at some distance the dancing fountains were displaying exquisite performances with best music of the world.

Some years back I had witnessed the Dying Swan ballet performance of Bolshoi theatre of Moscow. The performance of the ballet forms of this dancing fountain was no less exquisite. Hodu explained that these fountains can and regularly do perform to the best music composers of the world (and he rattled off the names at random: Wagner, Beethoven, Mozart, Tchaikovsky and Hans Christen Anderson, many others including Jazz, Rap and all music forms). It is shameful that the dancing fountain of Akshardham Temple of Delhi is no match to the fountain in Hamburg, even though the fountain in Delhi is supposed to be more modern and more costly. Hodu loudly proclaimed his verdict on brains of the Germans and, in this case I agreed with him in full. Though performance of the fountain was top class, but civic administration of Hamburg had put the speakers on poles erected in front of the viewing stand. These vertical poles were great nuisance to the spectators. Hodu loved most two countries – Germany and India – and he reserved the right to criticize both ceaselessly; I do not know his opinion about India fully, as I did not have opportunity to spend much time with him in India but he must have also concluded that "These Indians have amputed brains"! He spent all his adult life in Germany, mostly in Hamburg, having left India at the age of 16 and was very popular there as his walk to the station every morning was a long duration one as he deemed it necessary to greet and talk to many of his neighbours and acquaintances and he, confident that his German friends will stand in, could walk out of his office whenever we wanted him to accompany us anywhere. He came to India in one of his occasional visits to die prematurely of cardiac arrest, leaving his friends and relations forlorn.

48 As defined by my NDC course mate (star story/ribald joke teller of the course, late Major General PP Singh, who retired as the Delhi Area Commander), once during a course seminar defined a consultant as a castrated bull. He narrated that once a massive bull was advising a much younger novice bull about the proper way of servicing the whole herd of eligible cows. When asked why he himself was not servicing the cows, the older bull explained that one day, when in full heat, he tried to jump over a fence and his testicles got caught in the barbed wire. Since then he has become an authority and has become a well known revered consultant/adviser.

[49] *HT*, 16.11.2007, in front page headlines reported: "FORBES LIST: TOTAL WORTH DOUBLE TO OVER $350 BILLION IN JUST 1 YEAR. 'Stocks rising for India's billionaires'.

[50] Somewhat this is the line that Bangladesh (earlier East Bengal, then East Pakistan and then Bangladesh – God only knows what name it will adopt after one more decade, if its current virulently communal and irreligious approach continue!) writer, Taslima Nasreen, has been taking for which she has been hounded out of Bangladesh and then from Indian portion of Bengal in Nov 2007 by the Brahmin (a disgrace to Brahmanism) communist Chief Minister, Buddhadev Bhattacharya, because fundamentalist Muslims created mayhem in Kolkata to divert attention from Buddha's diabolical schemes for Nandigram and Singur, where West Bengal government tried to usurp agricultural lands for providing profiteering opportunities to big businesses like (sovereign?) TATA Empire and people there were actively opposing these. Buddha had suffered loss of face and support and badly needed a diversion, for which Taslima Nasreen had to bear the cost of attack on human rights and dignity by Buddha, his party and henchmen.

[51] *Outlook* magazine, in 20th April 2006, issue

[52] Published in 'Nippon no dogi', Jiyu, April, 1974, pp 18-31; Translation by Wayne Root and Takeshi Manabu: 'The Japan Interpreter', Vol. 9, 1974-1975.

[53] The author is acutely aware that this prescription is itself a Semitic option of assigning God-like authority on an ordinary mortal like this author. But this is necessary as you often need a bitter medicine to cure a serious illness! Further, this limitation will vanish after the appropriately amended constitution is put in place.

REFERENCES

Advaita Ashrama (Publication Department). 2000. Letters of Swami Vivekananda. Calcutta 700014: 5, Dehi Entally Road. Eleventh Impression

Bakshi PM: Selective Comments. 1993. The Constitution of India.

Delhi 110054: Universal Book Traders, 80, Gokhale Market, Delhi.

BAJAJ JITENDRA. 1993. Ayodhya and the Future India. Edited by Jitendra Bajaj: Çentre for Policy Studies.

DAS VEENA. Editor. MIRRORS OF VIOLENCE: Communities, Riot and Survivors in South Asia. Oxford OX2 6DP: Oxford University Press, Walton Street.

BASHAMA L. The Origins and Development of Classical Hinduism. Edited and Annotated by KENNETH G. ZYSK. Oxford OX2 6DP: Oxford University Press, Great Clarendon Street.

BASU KAUSHIK. 1998. Analytical Development Economics: The Less Developed Economy Revisited. New Delhi110001: Published in India by Oxford University Press, YMCA Library Building, Jai Singh Road, New Delhi.

BHADURI AMIT. On the border of Economic Theory and History, New Delhi 110001 : Published in India by

Oxford University Press, YMCA Library Building, Jai Singh Road, New Delhi

BHAGAWATI JAGDISH. IN Defense of Globalization, New York, 10016: Published by Oxford University Press, Inc. 198, Madison Avenue.

CENTRAL GOVERNMENT (of India). Budget Documents 1999-2000, 2001-2002, 2002-2003, 2003-2004, 2004-2005, 2006-2007

CHANDRA BIPAN, TRIPATHI AMALES, DE BARUN. FREEDOM STRUGGLE. National Book Trust, India. A-5, Green Park, New Delhi.

CHOMSKI NOAM. 1999. Profit over People: Neoliberalism and Global Order. Madhyam Books, 142, Maitri Apartments, Plot No. 28, Patparganj, Delhi-110092. Published by arrangement with Seven Stories Press, New York.

DASGUPTA, R K. Swami Vivekananda's Vedantic Socialism, Calcutta 700029, India: Published by Swami Lokeswarananda, Secretary, The Ramakrishna Mission Institute of Culture.

DESAI A R. 1960. Recent Trends in Indian Nationalism. Popular Prakashan Private Ltd., 35C, Pandit Madan Mohan Malaviya Marg, Tardeo Mumbai 400034.

DOBSON STEPHEN AND PALFREMAN SUSAN. Introduction to Economics. Oxford University Press Inc. New York, United States.

ENGELS F. 1884. The Origin of the Family, Private Property and the State. In the light of the Researches of Lewis H. Morgan. Union of Soviet Socialist Republics: Progress Publishers, Moscow: Printed in 1948 in English and reprinted many times thereafter. First Edition, Zurich, 1884.

Economic Survey 2004-2005, 2002-2003, 2000-200I, 1999-2000. Economic Division: Ministry of Finance Government of India.

HUNTINGTON SAMUEL P. The Clash of Civilizations and the Remaking of World Order. Simon & Schuster,

Rockefeller Center, 1230 Avenue of the Americas. New York, NY 10020.

JOSHI DR. MURLI MANOHAR: Former Union Minister for Human Resource Development, Science and Technology and Ocean Development. 2003. Seventh Dr. Sarvapalli Radhakrishnan Memorial Lecture, 26 June 2003. Indian Institute of Advanced Studies, Shimla

__________. 2000. Sustainable Consumption - Towards a Vision. Address to Moscow University on 5th July, 2000.

__________. 2002. Technology Capacity Building for Climate Change. Inaugural address. New Delhi: International Conference on Science and Technology (October 20-22, 2002)

__________. 2002. Sustainable Consumption: Issues of a Paradigm Shift. ICSSR Occasional Monograph Series, 2002, No.1

JOSHI A P, SRINIVAS M D, Bajaj J K. 2003. Religious Demography of India. Centre for Policy Studies, Chennai.

LANDES DAVIS S. 1999. The Wealth and Poverty of Nations: Why Some Are So Rich and Some So Poor. WW Norton & Company, Inc., 500 Fifth Avenue. New York, NY10110.

MITCHELL RICHARD H. Thought Control in Prewar Japan. London W1Y 1AA: Published in the United Kingdom by Cornell University Press, 2-4 Brook Street

NANDY ASHIS, TRIVEDI SHIKA, MAYARAM SHAIL, YAGNIK ACHYUT Creating A Nationality: The Ramjanmabhumi Movement and Fear of the Self. Oxford OX2 6DP: Oxford University Press, Great Clarendon Street.

PRASAD RAMANUJ. 2003. Know the Upanishads. Delhi 110006: Pustak Mahal, 6686, Khari Boli.

RAJAN RAGHURAM G. & ZINGALES LUIGI. 2003. SAVING CAPITALISM FROM THE CAPITALISTS: Unleashing The Power of The Financial Markets To Create

Wealth And Spread Opportunity. New York: Published by Crown Business.

RESERVE BANK OF INDIA. REPORT ON CURRENCY AND FINANCE 1998-99, and REPORT ON CURRENCY AND FINANCE 1994-95, Volume I: ECONOMIC REVIEW

RESERVE BANK OF INDIA. Handbook of Statistics on Indian Economy.

SADHU MUKUNDCHARANDAS. 2005. Rishis, Mystics and Heroes of India. Ahmedabad, India: Swaminarayan Aksharpith, Shahibaug Road.

SARAH ANDERSON, ed. Essays by Martin Khor, Walden Bello, Vandana Shiva, Dot Keet, Sara Larrain & Oronto Douglas VIEWS from the South: THE EFFECTS OF GLOBALIZATION AND THE WTO ON THIRD WORLD COUNTRIES. San Francisco, CA 9410: Produced and Published by the International Forum On Globalization (IFG), 1555 Pacific Avenue.

SACHS JEFFREY D. 2005. The End of Poverty: Economic Possibilities of our Time. New York, 1001 USA: Published by the Penguin Press, 375 Hudson Street, 4.

SEN, PROFESSOR AMARTYA. 1999. On Economic Inequality. New Delhi 110001: Oxford University Press, YMCA Library Building, Jai Singh Road, Expanded edition, paperback.

______. 2000. Development as Freedom. New Delhi 110001: Oxford University Press, YMCA Library Building, Jai Singh Road, paperback.

______. 2005. The Argumentative Indian: Writings on Indian Culture, History and Identity. London and other places: Penguin Books, Printed by Penguin Group, 80, Strand, London, WC2R ORL.

SHOURIE ARUN. 1997. Worshipping False Gods: Ambedkar and the facts which have been erased. ASA Publications.

SHRI (RISHI) AUROBINDO. 1971. The Foundations of Indian Culture. Pondicherry, Shri Aurobindo Ashram Trust, India.

STIGLITZ JOSEPH. 2002. Globalization and Its Discontents London and other places: Penguin Books, Printed by Penguin Books Ltd. 80, Strand, London, WC2R ORL.

SWAMI MUMUKSHANANDA. July 2000. My Master. Calcutta 700014: Advaita Ashrama Publication Department, 5, Dehi Entally Road. Eleventh Impression.

_______. MAY, 1989. State, Society and Socialism. Calcutta700014: President, Advaita Ashrama Publication Department, 5, Dehi Entally Road. Second reprint July, 1995.

SWAMI VIDYATMANANDA, ed. What Religion IS. Calcutta 700014: Published by Swami Mumukshananda, President, Advaita Ashrama, Publication Department, 5, Delhi Entally Road.

United Nations Development programme (UNDP) 2002. Human Development Report 2002: Deepening democracy in a fragmented world. New Delhi: Oxford University Press.

World Bank. 2002. World Development Report 2000/2001: Attacking Poverty. New York, NY 10016: Oxford University Press, Inc., 200 Madison Avenue.

INDEX